# A PHILOSOPHY OF BEAUTY

# A Philosophy of Beauty

## SHAFTESBURY ON NATURE, VIRTUE, AND ART

*Michael B. Gill*

PRINCETON UNIVERSITY PRESS
PRINCETON & OXFORD

Copyright © 2022 by Princeton University Press

Princeton University Press is committed to the protection of copyright and the intellectual property our authors entrust to us. Copyright promotes the progress and integrity of knowledge created by humans. By engaging with an authorized copy of this work, you are supporting creators and the global exchange of ideas. As this work is protected by copyright, any reproduction or distribution of it in any form for any purpose requires permission; permission requests should be sent to permissions@press.princeton.edu. Ingestion of any IP for any AI purposes is strictly prohibited.

Published by Princeton University Press
41 William Street, Princeton, New Jersey 08540
99 Banbury Road, Oxford OX2 6JX

press.princeton.edu

GPSR Authorized Representative: Easy Access System Europe - Mustamäe tee 50, 10621 Tallinn, Estonia, gpsr.requests@easproject.com

All Rights Reserved

First paperback printing, 2025
Paperback ISBN 978-0-691-22668-2
Cloth ISBN 978-0-691-22661-3
ISBN (e-book) 978-0-691-22669-9

Library of Congress Control Number: 2022939301

British Library Cataloging-in-Publication Data is available

Editorial: Ben Tate and Josh Drake
Production Editorial: Karen Carter
Jacket/Cover Design: Chris Ferrante
Production: Danielle Amatucci
Publicity: Charlotte Coyne and Alyssa Sanford
Copyeditor: Karen Verde

Jacket/Cover art: Portrait of Anthony Ashley Cooper, 3rd Earl of Shaftesbury, from frontispiece to *Characteristicks of Men, Manners, Opinions, Times*, 2nd edition (1714), line engraving by Simon Gribelin, after John Closterman. Chronicle / Alamy Stock Photo

This book has been composed in Miller

For my mother, Carol Gill, a truly beautiful soul.

CONTENTS

|  | Introduction | 1 |
|---|---|---|
| CHAPTER 1 | Nature and God | 19 |
| CHAPTER 2 | Virtue | 59 |
| CHAPTER 3 | Art | 112 |
| CHAPTER 4 | Painting | 143 |
| CHAPTER 5 | Writing | 170 |
|  | Conclusion | 185 |

*Acknowledgments* · 189
*Notes* · 191
*Bibliography* · 221
*Index* · 233

A PHILOSOPHY OF BEAUTY

# Introduction

SHAFTESBURY'S *Characteristicks of Men, Manners, Opinions, Times* was one of the most important philosophical works of the first part of the eighteenth century. It played a momentous role in turning European thought away from the negative and toward the positive—in nature, religion, morality, and art.

In the seventeenth century, many thought wilderness was grotesque and frightful. Shaftesbury argued that all aspects of nature unaltered by human activity are part of a singular beautiful system. It subsequently became increasingly common to cherish wild nature as the pinnacle of beauty.

In the seventeenth century, many thought the essence of religion was obedience to a God with the terrible power to punish. Shaftesbury argued that true religion consists of disinterested love of God's beautiful mind. It subsequently became increasingly common to place love of God's goodness, rather than fear of God's wrath, at the center of true religion.

In the seventeenth century, many took morality to be a set of commands designed to combat human sin and selfishness. Shaftesbury argued that virtue is an internal beauty that is the truest expression of human nature. It subsequently became increasingly common to identify morality with a beautiful soul attuned to the good of humanity.

In the seventeenth century, in Britain at least, visual arts were often considered mere physical productions of questionable moral status. Shaftesbury argued that appreciation of beautiful art is of exquisite value. It subsequently became increasingly common to glorify artists and their creations.

These shifts away from the negatives of fear and hostility toward the positives of admiration and love involved the ideas of numerous early modern thinkers. But none played a bigger role than Shaftesbury's philosophy of beauty.

For twenty-first-century readers expecting a typical philosophical text, however, coming to *Characteristicks* can be a strange experience. *Characteristicks* starts with an emphatic denunciation of prefaces—an antipreface. It then dives into "A Letter," which begins like an actual letter and goes on to describe the writer's recent visit to a London meetinghouse, where he witnessed a religious fanatic speak in tongues. We then enter an epistolary essay on "wit and humour," in which the writer assures his correspondent that he was serious the other day when he praised ridicule; a "soliloquy" that gives advice to advice-givers; a "rhapsody" that begins in a city park, moves to a stately home, and concludes in the wild woodlands; a series of "miscellaneous reflections" that are almost post-modern in their self-referentiality.

Shaftesbury's purpose in deploying these literary techniques was to make his ideas accessible to the educated readership of his day. But on a contemporary reader they can have exactly the opposite effect; they can be off-putting. My goal in this book is to elucidate for contemporary readers the great intellectual achievement of Shaftesbury's philosophy of beauty, as well as reveal the vexatious beauty of Shaftesbury's writing.

In the rest of this introduction, I recount Shaftesbury's life, the rise and fall of his philosophical influence, and the challenges and rewards of reading his characteristic prose. In the chapters that follow, I explain his views of the beauty of nature and God (chapter 1), of virtue (chapter 2), of art in general (chapter 3), of painting (chapter 4), and of writing (chapter 5).

## *Life*

"Shaftesbury" was his title.[1] His name was Anthony Ashley Cooper, which was also the name of his father and grandfather. When he was born in 1671, his grandfather was soon to become the first Earl of Shaftesbury, and his father was Lord Ashley. When his grandfather died in 1683, his father became the second Earl of Shaftesbury and he became Lord Ashley. When his father died in 1699, he became the third Earl of Shaftesbury. If I didn't think it could have seemed affected and cause classification confusion, I might have called him "Cooper" throughout this book. Cooper was always his name. Cooper might have been more effective at evoking a singular writer rather than any of the roles he occupied. And Cooper suggests that one of his ancestors was a craftsman, a maker of barrels, which is, as we'll see in chapter 2, a job interestingly attuned to his concept of beauty. That said, if there was a craftsman-ancestor, he would have had to have lived a very long time ago. From at least the fourteenth century, both sides of his family had been landed gentry, knights, and baronets.

His grandfather was named first Earl of Shaftesbury in 1672, when he was serving as Lord Chancellor and was one of the most powerful politicians in the country. In the years that followed, his grandfather opposed the Stuart monarchy, which he believed was leading to Catholic and absolutist rule. His grandfather also helped found the Whig Party and advanced the Exclusion Bill, through which he sought to expand the power of Parliament and ensure a Protestant succession to the throne. As a result, he was arrested in 1677 and imprisoned in the Tower of London until 1678. In 1681, he was arrested for high treason and sent again to the Tower. The treason charge was dropped, but, fearing further persecution from Royalist Tories, he fled in 1682 to Amsterdam, where he died in 1683.

When Anthony—the one who would grow up to be a philosopher—was four years old, he was sent to live with his grandfather, at St. Giles's House in Dorset. John Locke was his grandfather's right-hand man, and it was Locke who oversaw Anthony's early education. Anthony and Locke had great affection for each other, in the way of a close nephew-uncle relationship. Anthony gained from Locke a philosophical training of uncommon value, even if he would eventually come to disagree ardently with many of Locke's ideas.

After his grandfather died, Anthony (now Lord Ashley), age 12, was sent to private boarding school. He loathed it. Part of the reason seems to have been that students from Tory families opposed to his grandfather inflicted on him ridicule and scorn. But he had other reasons as well. He thought the behavior of the student body was boorish and decadent, and that the educational quality was dreadful. As someone who cherished his solitude and privacy, he also just seemed to be fundamentally ill-suited to the intensely communal life of a boarding school.

It's not clear how many years he spent at boarding school. But he had certainly left by 1687, when, shortly before his sixteenth birthday, he began his grand tour of Europe. His companions were Daniel Denoune, an excellent and admired tutor, and John Cropley, one of his closest friends. His first stop was an extended visit with John Locke in the Netherlands, where Locke had fled to avoid Tory persecution. Then to Paris. Then, for the longest period, to cities throughout Italy. On the trip back north he visited Vienna, Prague, Dresden, Berlin, and Hamburg. The time he spent on his grand tour—especially in Italy—inspired in him a deep and abiding love of classical culture and art. On his trip through the

Alps and in scenic spots throughout Italy, he was also moved by the beauty of natural landscapes.

He returned to England in 1689. His father suffered from a degenerative malady that made him a virtual invalid, so, at age 18, he assumed many of the responsibilities that might have been expected to fall to his father. He did not enjoy it. There were painful family disputes. There was illicit burnbeating and hunting on his family's land, which he had to try to stop. There were legal battles with neighbors, whom he suspected of being encouraged by Tory enemies of his grandfather. His handling of these matters was characterized both by a powerful sense of duty that led him to work assiduously to address the problems and by an equally powerful animosity toward those who caused the problems. In years to come he would develop a more sanguine attitude toward humanity, but in his late teens and early twenties he bore prodigious contempt for people both near and far. He did write approvingly of the honesty and ability of laborers, and of the natural goodness of native Americans, but even then, his emphasis seemed to be on the contrasting mendacity of the upper classes and the stupid cruelty of English colonists.[2] He chafed at the public and social roles he was expected to occupy.

Even during the period in his twenties when he was at his most misanthropic, however, he had close friends about whom he cared deeply. In a letter from 1705 he wrote, "I never yet Lov'd any Soul in any degree that I could afterwards cease to love, or love but in a Less . . . In Friendship I must abide the Choice. Friends I have thus taken, are with Me *for better for wors* . . . I may loose Friends but they can never loose me."[3] He was in his thirties when he wrote that letter, but the sentiment had been and always would remain true of him. His friendships were for him of the utmost importance and the greatest joy.

In his late teens and early twenties, he was also reading, writing, and talking about philosophy. Although he and Locke interacted less as the years went by (to Locke's disappointment), the two did continue their philosophical discussions, by letter and in person. When he visited Locke, their conversation was joined by Damaris Cudworth (Lady Masham), at whose Essex estate Locke spent the final years of his life. At least by 1694, he had written "an Essay of my own," which was probably an early draft of the *Inquiry Concerning Virtue*.[4] When Locke sent him the second edition of the *Essay Concerning Human Understanding*, Locke asked to see a copy of his essay, but he refused, explaining that he "should be verry sorry to be Oblig'd for an Agreable Present made mee, to Return so Bad a one as a Bundle of such Thought as mine."[5] One can only imagine what it would be like to be asked, at age 23, to exchange an unfinished manuscript with the author of the *Essay Concerning Human Understanding*.

One of the unpleasant responsibilities he assumed from his father in the 1690s was participation in the administration of the Carolina Colony. He identified egregious mismanagement there, and was incensed by the ill treatment of the native Americans. But the Carolina Colony was also one of the most significant sites of African slavery, of which he would have been aware, and I know of no indication that he objected to that. Several decades later, Francis Hutcheson would use moral ideas with deep roots in Shaftesbury's philosophy of human nature to condemn African slavery. But as far as I know, he himself never drew that connection. There is, to my knowledge, no evidence that he was anything but complicit in African slavery in the colony he helped oversee.[6]

In 1695, he was elected a member of Parliament, where he served until 1698. During his time in Parliament, he promoted a bill to guarantee rights to defendants in treason cases (the charge of treason against his grandfather undoubtedly influencing this course of action). He supported a bill that restricted the franchise and excluded the non-affluent from running for office. He was generally a supporter of King William, but he also was in favor of disbanding William's standing army once the war with the French ended in 1697.

Because of his grandfather, he would always be closely associated with the Whig Party. And he certainly hewed throughout his life to certain Whig commitments, such as Protestant succession, religious toleration, and the power of Parliament. But he didn't toe the party line. As he saw it, he followed his principles, wherever they led, regardless of party.[7] As a result, he was the object of "constant criticism . . . for his lack of party spirit."[8] In 1696, he complained that there was a "bitter sentence" passed on him every day because he acted on principle rather than obedience to party. Tories never warmed to him when he sided with them. And the Whigs he disagreed with, according to his sometime-collaborator John Toland, "cou'd not endure him." Toland provides a vivid description of how Apostate-Whigs maligned him for his departure from strict party loyalty:

> They gave out that he was splenetick and melancholy; whimsical and eaten up with vapors: whereas he was in reality just reverse, naturally cheerful and pleasant, ever steddy in his Principles, and the farthest in the world from humorsom or fantastical. But becoming an Eyesore to them, as being an eternal reproach upon their conduct . . . they gave out that he was too bookish, because not given to Play, nor assiduous at

Court; that he was no good Companion, because not a Rake nor a hard Drinker, and that he was no Man of the World, because not selfish nor open to Bribes.[9]

In addition to providing some indication of his political status in the late 1690s, this letter offers a glimpse of what he was like as a person. There may have been disagreement about whether he was splenetic and melancholy, or cheerful and pleasant; my guess is that he behaved in ways that lent support to both assessments. But it seems that both sides would have agreed that he preferred books to "play," that he did not enjoy court events, that he was not a rake or a big drinker. The letter also suggests that the social dynamic he found at Parliament echoed the one he had encountered at boarding school.

When Parliament was in session, he lived in Chelsea rather than Dorset. The smoke of the city damaged his health, causing or exacerbating respiratory illness. He also developed eye problems and frequent fevers. These health issues forced him, in 1698, to retire from Parliament, withdraw from many other of his responsibilities, and move to the Dutch city of Rotterdam. Recovering his health was certainly the principal reason. But the move also satisfied his long-standing desire for solitude, privacy, and the time and space to think, read, and write. Though his health might have forced it, he couldn't have been entirely disappointed to have put some distance between himself and the political and familial entanglements of the previous nine years.

The Netherlands was an intellectual hotbed at the time, and he conversed regularly with other thinkers and writers. Among them was Pierre Bayle, who would become his good friend and one of his most important philosophical interlocutors. In a letter he wrote after Bayle's death, he says that Bayle's skepticism was the most valuable test for his thoughts, and that his own ideas dramatically improved as a result of Bayle's scrutiny, debate, and argument.[10] "Whatever Opinion of mind stood not the Test of his piercing Reason, I learnt by degrees either to discard as frivilouse, or not to rely on, with that Boldness as before: but That which bore the Tryall I priz'd as purest Gold."[11] He also says that while "different opinions" in religion and philosophy "usually create not only dislike but Animosity and Hatred," it "was far otherwise between Monsieur Bayle & my Self."[12] "[T]he continuall differences in Opinions and the constant disputes that were between us, serv'd to improve our Friendship."[13] He could not have hoped for anyone better than Bayle with whom to discuss philosophy.

There's some evidence that he had a notion of living the kind of life of the mind he had in Rotterdam for the rest of his days.[14] But various people in England persuaded him that responsibilities at home required his urgent attention. As well, his father was very sick. He returned to England in the middle of 1699, after living away for nine months. In November, his father died at age 46, and he assumed the Earlship.

In the years that followed, Shaftesbury saw to many matters of family and estate. He oversaw the important business of arranging marriages for his sisters. He set up a school, and helped fund education for poor children in his parish, as well as initiate action against those who were not caring properly for their children. He supervised the running of the large Shaftesbury household. He was landlord to the tenants on the family land in Dorset, working hard to manage rents, hunting, woodlands, and rabbit warrens. He was particularly attentive to how farming on his property was done, with a keen interest in land usage and horticulture. He bought a house near London, which he renovated and decorated. He commissioned artists to execute statues and family portraits. He built a "Philosopher's Tower" near St. Giles. He took a leading role in designing the gardens for his homes.

And he continued to be involved in politics. As Earl, he served in the House of Lords. He also worked to elect Whigs to Parliament, especially in the 1701 election. Whatever the difficulties of his relationship with some elements of the Whig Party, Shaftesbury never wavered in his hostility to certain Tories. In a letter discussing the 1701 election, he says that he had "the strongest Obligation on Earth" to "act with vigour" to defeat "the most inveterate of the Advers Party," and explains how pleased he is that "my Brother & his Friend" now sit in Parliament "instead of 2 inveterate Toryes."[15] At about this time, King William asked Shaftesbury to serve as Secretary of State. Shaftesbury declined. He was determined to be "active for the support of [William's] Government & for the Establishment of the Protestant Succession."[16] But he "resolv'd absolutely against taking any Employment at Court," thinking he "could best serve Him & my Country" behind the scenes.[17]

But when William died and Anne assumed the throne in 1702, Shaftesbury's political fortunes soured. Anne viewed him with suspicion. Shortly after her succession, he was stripped of the vice-admiralty of Dorset. The position was largely ceremonial, but it had been in the Shaftesbury family for generations, and it signaled the hostility of Anne's government. Tories were also threatening to punish him for his role in the parliamentary elections. At the same time, his health took a significant turn for the worse. He once again began to crave privacy and solitude. To top it off, his estate was in financial difficulty. His response to all these problems was to close down his Dorset household as much as possible, keeping only minimal staff, and withdraw to his home near London. That year he wrote: "My Efforts in time of Extreamity, for this last year or two, have been so much beyond my Strength in every respect, that not only for my Mind's sake (which is not a little, to one that loves Retirement as I do) but for my Health's sake & on the Account of my private Circumstances I am oblig'd to give myself a Recess."[18] Apparently, however, the home near London did not offer the comfort, privacy, and other recuperative qualities Shaftesbury sought. He soon began planning another trip to the Netherlands. In August 1703, he traveled again to Rotterdam.

Shaftesbury engaged in far less socializing during his second period in Rotterdam than during the first. He conversed regularly with Bayle and hardly anyone else. He wanted to conserve energy, to restore his health. He was determined to be frugal, to remedy his estate's financial situation. But he was also concentrating hard on writing philosophy. It seems likely that his energies were focused on *The Sociable Moralist*, which was completed by 1704. A revised version of that work, renamed *The Moralists*, would become central to his thought as a whole.

Shaftesbury returned to England in the summer of 1704. Unfortunately, his ship hit disastrously bad weather, and his respiratory illness flared dangerously, curtailing his activity for many months. But by the end of 1705, he was once again fully in charge of family and estate. In the several years that followed, he went to London occasionally, and still had his hand in political endeavors (albeit surreptitiously; he now sought to conceal his influence more than ever). But most of the time he lived in Dorset, where there were as many domestic issues to deal with as there had been before his second retreat. He also made time for philosophy. He completed his *Letter Concerning Enthusiasm* by September 1707, and turned *The Social Enthusiast* into *The Moralists* at about the same time. *Sensus Communis* appeared in 1709.

Shaftesbury felt keenly the importance of continuing the family line. But he did not want to get married. In 1708 he tried to pressure his younger brother Maurice into doing it. When that failed, he saw no choice but to look for a wife himself. "My only Brother," he wrote in a letter, "refuses to think of Marriage & leaves the heavy part upon me."[19]

Shaftesbury's first courtship was to a beautiful woman from a rich family. It did not succeed. He then resolved, he writes in 1709, to settle for "a Breeder out of a good Family, with a right Education, befitting a mere Wife, and with no advantages but simple Innocence, Modesty, and the plain Qualities of a good Mother."[20] The person he chose was Jane Ewer, the youngest daughter of a family that was "well born," although not wealthy, and of "worthy, virtuouse and good Parent's."[21] He had not seen the Ewer daughters for eight or nine years, but he had this information about them: "They are a healthy sound Breed, and the Youngest (they tell me) is the strongest Constitution of all, well proportion'd, and of good make. No Beauty."[22] He made the arrangements for the marriage. When everything with the Ewer family was settled, he finally met Jane. With joy, he immediately changed his tune. Writing to the same correspondent, he says, "But I can now tell you (which I cou'd not before) that I have seen the Young Lady and I protest I think she is injur'd in having been represented to me as *no Beauty* for so I writ you word before I had seen her . . . [L]et me tell you I think I was wrong when I said from common Report, that she was *no Beauty*. For I think her a *very great Beauty*."[23] They married in August 1709. All the evidence suggests it was a happy union for both of them. (As it happened, younger brother Maurice got married shortly after Shaftesbury did, in a match Shaftesbury severely disapproved of.)

Upon getting married, Shaftesbury sold his house in Chelsea and moved with Jane to a new home in Reigate, south of London. Hoping to put the family finances on a stable footing, he scaled back the household at St. Giles's House in Dorset. He and Jane spent almost all of 1710 in Reigate.

Shaftesbury was now less involved in politics than he had been in previous years. But Robert Harley, the Lord High Treasurer and most powerful politician of the period, thought Shaftesbury's influence was still important enough to warrant seeking his support. Seventeen-ten was also the year the Anglican clergyman Henry Sacheverell was put on trial for the fiery anti-Whig sermon he had delivered the previous Fifth of November, and Shaftesbury fully endorsed the resulting governmental action against Sacheverell, although he was not directly involved in it. One of the few times Shaftesbury left Reigate in 1710 was to travel to Dorset to deal with local ferment caused by the Sacheverell affair.

Shaftesbury's main focus at the time was philosophy. He completed *Soliloquy* in 1710, and then dedicated himself to forming that and his most important previous writings into a single unified work. He revised several other essays, and made especially extensive changes to the *Inquiry*. He wrote what he called "Miscellaneous Reflections," over 50,000 words of commentary that connected and extended the ideas of the other essays. He added footnotes, with copious cross-references to emphasize the consistency of thought throughout. He compiled an index, which is noteworthy because at the time almost no books written in English had indexes.

Shaftesbury must have devoted a tremendous amount of time and energy to such efforts. It seems that he had now decided that his greatest legacy would be his philosophy, as delivered in a magnificent book. He chose for the title of his magnum opus: *Characteristicks of Men, Manners, Opinions, Times*.

Shaftesbury's devotion to philosophy can also be seen as making a virtue out of necessity. His poor health left him increasingly unfit for other activities. Toward the end of 1710, his health was so poor that it was decided that his survival depended on leaving England for the more salubrious climate of Italy. His wife Jane was pregnant, however, and they could not leave until she gave birth.

His son was born in February 1711. In the months that followed, Shaftesbury shepherded *Characteristicks* into publication, while also seeing to the complex arrangements for the trip to Italy. The three-volume *Characteristicks* came out at the beginning of June. His son was brought to stay at the home of Shaftesbury's sister Anne. Then, at the end of June, Shaftesbury and Jane—along with Shaftesbury's secretary, Jane's two companions, six servants, and four hundred pounds of luggage—embarked on the grueling trip to Naples.

On the day of departure, Shaftesbury wrote a note telling himself that a firm, uncompromising choice had to be made between philosophy and politics. He had to be "wholly *in*" one of them, and "wholly *out*" of the other.[24] He must not try to "engage anew in both Parts." And philosophy was what he resolved to do, with a determination to resist any distraction from the other, even in the unlikely event that he was "restor'd" to health. More than four months after leaving England, in November 1711, his party finally arrived in Naples. Once there, Shaftesbury largely kept to his resolution. Although significantly (and sometimes drastically) limited by poor health, he conversed with Napolitano intellectuals, he cultivated his interests in painting and sculpture, he patronized the arts, and he worked on his philosophy.

One of his priorities was a second edition of *Characteristicks*. The most conspicuous new element was to be a set of engraved illustrations, every detail of which Shaftesbury sought to control completely. In an outstanding article from 1974, Felix Paknadel writes, "[H]is notes and correspondence dealing with them are much more abundant than those about the revision of the text of *Characteristics* . . . [T]hese illustrations were not for him mere ornaments. They were to convey in another medium the main points of his written work, to 'instil some thoughts of virtue and honesty, and the love of liberty and mankind.' They were an 'underplot' working in perfect harmony with the main plot."²⁵ Shaftesbury was also meticulous—obsessive, even—about other aspects of the book's appearance, sending the printer voluminous instructions about all aspects of layout and ornamentation. The result was, according to his biographer Robert Voitle, a strikingly "beautiful book at a time when English books were about the ugliest produced anywhere."²⁶

Shaftesbury was also engaged in new writing. His goal was to produce a second major work, which would be called *Second Characters, or the Language of Forms*. The topic would be fine art and what we now call aesthetics. It "was planned as a collection of four treatises . . . to be linked by cross-references and thus interconnected in the same way as the essays comprising his *Characteristicks*."²⁷ Shaftesbury completed two of the four treatises: a treatise on painting, and a discussion of public support for the arts. The third planned treatise was to be an analysis of a mythological image that represented all of human life; as far as we know, Shaftesbury did not make a significant start on that one. The fourth treatise, projected to develop a fundamental theory of the visual arts, was never completed, although there are enough notes, sketches, and fragments to indicate what Shaftesbury had in mind.

Shaftesbury died in Naples in February 1713. His body was sent to St. Giles in Dorset and buried there in June. Jane returned to England to raise their son. The beautiful revised edition of *Characteristicks* appeared in 1714.

## *The Rise and Fall of Shaftesbury's Influence*

In the first half of the eighteenth century, Shaftesbury was a giant on the philosophical scene. Astell (1709),²⁸ Mandeville (1723),²⁹ Balguy (1726),³⁰ and Berkeley (1732)³¹ all wrote books largely devoted to refuting him. The title of Hutcheson's first major publication (1725) was: *An Inquiry into the original of our ideas of beauty and virtue; in two treatises. In which the principles of the late Earl of Shaftesbury are Explain'd and Defended*. In his introduction to *Fifteen Sermons* (1726), Joseph Butler singled out Shaftesbury for extended discussion (arguing that although his theory gets some important things right, it ultimately fails because it does not account for the authority of the reflective moral capacity).³² A host of other writers also published refutations and defenses of Shaftesbury in this period. Harris suggests that reading Shaftesbury was perhaps the single most important event of Hume's early intellectual life.³³ Rivers maintains that Shaftesbury was "the key influence on Scottish moral philosophy in the

1720s and 30's."³⁴ Den Uyl says that Shaftesbury was "second only to Locke in terms of influence during the eighteenth century."³⁵

Eleven editions of the three-volume *Characteristicks* were published by 1790. Its influence extended beyond philosophy. Along with Joseph Addison, Shaftesbury paved the way for a new approach to English writing, pioneering a kind of polite and entertaining essay aimed at the educated classes.³⁶ Shaftesbury was a significant influence on eighteenth-century British poetry. According to Moore, his view of morality directly inspired James Thomson in the writing of his *Seasons* (1276–1730); Mark Akenside, whose *Pleasures of the Imagination* (1744) "versifies" *Characteristicks* in an attempt to defend Shaftesbury from the attacks of Mandeville; and James Harris, who renders Shaftesbury's theory into verse in *Concord* (1751).³⁷ Moore claims that Shaftesbury's influence—"not only in idea, but also in phrasing"—can be found in Fielding, Lyttelton, Armstrong, and a host of others.³⁸ Robertson claims that Alexander Pope's *Essay on Man* is "in large part pure Shaftesbury filtered through Bolingbroke."³⁹ Shaftesbury influenced the writings of Yeats,⁴⁰ Burke,⁴¹ and Wordsworth.⁴²

Shaftesbury's influence was also immense on the continent, especially in Germany. Boyer writes, "Shaftesbury shaped eighteenth-century German thought to a degree that can now seem quite astonishing."⁴³ Leibniz said that Shaftesbury was an "excellent and sublime" mind who went even "beyond Plato and Descartes." Leibniz bestowed exorbitant praise on almost every part of *Characteristicks*, maintaining that "There are few works in which soundness and elegance are so well combined."⁴⁴ Leibniz was particularly impressed by *The Moralists*, which he called "the most sublime philosophy" whose "grandeur and beauty" of ideas "ravished me and brought me to a state of ecstasy."⁴⁵ Shaftesbury was instrumental to the philosophical development of Mendelssohn, Hamann, Jacobi, and Wieland.⁴⁶ Lessing's aesthetics bear strong connections to Shaftesbury's views on art.⁴⁷ Herder called Shaftesbury "the beloved Plato of Europe" and the "virtuoso of humanity."⁴⁸ Goethe's views of nature bear clear marks of Shaftesbury's influence.⁴⁹ Shaftesbury's ideas helped shape the thought of Schiller and Schleiermacher.⁵⁰ In France, Voltaire called Shaftesbury "one of the boldest of English philosophers."⁵¹ Montesquieu ranked him as one of the four greatest poets, along with Plato, Malebranche, and Montaigne.⁵² Diderot published a translation of Shaftesbury's *Inquiry concerning Virtue*.⁵³

In Great Britain, however, Shaftesbury's star dimmed considerably in the second half of the eighteenth century. Shaftesbury's writing had always been polarizing. Brown wrote in 1751:

It has been the Fate of Lord Shaftesbury's *Characteristics*, beyond that of most other Books, to be idolized by one Party, and detested by another. While the first regard it as a Work of *perfect Excellence*, as containing every Thing that can render Mankind wise and happy; the latter are disposed to rank it among the most pernicious of Writings, and brand it as one continued Heap of *Fustian Scurrility*, and *Falsehood*.[54]

The literary critic Horatio Walpole wrote in a work published in 1806:

Few writings have attracted more attention, or excited more discussion, than the works of this noble author; who has been applauded and condemned with equal extravagance . . . For a considerable time he stood in high repute as a polite writer, and was regarded by many as the standard of elegant composition: his imitators, as well as admirers were numerous, and he was esteemed the head of the school of sentimental philosophy. Of late years he has been as much depreciated as he was before extolled, and in both cases the matter has been carried to an extreme.[55]

A century after Brown's assessment of the reaction to Shaftesbury, and a half century after Walpole's, Shaftesbury's thought had drifted far from the center of the philosophical conversation. In the 1720s and '30s, it was very likely that a British philosopher concerned with morality and religion would at some point reckon seriously with Shaftesbury. By 1861, John Stuart Mill could develop philosophical views that overlap considerably with those expounded in *Characteristicks* without any indication of having given Shaftesbury any significant thought at all.

Shaftesbury's style was a major factor in his fall from philosophical grace. The way he wrote, which so many in his own day found enchanting, did not age well. Representative of this attitude is a 1758 letter the poet Thomas Gray writes to a friend who "cannot conceive how Lord Shaftesbury came to be a Philosopher in vogue."[56] Among the reasons Gray gives for Shaftesbury's baffling popularity is that Shaftesbury was "vain," that he "seemed always to mean more than he said," and that "men are very prone to believe what they do not understand." Shaftesbury thought it was "graceful, half to cover and half conceal the mind," but "an interval of about forty years has pretty well destroyed the charm." Gray accused Shaftesbury of writing with a coronet on his head.

Adam Smith's assessment was equally negative. In *Theory of Moral Sentiments*, Smith deigns to mention Shaftesbury only once, in passing, despite the significant similarities between their views.[57] Smith does discuss Shaftesbury in his university lectures on rhetoric. But there he is critical to the point of dismissiveness, using Shaftesbury as an example of stylistic failure. Shaftesbury, Smith says, is a "much inferior" writer.[58] His style leads him "frequently into a dungeon of metaphorical obscurity."[59] His modes of expression "often become so obscure that their meaning is not to be discovered without great attention and being altogether awake."[60] Sometimes Shaftesbury "designs to banter and laugh at his adversary," but he seldom manages to pull it off: "he hardly ever makes us laugh, only in two places in the whole characteristicks."[61] Other times Shaftesbury "is disposed to be in a Rapture," but with no greater success, his attempts "always unbounded, overstretcht, and unsupported by the appearance of Reason."[62]

De Quincy, more succinctly, rated Shaftesbury "the most absolute and undistinguished pedant that perhaps literature has to show."[63]

## *Reading* Characteristicks

Annoyance with Shaftesbury's style is understandable. The problem is not that his writing is turgid or dense. It's that it can often seem perversely indirect, overly elaborate, meretricious. Cogent ideas sometimes appear in danger of being strangled by pomposity and cleverness.

But *Characteristicks* is, nonetheless, well worth the effort. I'll try to make that case in the chapters to come. At several points, I'll discuss his style, explaining why Shaftesbury wrote the way he did. I'll explain how he intended for the literary aspects to serve philosophical purposes, which we can identify by locating his different authorial voices and metaphoric flights of fancy within the larger context of his thought as a whole. First, though, let's look at several examples of passages from *Characteristicks* that Gray, Smith, and De Quincey might have had in mind when criticizing him.

Here's a typical passage from the third volume of *Characteristicks*.

> I have often known *Pretenders to* WIT break out into admiration, on the sight of some raw, heedless, unthinking Gentleman; declaring on this occasion, That they esteem'd it the happiest Case in the World, "Never *to think*, or trouble one's Head with *Study* or *Consideration*." This I have always look'd upon as one of the highest Airs of Distinction, which the self-admiring Wits are us'd to give them-selves, in publick Company. Now the *Echo* or *Antiphony* which these elegant Exclaimers hope, by this Reflection, to draw necessarily from their Audience, is, "That they themselves are over-fraighted with this Merchandize of

Thought; and have not only enough for *Ballast*, but such a *Cargo* over and above, as is enough to sink 'em by its Weight." (C 3.183–184)*

This prose would not delight Strunk and White. But when we expend the energy necessary to parse it, we see that it succeeds at the worthwhile task of nailing the phenomenon of the humblebrag. It describes a person who is apparently disparaging himself for being too reflective, but who in actuality is boasting of great intellect.

Here's another bit of prose I wouldn't call exactly pellucid:

> 'Tis esteem'd the highest Compliment which can be paid *a Writer*, on the occasion of some new Work he has made publick, to tell him, "That he has undoubtedly *surpass'd* HIMSELF." And indeed when one observes how well this Compliment is receiv'd, one wou'd imagine it to contain some wonderful *Hyperbole* of Praise. For according to the Strain of modern Politeness; 'tis not an ordinary Violation of Truth, which can afford a Tribute sufficient to answer any common degree of *Merit*. Now 'tis well known that the Gentlemen whose Merit lies towards *Authorship*, are unwilling to make the least abatement on the foot of this Ceremonial. One wou'd wonder therefore to find 'em so entirely satisfy'd with a Form of Praise, which in plain sense amounts to no more than a bare Affirmative, "That they have in some manner differ'd from themselves, and are become somewhat *worse* or *better*, than their common rate." For if the vilest Writer grows *viler* than ordinary, or exceeds his natural pitch on either side, he is justly said *to exceed*, or *go beyond himself*. (C 1.173–174)

I had to re-read this multiple times before I could make sense of it. But the point is straightforward enough. The narrator is wondering why writers are so pleased with the assessment "He has surpassed himself." If a writer has written well in the past, it implies that his current work is even better. But if a writer has written poorly in the past, it implies that his current work is even worse. So why does everyone take it to be such high praise? In the next paragraph the narrator gives an answer. People take "You have surpassed yourself" to mean that they have acted more fully in accord with their "true" selves than they ever have before. And people believe that while they may have some faults, their "true" selves are worthy and

---

\* I use 'C' to refer to Shaftesbury's *Characteristicks of Men, Manners, Opinions, Times, with A Notion of the Historical Draught, or Tablature of the Judgment of Hercules and a Letter Concerning Design*, in three volumes (Indianapolis: Liberty Fund, 2001), with the first number following referring to the volume and the second to the page.

deserving. In addition to their flaws and sins, people are convinced they have within "the Reality of *a better* SELF" (C 1.174). The narrator goes on to explore this belief that one's *"genuine, true,* and *natural* SELF" is entirely worthy and deserving (C 1.174). He eventually arrives at this conclusion: we identify the true self with internal moral principles, with values. To act in line with one's moral principles is thus to act in line with who one really is. To surpass oneself is to realize one's own values more fully than one has done before. The narrator expands on this conclusion in another passage that requires non-trivial effort to parse.

> Shou'd an intimate Friend of ours, who had endur'd many Sicknesses, and run many ill Adventures while he travel'd thro' the remotest parts of the East, and hottest Countrys of the South, return to us so alter'd in his whole outward Figure, that till we had for a time convers'd with him, we cou'd not know him again to be the same Person; the matter wou'd not seem so very strange, nor wou'd our concern on this account be very great. But shou'd a like Face and Figure of a Friend return to us with Thoughts and Humours of a strange and foreign Turn, with Passions, Affections, and Opinions wholly different from any thing we had formerly known; we shou'd say in earnest, and with the greatest Amazement and Concern, that this was *another Creature*, and not *the Friend* whom we once knew familiarly. (C 1.176)

Maybe this paragraph's syntax could have been simpler. But the central claim is not recherche: we think people's deep psychological principles are more essential than their physical characteristics. It's a claim that has affinities with Strohminger and Nichols's 2014 finding that our "notions of personal identity are largely informed by the mental faculties affecting social relationships," while "purely physical traits" have a "tenuous connection to identity."[64] Shaftesbury doesn't anticipate perfectly Strohminger and Nichols's results. At the same time, he's not a million miles away. While the writing style might be baroque, the thought remains surprisingly fresh.

Another passage has as its central figure "a native of ETHIOPIA" who has never seen anyone with a *"fair* Complexion." A racial example such as this is going to strike us as problematic. Shaftesbury criticized severely those who told and believed travel stories about the moral barbarity of Africans and native Americans. He argued that all humans had the same natural moral sense, and that, if anything, it was the Europeans who were likely to be morally worse than the Africans or native Americans. But still: he was very far from being a champion of racial equality. Most telling in this regard is his oversight of the Carolina Colony during the time of a terrible growth in slavery. He also seemed to be as comfortable trafficking in racist stereotypes as other writers of his day. To give an indication of how he wrote about people of other races is one reason to look at this passage. But I also want to suggest that this passage introduces a philosophical point that is separable from the racial elements, as well as from the complicated syntax.

> If a Native of ETHIOPIA were on a sudden transported into EUROPE, and placed either at PARIS or VENICE at a time of Carnival, when the general Face of Mankind was disguis'd, and almost every Creature wore a Mask; 'tis probable he wou'd for some time be at a stand, before he discover'd the Cheat: not imagining that a whole People cou'd be so fantastical, as upon Agreement, at an appointed time, to transform themselves by a Variety of Habits, and make it a solemn Practice to impose on one another, by this universal Confusion of Characters and Persons. Tho he might at first perhaps have look'd on this with a serious eye, it wou'd be hardly possible for him to hold his Countenance, when he had perceiv'd what was carrying on. The EUROPEANS, on their side, might laugh perhaps at this Simplicity. But our ETHIOPIAN wou'd certainly laugh with better reason. 'Tis easy to see which of the two wou'd be ridiculous. For he who laughs, and is himself ridiculous, bears a double share of Ridicule. However, shou'd it so happen, that in the Transport of Ridicule, our ETHIOPIAN, having his Head still running upon *Masks*, and knowing nothing of the *fair* Complexion and common Dress of the EUROPEANS, shou'd upon the sight of a natural Face and Habit, laugh just as heartily as before; wou'd not he in his turn become ridiculous, by carrying the Jest too far; when by a silly Presumption he took *Nature* for mere *Art*? (C 1.52–53)

An Ethiopian is transported to carnival in Europe. Not having any reason to think that an entire population would wear masks, he assumes the ridiculous masks people are wearing are their natural faces. The Europeans laugh at him for this mistake. When he realizes they're wearing ridiculous masks, he laughs at them. And he laughs with better reason. His mistake about what the carnival-goers' natural faces were like was perfectly reasonable. It's the carnival-goers who are ridiculous—for laughing at his reasonable mistake, and for wearing ridiculous masks in the first place. But then he sees a natural European face, and he laughs at it because he thinks it's one more ridiculous mask. His first mistake was thinking that faces that were in fact ridiculously artificial were natural. His second mistake is thinking that a face that is in fact natural is artificial.

The story might betray the view that Ethiopians are of lesser intelligence, or the view that Europeans are more natural and beautiful (although I do not think it's clear the passage suggests either of those). In what follows the passage, however, it emerges that Shaftesbury tells the story to make a point about the destructive power of enforced religion (C 1.53–54). In ancient times, authorities demanded only that people fulfill their civic duties; they didn't care about the religious beliefs people held. In modern times, authorities do demand that people hold certain religious beliefs. It's impossible, however, to hold a belief just because one has been commanded to. Moreover, those in authority keep changing, so the commands keep changing as well. In response to these impossible and changing demands, people adopt grotesque rites and rituals that distort their natural moral sense. The result is analogous to the carnival: an entire population whose conduct is as artificial and ridiculous as the masks of the carnival-goers. As the Ethiopian had good reason to laugh at the carnival-goers, we have good reason to laugh at people engaged in such ridiculous religious masquerades. But just because some outward appearances are unnatural and worthy of ridicule, we shouldn't jump to the conclusion that all of them are. Some conduct may manifest what is good and moral in human nature. It's a mistake to think that artificial and insincere rites and rituals are reflections of human nature. Such rites and rituals deserve ridicule. But it's also a mistake—a mistake akin to the Ethiopian's belief that a "*fair* Complexion" is a mask—not to recognize natural human virtue and love of God when it does present.[65]

Shaftesbury may not be right about religion and morality. His use of the Ethiopian may be objectionable. I think, nonetheless, his point is profound, and the story is a vivid metaphor for it.

In this book I quote from Shaftesbury a lot. Sometimes I use longish block quotes. I try to explain in my own words the content of the block quotes. My goal is to make it possible for you to understand my view of Shaftesbury's position even if you skip over the block quotes. So skipping over them is something you can do. But there are two reasons I hope you read them anyway. One reason is to check my view against Shaftesbury's text; my interpretations may be incorrect, or at least different from yours. The other reason is that the way Shaftesbury expresses his thought is essential to what makes him a fascinating writer. Skipping over the block quotes would be rather like reading the lyrics without playing the record.[66]

CHAPTER ONE

# Nature and God

## 1. Burnet's Ruin and Locke's Wasteland

At the turn of the eighteenth century, one of the most controversial books in Europe was Thomas Burnet's *The Sacred Theory of the Earth*.[1] First published in English in two volumes in 1684 and 1690, Burnet's *Theory* was at the storm center of the era's disputes about religion and science in the same way Galileo's work had been decades before.

Burnet argued that the common understanding of Noah's flood was fundamentally mistaken. There was, on the common understanding, a 40-day "Deluge of Water" that "over-spread the Face of the Whole Earth, from Pole to Pole, and from *East* to *West*, and that in such Excess, that the Floods over-reacht the Tops of the highest Mountains."[2] Eventually, the waters subsided, the mountains and fields reappeared, and Noah's descendants began to re-inhabit the world that had been temporarily flooded.

That story couldn't be true, Burnet argued, because there simply wasn't enough water.

If the flood reached above all the highest mountains of the entire world, there would have had to be unbroken global ocean that was more than a mile higher than current sea levels. The volume of water, moreover, would have had to increase its rate of growth as sea levels rose, since the surface area of a sphere increases as the sphere expands. Burnet calculated that this would require "a Quantity of Water eight times as great" as what all the oceans currently contain.[3] But where would all this water come from?

There are two sources on our planet: bodies of water such as seas and lakes, and clouds. The seas and lakes could not contribute to the rise in sea level, since any water moved from one body of water would have to be replaced by water from somewhere else. "If you have two Vessels to fill, and you empty one to fill the other, you gain nothing by that, there still remains one Vessel empty."[4] The clouds supply rain, but no rate of cloud-fed rainfall could produce eight oceans of water in 40 days. That would take a constant torrent of at least 40 years, which the clouds could not contain.

There's another problem as well. Even if we suppose that much water did fall on the earth, there can be no accounting for where it all went. According to the common understanding, "the Earth was dry and habitable" only four or five months later.[5] But there would have been no place for the water to drain into, since every cavity and channel would already have been inundated. The story is thus "impossible and unintelligible upon a double Account, both in requiring more Water than can be found, and more than can be disposed of if it was found."[6]

After establishing that the common understanding of Noah's flood conflicts with what science plainly tells us, Burnet draws the only logical conclusion: at the time of Noah's flood, the entire surface of the earth must have been perfectly "smooth and uniform"—like an egg—so that it could "easily be overflowed, and the Deluge performed with less Water."[7]

Before the flood, a person who had traveled all over the world would "not meet with a Mountain or a Rock."[8] "[T]here was no Sea there, no Mountains, nor Rocks, nor broken Caves, 'twas all one continued and regular Mass, smooth, simple, and compleat, as the first Works of Nature use to be."[9] Everything was as flat as "the face of the calmest Sea."[10] Burnet calls his theory of antediluvian geography the "Doctrine of the *Mundane Egg*."[11] Before the flood, the ground everywhere was as even and regular as the shell of an egg, with all the world's water encased underground (like an egg's albumen) between the flat surface and a hard inner core.

The mundane egg was a marvel of divine architecture, the "whole Globe of the Water vaulted over, and the exterior Earth hanging above the Deep, sustain'd by nothing but its own Measures and Manner of Construction: A Building without Foundation or Corner-stone."[12] The era of egg-world was most wonderful, a golden age of human history.

> In this smooth Earth were the first Scenes of the World, and the first Generations of Mankind; it had the Beauty of Youth and blooming Nature, fresh and fruitful, and not a Wrinkle, Scar or Fracture in all its body; no Rocks nor Mountains, no hollow Caves, nor gaping Channels, but even and uniform all over. And the Smoothness of the Earth made the Face of the Heavens so too; the Air was calm and serene; none of those tumultuary Motions and Conflicts of Vapours, which the

Mountains and the Winds cause in ours: 'Twas suited to a golden Age, and to the first Innocency of Nature.[13]

Egg-world was paradise. And egg-world was beautiful: proportionate, regular, uniform, ordered, simple, geometrically perfect.

But humans were sinful, and punishment followed. The smooth outer shell cracked. "[T]he Frame of the Earth was torn in pieces, as by an Earthquake."[14] Massive fragments fell onto the water that had been beneath the surface, causing tsunamis so large and widespread that for a time the entire planet was covered by water. When the waters later rushed in to fill the lower places, they swept "Woods, Buildings [and] Living Creatures" with them, carrying it "all headlong into the great gulph."[15] This created scars on the land, and additional debris. Massive fragments came to rest in all sorts of postures, chaotically, some close to upright, others at different angles, forming mountains and canyons, islands, rocks, and crevices.

The geological features we see today are the consequences of that cataclysm. By that "fatal Blow, the Earth fell out of that regular Form, wherein it was produced at first, into all these Irregularities which we see in its present Form and Composition."[16] Everything on the face of the planet that is a departure from egg-like smoothness is the result of God's punishment of "the Wickedness and Degeneracy of Men."[17]

Egg-world was beautiful. Our world is not. What we inhabit is rough and unsightly, monstrous, rude and irregular, disordered, disproportioned, ghastly. We traverse a scene of dislocation and dissolution, with broken pieces of the earth "scatter'd like Limbs torn from the rest of the Body."[18] Nature is a vast array of deformity, ugliness caused by human sin. Our mountains and valleys and seas and chasms "have the true Aspect of a World lying in its Rubbish."[19] "[S]ay but they are a *Ruin*, and you have in one Word explained them all."[20]

John Locke didn't cherish wilderness any more than Burnet. In 1690, about the same time as Burnet's *Sacred Theory*, Locke published his *Second Treatise of Government*. Chapter V of the *Second Treatise* addresses a crucial question. God gave the earth to all of humanity. The land's benefits were originally bestowed on every human. But the land is now owned by some and not by others. A few rich individuals control huge swaths, from which the multitudes of poor are excluded. If God gave the land in common to all of humanity, how can the current state of land ownership possibly be justified?

It can be justified, according to Locke, because God intended for the earth to be of maximal benefit to all humans. And, crucially, the earth produces its greatest benefits when cultivated. People thus do God's will when they work the land—when they "subdue the Earth" and by so doing "improve it for the benefit of life."[21] And it is by working the land that a person gains ownership of it. For every person owns himself, owns his body. It follows that every person owns the labor of his own body. When a person works the land, he mixes his labor into it. Cultivated land contains the labor of the person who cultivated it. Since the person owns his labor, it follows that he now owns the land. The prospect of gaining ownership of the land by cultivating it is, as well, a salutary incentive to improve the land for humanity's benefit.

There is much to say about Locke's theory of land appropriation. The point I wish to highlight is that on his view, land is valuable just to the extent that it benefits human beings. The more benefits the land produces—the more "conveniences" or "provisions" it provides—the more valuable it is. Land's value "depends only on [its] usefulness to the life of man."[22] And the benefits of wilderness are miniscule in comparison with the benefits of land that is cultivated. An acre of farmland in Devonshire is a hundred times more valuable than an "equally fertile" acre of "wild woods and cultivated waste of America, left to nature, without any improvement, tillage or husbandry."[23] Wilderness is "almost worthless."[24] The "benefit of it amount[s] to little more than nothing."[25] "Ninety-nine-hundredths" of the value of land is "wholly to be put on the account of labour" rather than to what "is purely owing to Nature."[26]

When Burnet looked at wilderness he saw deformity—an originally beautiful earth that had been ruined by sin. Locke didn't seem to care about beauty or ugliness. The land's productivity was all that mattered to him. But Locke too denigrated wilderness. The pejorative distinctive of Burnet's attitude toward nature was "ruin." The pejorative distinctive of Locke's was "waste." A place that has not been "improved" by human cultivation is a "waste land."[27] "Land that is left wholly to nature, that hath no improvement of pasturage, tillage, or planting, is called, as indeed it is, waste."[28] All the wild woods of America are but "uncultivated waste."[29] Locke recognized nothing to cherish in wilderness. Uncultivated nature was wasted, something God wished us to alter for human benefit.[30]

Many today hold views of nature diametrically opposed to those of Burnet and Locke. Many today think of rugged mountains, old growth forests, and ancient grassland as the earth's most precious places. Wilderness is not a ruin, not a waste. It is unspoiled. Uncultivated nature, at least in certain circles, has enjoyed a 180-degree revaluation. It is now taken to be of great intrinsic value, the height of beauty.

This contemporary appreciation of nature has a rich philosophical heritage: from the contemporary view of positive aesthetics, which affirms the beauty of all things wild; to the environmental philosophies of Leopold and Muir; to the transcendentalism of Emerson and Thoreau; to Humboldt's scientific holism; to the Romanticism of Wordsworth in England and Goethe in Germany.

Shaftesbury was instrumental in initiating this modern revaluation of nature. Shaftesbury knew well the works of Locke and Burnet.[31] But Shaftesbury's attitude toward nature was like ours, not theirs. He loved the "original Wilds" (C 2.217). He thought all things untouched by human influence were "beauteous in themselves" (C 2.217). Everywhere he looked he saw "*Master-pieces* in NATURE," sources of intense "Delight" (C 2.224; 2.164). As one of his characters puts it, "The Wildness pleases" (C 2.217).

In this chapter we look at Shaftesbury's pivotal view of nature. We'll see that his view emerged as a solution to a problem he took to be of the deepest philosophical and personal importance: the problem of how worship of God can be both transportingly emotional and entirely rational.

I first explain Shaftesbury's problem, describing in section 2 his view of religious emotion and in section 3 his view of religious rationality. I then explain Shaftesbury's solution, describing in section 4 his view of beauty in general and in section 5 his view of the beauty of nature. In section 6 I raise the question of what happens when Shaftesbury's view meets Darwin.

## 2. *Emotional Religion: The First Part of Shaftesbury's Problem*

Shaftesbury explored the psychology of religion throughout his writings, in discussions of self-interest, enthusiasm, zealotry, the spirit of faction. His most systematic treatment comes in the first part of *Inquiry concerning Virtue, or Merit*, where he catalogs the emotional effects of religious belief. The three main categories he discusses are: atheism, the belief that there is no god; daemonism, the belief that there is a god who is not perfectly moral; and theism, the belief that there is a god who is perfectly moral.[32]

Atheism is grim. The atheist's experience of reality is of "a vast and infinite Deformity," a "Pattern of *Disorder*" with "neither *Goodness* nor *Beauty*" in it (C 2.40). "There is nothing good or lovely which presents it-self," nothing to raise "any passion besides that of Contempt, Hatred, or Dislike" (C 2.40). Shaftesbury's atheist resembles Sartre's authentic existentialist, whose realization of the non-existence of God condemns him to a state of abandonment, anguish, despair, and profound aloneness. "Nothing indeed," Shaftesbury writes, "can be more melancholy, than the Thought of living in a distracted Universe" (C 2.40). To the atheist all is amoral and ugly. When the world accommodates his wishes, there is nothing about it that deserves his "Admiration and Love" (C 2.40). For it is merely the result of "what *Atoms and Chance* produce" (C 2.42). All too often, moreover, the world does not accommodate his wishes. Its storms and diseases and biting things produce "many Ills" (C 2.40). And while in theory the random movements of atoms don't deserve "Anger, and Abhorrence" any more than admiration or love, in practice an atheist will find it almost impossible not to rage at the meaningless suffering they cause. "[U]pon disastrous Occasions, and under the Circumstances of a calamitous and hard Fortune, 'tis scarce possible to prevent a natural kind of Abhorrence and Spleen, which will be entertain'd and kept alive by the Imagination of so perverse an Order of Things" (C 2.42).

Shaftesbury thinks it's possible for an atheist to be virtuous. But just barely. Human psychology and the events of a life being what they are, it's likely that an atheist's commitment to morality will wither. Good people suffer. Bad people prosper. Virtue seems to be an *"Enemy to Happiness"* (C 2.41). The world is a vast disorder. This presentation of reality will produce in the atheist a dark attitude that "affects the Temper, and disturbs that easy Course of the Affections on which Virtue and Goodness so much depend" (C 2.42). Unless a person has almost superhuman moral fortitude, atheism will "by degrees imbitter the Temper, and not only make the Love of Virtue to be less felt, but help to impair and ruin the very Principle of Virtue, *viz. natural* and *kind Affection*" (C 2.41).

As grim as atheism is, the effects of daemonism are worse. Daemonists believe in a god who is immoral. This belief corrupts their sense of right and wrong. It accommodates them to atrocity. This corruption occurs as a result of a deity's being represented as performing "odious and abominable" acts (C 2.27). Shaftesbury gives several examples. Jupiter seduces and rapes. The god of another sect (Calvinism) "arbitrar[il]y and without reason" destines some people "to endure perpetual Ill, and others as constantly to enjoy Good" (C 2.29). The god of still another sect (Judaism) has a character that is "captious and of high resentment, subject to Wrath and Anger, furious, revengeful . . . encouraging Deceit and Treachery amongst Men, favourable to a few, tho for slight causes, and cruel to the rest" (C 2.28). People's innate sense of right and wrong would naturally lead them to condemn such conduct. But religions teach their adherents to esteem and honor their gods, to worship and adore them. When a religion succeeds in inculcating "Love and Admiration" for an odious and abominable god, it warps the moral sense to conform to conduct that is in reality "horrid and detestable" (C 2.27). As a believer becomes "more and more reconcil'd to the Malignity, Arbitrariness, Partiality or Revengefulness of his believ'd DEITY; his Reconciliation with these Qualitys themselves will soon grow in proportion; and the most cruel, unjust, and barbarous Acts, will, by the power of this Example, be often consider'd by him, not only as just and lawful, but as divine, and worthy of imitation" (C 2.28–29). Jupiter's followers end up delighting in "amorous and wanton Acts." Followers of another god become captious, resentful, and deceptive. Members of another sect self-righteously pursue arbitrary punishment. "And thus it appears, that where a real Devotion and hearty Worship is paid to a supreme Being, who in his History or Character is represented otherwise than as really and truly just and good; there must ensue a Loss of Rectitude, a Disturbance of Thought, and a Corruption of Temper and Manners in the Believer. His Honesty will, of necessity, be supplanted by his Zeal, whilst he is thus unnaturally influenc'd and render'd thus immorally devout" (C 2.29). Worship of an immoral god inevitably produces immoral character.

"Immorally devout." That's just one of Shaftesbury's scathing descriptions of the fervidly religious. He calls them *"servile"* (C 2.32). He condemns their "Wretchedness and Meanness" (C 2.32). He speaks of the "Narrowness of Spirit . . . peculiarly observable in the devout Persons and Zealots of almost every religious Persuasion" (C 2.34). Shaftesbury loathed people of aggressive pieties. His attitude toward atheism is benign in comparison. Atheism is a melancholy condition, but atheists know what's right and what's wrong, and they may struggle toward virtue, difficult though it is for them to achieve. Deamonism is an inexorable slide to viciousness.

At the other end of the spectrum is theism, belief in a perfectly good god. The theist believes "everything is govern'd, order'd, or regulated *for the best*, by a designing Principle, or Mind, necessarily good and permanent" (C 2.6). There is, the theist believes, a "divine Providence and Bounty" that extends to all living things. God loves everyone and everything, and he has designed the world accordingly (C 2.29–30).

Our moral sense naturally approves of love for humanity as a whole. Religions prescribe approval of their deities. When a religion represents its deity as acting in conflict with love for humanity, something has to give. An embrace of the religion must result in a deforming of the moral sense.

But the deity of the theist acts in perfect accord with love for humanity as a whole. So while other religious views deform our moral sense, theism reinforces its natural shape.

And theism does more than stabilize judgments of right and wrong. The great goodness of the theist's god inspires by example. When the deity is represented as "good and excellent, [with] a Concern for the good of *All*, and an Affection of Benevolence and Love towards *the Whole*; such an Example must undoubtedly serve (. . .) to raise and increase the Affection towards Virtue, and help to submit and subdue all other Affections to that alone" (C 2.32–33). Contemplation of an omnibenevolent god produces feelings of gratitude, admiration, and awe. These feelings motivate us to godly emulation. The positive emotions of theism encourage expansive love. God's "excellency and worth" leads the theist to aspire to "the Perfection of Nature to imitate and resemble him" (C 2.31).

Belief in a perfect god promotes virtue in another way as well. Theists believe there is a god that is conscious of everything everyone thinks and does. Even in the "deepest Solitude, there must be *One* still presum'd remaining with us; whose Presence singly must be of more moment than that of the most august Assembly on Earth" (C 2.33). Belief in the constant presence of this ideal observer can spur us to virtue because of our wish to avoid the shame of being observed acting badly. But Shaftesbury places more emphasis on the positive boost the ideal observer's presence can give to our desire to do what is honorable "even under the unjust Censure of a World" (C 2.33). When an atheist would feel utterly alone and abandoned, perfect theists will have the company of someone who completely understands their circumstances and fully appreciates their good deeds.[33]

Shaftesbury contends that believing in a god merely because of the benefits it will win you is a pernicious mistake. But he's willing to allow that virtue may be rewarded and vice punished in an afterlife (even if he doesn't give full-throated endorsement to the possibility). And these thoughts of reward and punishment can be useful, so long as they flow from belief in a morally perfect god. For if reward and punishment are correctly administered—by a wise parent, a judicious magistrate, a perfect god—they can be morally instructive, inculcating esteem for virtue and detestation of villainy in a way that penalties and bribes do not. The crucial thing is that the administrators themselves be virtuous. For "it is *Example* which chiefly influences Mankind, and forms the Character" (C 2.37). It's not the rewards and punishments themselves that are important. What's important is that they express the commitment to virtue of the person who is doing the rewarding or punishing. Thoughts of reward and punishment can be beneficial to virtue, but only to the extent that they ultimately inspire love of virtue for its own sake. Such inspiration is exactly what theism produces.

The atheist is a melancholy figure. Adherents of most established religions are angry and bigoted. But the personality of the theist is blue skies and sunshine. Theists love all of creation. They think everything has been designed for the best. Elevated by the example of the deity's omnibenevolence, they feel expansive love for humanity as a whole. The world fills them with delight. They are serenely happy—paragons of positive emotion.

The *Inquiry* description of the theist might give the impression that belief in a morally perfect god produces loving worship as surely as night follows day. Shaftesbury knew all too well it was not that simple. While Shaftesbury believed in a perfectly good god, he himself was gloomy, pessimistic, bleak, anguished. This caused him meta-anguish: he lacked the positive emotions theism ought to produce, and he excoriated himself for lacking them.

Shaftesbury described the problem by comparing himself unfavorably to atheists. Depressed atheists are wrong not to believe in a perfectly good god. But at least their affective responses to the world are consistent with their lack of belief. Shaftesbury, in contrast, believed in a perfectly good god but failed to feel the love that should accompany such a belief. Which is more shameful, he asks himself: to hold the atheist's position,

> or thinking of Providence as thou dost, to be no otherwise affected than as thou art? Which of the two is the more absurd? To [be an atomist like Epicurus]; or, being consciouse of Deity, to be no otherwise moved by his presence than if He were not, or had no Inspection of our Thought or Action? This is, in the same manner, *to live without Deity*, and perhaps this last may be esteemed the greater Impiety.[34]

It's worse to believe in God but not feel the appropriate love for his creation than not to believe in God at all. It was the worse offense of which Shaftesbury found himself guilty.

Shaftesbury was convinced that God's "*Administration is intirely Just & Good.*"[35] He should, consequently, have felt the joy of being in the constant presence of the greatest being imaginable. But he didn't. Like Sartre's existentialist, he felt alienated, "*Alone*," "miserable."[36] "Is this thy Conception & Belief of a Deity?" he sardonically asks himself. "This is, in effect, to believe, & not believe."[37]

Shaftesbury tried hard to instill in himself the loving worship appropriate to perfect theism. He resolved to consider as often as possible the perfection of God's design, with the hope that over time this would have elevating effects. "[E]nter into what is done," he told himself, "so as to admire that Grace & Majesty of things so Great & Noble. . . . Bring thy self as oft as thou canst into this Sense and Apprehension [of] what is chiefly Beautifull Splendid & Great in things."[38]

Shaftesbury rejected "vulgar Prayer," which he took to be the sycophantic act of begging God to bestow benefits.[39] We shouldn't ask God to change the world. God's creation is already perfect. We should love everything just the way it is. But Shaftesbury did write one prayer himself. It was a self-exhortation to develop the positive emotions he thought perfect theism should arouse.

In his prayer Shaftesbury asks for the "power of Reason" to overcome his impious tendencies. He wants to be rid of "those Monstrouse Thoughts, Absurd Imaginations Wild & Extravagant Suggestions of a Debauch'd Corrupted Mind, or a Discompos'd Entangled or Sick Reason, which are able att any time to make mee think of thy Being either Uncertainly, by falling into those Mazes of Atheisme, or Proposterously, by Superstition."[40] Instead of those monstrous thoughts, Shaftesbury tells himself to dwell on God's beautiful perfections. He hopes those pious thoughts will elevate him—to love everything and to act accordingly. Here are some examples of his self-exhortations:

> Lett this therefore bee my Purpose, to Learn how to think on Thee, and Know Thee more, that I may bee more in love with Excellence and Admire Ador & Love, what alone is worthy to bee admird Ador'd & Lov'd.[41]

> Lett mee . . . Consider every thing with a respect to the Excellence & Perfection of Thy Government & Rule.[42]

> [L]ett thy mighty Image in my Mind and right sence of thy Goodness, & of the Excellence of this high advantage thou hast bestow'd, support mee in the Work of making my self a worthy Spectatour of Things so Goodly to Contemplate, and not only a Spectatour, but an Actor such as thou wouldst have mee to bee on this thy Theater.[43]

In his prayer, as in his notebooks in general, Shaftesbury engages in intensely reflective self-work. He meditates on God's goodness to try to inculcate in himself the emotions he takes to be appropriate responses to God's creation.

Shaftesbury's characters in *The Moralists* also voice concern about not feeling the love that belief in a perfect god should produce. They attribute this failing to adherents of "modern DEISM" (C 2.151). True religion "is not dry, and barren; but such Consequences are necessarily drawn from it, as must set us in Action, and find Employment for our strongest Affections" (C 2.152). But while modern deists affirm the existence of a *"supreme* NATURE, an *infinite Being*, and a DEITY," they lack any motivationally efficacious *"Love of* GOD" (C 2.152–153). As a result of their purely intellectual approach, they have in effect "given up Devotion; and in reality had left so little of Zeal, Affection, or Warmth, in what they call their *Rational Religion*, as to make them much suspected of their Sincerity in *any*" (C 2.153). The modern deists' notion of God has no emotional power. Without that, religion is worthless.

Philocles, the narrator of *The Moralists*, expresses similar concerns about himself. Like Shaftesbury in the notebooks, Philocles worries that he's incapable of the elevated, "Mystical Love" perfect theism should inspire (C 2.137). "[T]his *complex universal* sort," he confesses, "was beyond my reach." The other main character of *The Moralists* is Theocles. He is a paragon of Shaftesbury's religious ideal—someone who is emotionally transported by God's creation, a true perfect theist. The core of *The Moralists* is a conversation in which Theocles guides Philocles to the religious heights Theocles already occupies. Before we see how Theocles guides Philocles, let us turn to the other aspect of Shaftesbury's problem: his insistence that religion be entirely rational—his commitment to hold religion to a *"premeditated & stubborn Resolution to give every thing the Lye besides Reason only."*[44]

## *3. Rational Religion: The Second Part of Shaftesbury's Problem*

Shaftesbury's commitment to rationality is clearly evident in the positive arguments he gives for the existence of a perfectly good god. We'll discuss those arguments in section 5. In this section we examine the commitment to rationality in his negative arguments against religion. These negative arguments attack religion based first on self-interest and second on revelation.

To base religion on self-interest is to worship God not because you have rational grounds for believing God is worthy of worship but because you believe it will benefit you. Such worship, Shaftesbury argues, debases both God and yourself. It's "the most beggarly Refuge imaginable" (C 1.23).

Truthfulness is part of goodness. So a perfectly good god—a god worthy of worship—will value truthfulness. To value truthfulness is to endorse all and only those beliefs for which there are rational grounds. As a result, we conduct ourselves in accord with a perfectly good god's values when we believe all and only those things we have rational grounds to believe. We conduct ourselves contrary to the values of a perfectly good god when we affirm things we do not have rational grounds for. The consequence is that it is disrespectful to a good god to assume he would be pleased by worship based on self-interest rather than on what we have good reason to believe.

> When we are afraid to use our Reason freely, even on that very Question, "Whether He [God] really *be*, or *not*"; we then actually presume him *bad*, and flatly contradict that pretended Character of Goodness and Greatness; whilst we discover this Mistrust of his Temper, and fear his Anger and Resentment, in the case of this *Freedom of* INQUIRY. (C 1.21)

Any god that would be pleased by worship of selfish convenience would not be worthy of worship, for such a god would not value the truthfulness that is part of goodness. Only a thoroughly rational approach to religion accords with the values of a god worthy of worship—with the "Excellent Character of the God *of Truth*" (C 1.22).

As an example of self-interested basis for religion, Shaftesbury points to Pascal's Wager. Pascal places his bets on worship of God because he has everything to gain by worshipping, and nothing to lose. If God exists, Pascal thinks he will be better off if he worships than if he doesn't. If God doesn't exist, Pascal thinks he will be no worse off if he worships than if he doesn't. But according to Shaftesbury, to worship God for such self-interested reasons rather than to rationally investigate whether there is a God who is really worthy of worship is to "grow *worse* in our Religion" (C 1.23). It is to entertain a lowly, "injurious" opinion of the Deity (C 1.23). A truly good god would never punish a person for "an impartial Use of his Reason, in any matter of Speculation whatsoever," nor reward a person for "a mean *Denial of his Reason*, and an *Affectation of Belief*" (C 1.22). Shaftesbury compares Pascal to a shameless beggar who tries to manipulate passersby into coughing up alms by addressing every one of them as "My Lord" without any regard to whether or not the passerby is actually titled. The beggar falsely flatters his marks and debases himself. A god worthy of worship would not wish for similar "*Sycophants*" in Religion" (C 1.22). A god worthy of worship would see no merit in "mere *Parasites* of Devotion."

Shaftesbury makes the same point in his discussion of the Book of Job. After Job suffers his hardships, his friends try to persuade him to regain

God's favor by proclaiming God's goodness even though he lacks rational grounds for believing in it. But Job refuses to accede to anything simply because it is in his self-interest. He refuses to accede to anything for which he does not have fully rational grounds. Shaftesbury praises Job's rational steadfastness while condemning his friends' willingness to believe "at the very stretch of their Reason, and sometimes quite beyond it" (C 1.22).

Equally illegitimate is the second non-rational ground of religion: revelation. Shaftesbury's opponents here are those who would base religion on what revelation tells them—not because they grasp the rational cogency of the message but because what has been revealed to them possesses an inherent authority that transcends rational thought. A god worthy of worship, Shaftesbury argues, would see no value in such unreasonable submission. A god worthy of worship would never "assert his Being any other way to Men, than 'By revealing himself to their *Reason*, appealing to their *Judgment*, and submitting his Ways to their *Censure*, and *cool Deliberation*'" (C 2.187–188).

Shaftesbury attacks two kinds of revelation: direct revelation, immediate personal communication from God; and scriptural revelation, the written word of the Bible.

People who claim direct revelation believe God has spoken to them directly. Such people, call them vulgar enthusiasts, believe they've experienced God's voice first-hand. They know what the voice tells them is valid because it comes from God, not the other way around. Shaftesbury doesn't deny that vulgar enthusiasts have had powerful personal experiences. He denies that such experiences constitute justifiable grounds for belief.

We may be infallible authorities on what our experiences are like. But we are not infallible authorities on what has caused us to have those experiences. We can misdiagnose our own symptoms. We can suffer delusions. We can have strong reactions to events we have completely misinterpreted. The power of our responses is no guarantee of the accuracy of our beliefs about their stimuli.

To illustrate the fallibility of our perception of the causes of our own experiences, Shaftesbury tells a story of how Pan and a few fellows succeeded in repelling a troop of armed warriors. Pan waited until the warriors entered a narrow wooded valley amid rocky mountains. He and his company then clamored about "among the echoing Rocks and Caverns" (C 1.10). The resulting noises echoed and reverberated through the gloom, terrifying the warriors, who came to believe that they were surrounded by a massive army of ferocious beasts. Each saw the fear in the face of his comrades, which amplified his own. Terrified, they fled in all directions, in what "in after-times Men call'd *a Panick*" (C 1.10; see also see also 3.53–55).

The warriors really did have a powerful feeling of fear. But the power of their feeling did not make them any less mistaken about its cause. The same could very well be true of those who claim to have received direct revelation from God. No doubt these vulgar enthusiasts have had powerful experiences. But they may be as mistaken about the cause of their experiences as the warriors were about theirs. Rather than personal communication from God, the cause may have been decidedly more mundane. It may have been amazed confusion at "Storms, Earthquakes" or other unusual natural phenomena (C 1.11). It may have been frustration with "publick Calamitys"—amplified by feedback loops into furious hysteria (C 1.11). It may have been "Unwholesomeness of Air or Diet" (C 1.11).[45]

Even if you're not delusional, you still shouldn't base religious belief on perceptions that have not passed rational muster. If you were to climb a mountaintop, espy a shaft of golden light shining through the clouds, hear a thunderous voice booming from on high—if the voice's words were blazoned across the heavens or fired in legible characters unto stone—even then, Shaftesbury argues, you would not be justified in acceding to the message unless you had independent rational grounds for thinking its content "just and true."

> What tho the Sky shou'd suddenly open, and all kinds of Prodigys appear, Voices be heard, or Characters read? What wou'd this evince more than "That there were *certain* POWERS cou'd do all this?" But "*What* POWERS; Whether *One*, or *more*; Whether *Superior*, or *Subaltern*; *Mortal*, or *Immortal*; *Wise*, or *Foolish*; *Just*, or *Unjust*; *Good*, or *Bad*": this wou'd still remain a Mystery; as wou'd the true Intention, the Infallibility or Certainty of whatever *these* POWERS asserted. Their Word cou'd not be taken in their own case. (C 2.188)

The only rational conclusion you could draw from such an occurrence is that there exists a being with the power to produce spectacular events. But the power of such a being is no proof of the justice of its claims.

The upshot is that we have no more reason to believe what is purported to be directly revealed than we have to believe any other set of propositions. The drama of a statement's packaging does nothing to establish the cogency of its content.

The second kind of revelation is scriptural, the revealed word of the Bible. But scriptural revelation cannot legitimately supplant the primacy of reason any more than direct revelation can. Scripture is considered infallible because the individual who first produced the text is taken to have related the word of God as he experienced it through direct revelation.[46] We have just seen Shaftesbury argue against basing religion on direct revelation. But for the sake of argument, let's grant that the first relater did truly have a godly experience. Even so, the words the first relater delivers to us are not God's words. God would have expressed himself in "a Language and Grammar different from any of human Structure ... deliver'd down from Heaven, and miraculously accommodated to human Service and Capacity" (C 3.140). But the first relater has to write in a specific "*human Language*" with "grammatical Rules of human Invention" and arbitrary compositional mechanics (C 3.140). The words of even the very first version of Scripture are the result of translation decisions of a person subject to the same perils of meaning slippage all translators face.

Moreover, almost no one today reads the words of the original relater. People base their religion on a translated text (C 3.145). All the pitfalls of translation are thus compounded, further eroding confidence that what people are reading is an accurate representation of the thoughts of God. There are, as well, multiple translations to choose from. When people base their religion on one translation rather than another, they're putting their faith not in God alone, nor even in the first relater, but in the translation decisions of yet another fallible human.

Then there's the problem of what counts as Scripture. The texts that are now taken to be the sacred word of God are a mere subset of the many documents produced in ancient times. At some point, certain of those documents were designated canonical and others apocryphal. Some were authorized, others controverted, still others declared heretical. These decisions were not made by God. History plainly reveals that they were made by contentious groups of human beings with a full complement of interests, agendas, and grievances (C 3.195–197, 3.201–203).

The texts we have, furthermore, are copies of earlier texts. The centuries of iterated copying introduced even more variations, making it impossible to designate any one version as "the very *Original*, or a *perfectly true Copy*" (C 3.202). There have been "so many thousands of *Copys* that were writ by Persons of several *Interests* and *Persuasions*, such different Understandings and Tempers, such distinct Abilitys and Weaknesses, that 'tis no wonder there is so great *variety of Readings*:—whole Verses in *one*, that are not in *another*:—whole books admitted by *one* Church or Communion, which are rejected by *another*; and whole Storys and Relations admitted by *some* Fathers, and rejected by *others*" (C 3.197). But given that the texts have been passed down to us through "many Channels" and are "subject to so many Variations, of which [we] are wholly ignorant," it is ridiculous to unquestioningly place all our faith in the particular version of Scripture we happen to find in front of us (C 3.145).[47]

Even if there were grounds for complete confidence in the human-worded, human-translated, multiply human-copied text we happen to be using—even then—there's still the problem of interpretation. The Scriptures don't have a single clear and consistent meaning. Everyone acknowledges that they are "*of the most difficult Interpretation*" (C 3.141). Particularly unclear is whether various parts are supposed to be taken literally or figuratively (C 3.197–198). The difference between a literal and a figurative interpretation can have momentous implications. But the interpretation one accepts is once again the result of undivine, human thought.

Most fundamentally, Shaftesbury denies Scriptures are self-justifying. There is in their "Composition or Style nothing miraculous, or self-convincing" (C 3.144). That there is in Scripture the assertion of a proposition is in and of itself no more reason to believe it than there is to believe assertions in any other text. Whether to accede to a proposition in all these cases is a matter for rational judgment—a question of thinking critically about the intrinsic merits of the proposition and how well it fits with other things we know (C 3.140, 3.144–145, 3.193, 3.201).

Shaftesbury's scriptural skepticism stands out clearly when we compare him with other thinkers of his time who were considered religious rationalists. Burnet and Locke, for instance, saw themselves as being in the business of establishing the reasonability of Christianity. Indeed, Burnet and Locke met with intense criticism for giving reason too prominent a religious role. But reasonability in Burnet and Locke is beholden to the claims of Scripture in a manner Shaftesbury explicitly rejects.

For Burnet, it is a given that the events described in the Bible actually happened. His goal in *Sacred Theory of the Earth* is to rationalize Scripture—to show how reason can make sense of what Scripture tells us. We should think things through, by all means, but for Burnet that thinking-through consists of figuring out how to bring our other data into coherence with the fixed points of the Bible. He does not question the accuracy of scriptural history. If the Bible says there was a flood, there was a flood.

Locke may not have shared Burnet's belief in the literal truth of the events described in Genesis. But Locke's approach to the Gospels in *The Reasonableness of Christianity* is similar to Burnet's approach to the flood. Just as Burnet never entertains the question of whether the flood occurred, Locke never entertains the question of whether the Gospel accounts are true and morally perfect. Locke's task is to explain what the Gospel's truth and moral message amount to. Scripture is the fixed anchor from which all Locke's chains of reasoning begin, not a set of propositions that themselves need to answer to reason's demands.

Another example is Benjamin Whichcote. Shaftesbury's first publication, in 1698, was a collection of sermons by Whichcote, which Shaftesbury edited and wrote an effusive introduction to. Whichcote came under strong criticism from the Puritan establishment for his reliance—his perceived overreliance—on reason. "I oppose not rational to spiritual," Whichcote famously said, "for spiritual is most rational."[48] But Whichcote's commitment to rationality wavered in the face of moral claims found in Scripture. Whichcote took to be rationally undeniable the principle of ought-implies-can, according to which persons can legitimately be held accountable for failing to do only those things that they are capable of doing.[49] Whichcote also took Scripture to claim that the only way to achieve salvation is through acceptance of Christ.[50] He acknowledged, however, that people living in ancient times and distant lands had never heard of Christ and so were incapable of accepting Him.[51] There thus seemed to be a contradiction between the scriptural command to accept Christ and the rational principle of ought-implies-can. But Whichcote was unwilling to give up the scriptural command, choosing instead to attempt various convoluted reconciliations, in torturously turgid passages that stand in stark contrast to the plain lucid reasonability of the rest of his work.[52] None of those passages appear in the sermons Shaftesbury chose for his collection.[53]

A fourth example is John Toland, with whom Shaftesbury collaborated in the late 1690s and early 1700s. In his *Christianity not Mysterious* (1696), Toland proclaimed that he would show "That there is nothing in the Gospel Contrary to Reason, Nor Above it: And that no Christian Doctrine can be properly call'd A Mystery." Toland was widely condemned for subordinating religion to rationality. But *Christianity not Mysterious* contains defenses of scriptural claims reason alone would never produce.[54] Toland argues that Abraham's willingness to kill Isaac was justified because Isaac's birth (to Sarah, who was past child-bearing years) was a miracle.[55] The miracle of Isaac's birth warranted Abraham to believe that after the sacrifice, God would perform a second miracle and restore Isaac to life. *Christianity not Mysterious* offers similar defenses of the reasonability of believing in original sin and the resurrection.[56] The book's task is to explain the reasonability of what the Bible says, not to submit what the Bible says to reason's examination.

Shaftesbury eschews such rationalizations of Scripture. At the turn of the eighteenth century, many years before it was common, acceptable, or safe, he insists the Bible's claims be put to the same critical test as any other claim we encounter. As much as any other account, Scripture stands in need of support from "the collateral Testimony of other antient Records, Historians, and foreign Authors" (C 3.144). We should accept what the Bible tells us only to the extent that it fits best with things we learn from other sources.

In his published works Shaftesbury does on a few occasions speak approvingly of the moral message of certain biblical passages (C 1.28, 1.62–63, 3.74–76). But he treats those passages not as uniquely holy texts but as examples of morally perspicuous literature, of which he gives a great many more non-scriptural examples. Shaftesbury also points out that many of the actions the Bible attributes to its heroes are morally extremely problematic. He refers to Joshua's killing of the Canaanites, to Moses's advice to borrow gold and silver from the Egyptians just before fleeing, and to David's various misdeeds (C 1.220). No mortal author could morally reconcile us to such actions. Only a divinely inspired text, Shaftesbury says with razor-sharp irony, would be able to represent such actions as heroic and worthy of emulation.[57]

Biblical references are also conspicuously absent from Shaftesbury's private notebooks. He used those notebooks to explore what kind of person he wanted to be. This thinking of Shaftesbury's was inextricably bound up with his reading. He refers to other texts on almost every page. There are hundreds of quotations from Epictetus. Marcus Aurelius, Horace, Socrates, and Plato appear dozens of times each. But over many years of extensive writing of his most personal thoughts, Shaftesbury makes (so far as I can tell) only two references to the Bible, and both of those are to passages in Ecclesiastes to which he gives secular interpretations.[58] When he was doing his most personal thinking, Shaftesbury hardly ever had a Bible on his desk or on his mind.

It is reported that Alexander Pope said that "to his knowledge the *Characteristics* had done more harm to revealed religion in England than all the works of infidelity put together."[59] Pope definitely had a point.[60]

## 4. Beauty in General: The First Part of Shaftesbury's Solution

Shaftesbury wishes to be transported by love for God. But he is determined to remain entirely rational. How does he do it? How does he develop a worshipful attitude that is both rational and emotional?

This is where nature comes in. Shaftesbury reconciles the requirements of emotion and rationality by cultivating an attitude toward nature that is the polar opposite of what we saw in Burnet and Locke. The key is his concept of beauty. We'll look at that concept in general in this section. In the next section we'll see how Shaftesbury applies it to the natural world.

To be beautiful, according to Shaftesbury, is to possess "Unity of Design" (C 1.89). A beautiful thing is beautiful because all its parts "concur *in one*" (C 2.161), because it has the "Character of *Unity*" (C 3.229), because it is "*a Single Piece*" (C 3.214). A beautiful thing "constitutes a *real* WHOLE, by a mutual and necessary Relation of its Parts" (C 3.214). It is "a *Whole*, coherent and proportion'd in it-self" (C 1.129).[61]

Shaftesbury uses numerous words to refer to the property that all beautiful things possess: unity, harmony, regularity, proportion, order, symmetry, balance. He also uses *intire*, as when he says that beautiful entities "are, in themselves, *intire Systems*" and that a beautiful entity is "*One Intire Thing*" (C 2.161 and C 2.195). This is the adjectival form of "integrity," a word we generally use to get across the idea that people are internally consistent, in complete accord with themselves. Shaftesbury thinks that to be beautiful is to have this quality. Every part of a beautiful thing agrees with all the rest. All its elements work together to form a singularly perfect system.

Many different kinds of things can have this property. Music, painting, and poetry can have it. A well-proportioned building can as well. So can a piece of quality workmanship, such as a barrel or a wagon or a timepiece. Any of these can be beautiful because any of them can possess unity of design. In this, Shaftesbury's concept of beauty does not track our contemporary notions of aesthetic merit. A workaday object to which we might not think to give aesthetic consideration may possess the unity of design Shaftesbury identifies as beauty. A wildly original and provocative performance we judge artistically worthy may lack it.

Shaftesbury thinks we are naturally constituted to have an affectively positive response to beauty. We are "imprinted" with a "plain internal Sensation" in favor of it (C 2.161). For unity of design we have an instinctive "*Liking*" or "taste" (C 2.24–25). Imagine you hear a jumble of discordant notes. Then they come together to form the "truest harmony" (C 1.208). That moment will be an emotionally pleasant experience. You'll feel an "original Satisfaction," a "natural Joy" (C 2.60). Or imagine you come across a drawing of 350 degrees of a perfect circle. There are an infinite number of ways of connecting the two ends. They can be connected by a jagged lightning bolt. By a loop-de-loop swirl. By a random squiggle that travels the margins of the page, or even off the page and onto the table, before connecting up. But the perfectly curved completion of the circle will give you a feeling of satisfaction those other connections will not. The completion of the circle, and only that, will feel right.

For some types of beauty, we feel love at first sight. For other types, love grows out of thoughtful consideration. We experience love at first sight when we encounter *"simple* Beautys" (C 2.231). As examples Shaftesbury cites "the simplest of figures, as either a round *Ball*, a *Cube* or *Dye*." The beauty of such things "is immediately perceiv'd" (C 2.161). "[E]ven an Infant [is] pleas'd with the first View" of them (C 2.231). Recognition of their proportionality is instantaneous. "No sooner the Eye opens upon *Figures*, the Ear to *Sounds*, than straight *the Beautiful* results, and *Grace* and *Harmony* are known and acknowledg'd" (C 2.231).

For *"complicated Beautys*," in contrast, love develops as a result of rational examination (C 2.231; see also 1.209–210). The "true beauty and worth" of a thing is its fundamental structure, the harmony and order of all its parts (C 3.101). When an object is complex, an understanding of that structure may require plenty of "the antecedent *Labour* and *Pains*" of *"Examination* and *Search"* (C 2.224, C 3.102). Consider the beauty of *"Mathematicks."* Someone who understands mathematical principles feels "Admiration, Joy, or Love" for their *"Harmony, Proportion*, and *Concord"* (C 2.60). Such a person "receives a Pleasure and Delight" from the "Proportion, Order, and Symmetry" of mathematical discoveries. But this pleasure depends on mathematical understanding acquired by "progress in Science or Learning." The mathematician's delight grows out of "the exercise of his Mind." Or consider the movement of a sophisticated timepiece. Discerning how the parts—cogs, mainspring, balance wheel, escapement—slot perfectly into place, how they all combine to form a single, perfectly harmonious machine, is deeply satisfying, delightful, a joy. But the beauty of the mechanism is not "immediately perceived." An infant wouldn't see it, nor would the ignorant, nor the inattentive. It's a beauty you experience because of how the thing works. Your experience of this beauty is inextricably linked to your understanding of it.

This cognitive component of beauty underlies Shaftesbury's defense of art criticism. Some may think that first responses to works of art are the purest, that criticism is at odds with genuine aesthetic engagement, that to dissect is to kill. Shaftesbury rejects that thought. He contends that taste can and should be refined, and that such refinement grows out of well-informed criticism (C 3.101). Fully appreciating complex beauty involves moving beyond "those *regular Figures* and *Symmetrys* with which Children are delighted; and proceeding gradually to [more complex] Proportions" (C 3.112). It is a *"false Relish*, which is govern'd rather by what immediately strikes the Sense, than by what consequentially and by reflection pleases the Mind, and satisfies the Thought and Reason" (C 3.239). To appreciate complex beauty, a person first has to do the mental work of bringing "Truth and Nature to his *Humour*" (C 3.103). Love at first sight is nice enough, but only the superficial think it's the highest kind of love there is.[62]

Appreciation of architecture epitomizes the cognitive character of Shaftesbury's view of the experience of beauty (see C 3.112). There's an obvious way architectural beauty is not immediately perceivable: you can't see every facet of a building all at once.[63] More important, the architect's art consists of countless decisions that viewers will appreciate only if they possess some knowledge and understanding. Consider someone who on her way to work every day passes something that registers with her as nothing more than a black box office building. Then she joins an out-of-town friend on an architectural tour that includes the black box. The guide explains how the architect used new materials to create open spaces that before had been impossible in structures of that height. How the building's skin both reflects sunshine and emits interior lighting. How the exposed floor lines balance the building's verticality. How the spacing of the window struts echoes the rhythm of the I-beams. How the recessed and transparent ground-floor walls create the appearance of the building's being lifted skyward. And the person gets it. She grasps the elegance of the design. When she passes by the building now, she sees a perfectly proportioned structure that glows and floats. An entity that exudes light and lightness. Through her cognitive accomplishment she now experiences the building as beautiful.

Her new response to the building is emotional, but it's also rational. It flows from reflection and understanding, informed by the facts she learned from the tour guide. Her new response is more objective than her old response in the sense of being responsive to more of the real features of the object—in the sense of being more responsive to the object's real features.

Her new response to the building is rational, but it's also emotional. When she looks at the building now, she has an affectively positive reaction that she did not have before. The vision for her now is stirring. She does not merely notice new aspects. She feels a new joy.

## 5. Beauty of Nature: The Second Part of Shaftesbury's Solution

In *The Moralists*, Shaftesbury tries to make us see and feel the beauty of nature as a whole.

On the first of the two days that constitute the narrative of *The Moralists*, Philocles, Theocles, and two other guests take a stroll in the cultivated fields outside Theocles's manor. The other guests note the appearance of the plants. This spurs Philocles, who is an expert in biology, to expound on how each thing works. Having acquired "Insight into the nature of Simples," Philocles is able to explain the unity of design of each organism, how its various parts fit together to form a single harmoniously functioning unit (C 2.159). The two guests "mightily" approve Philocles's explanations. They appreciate the structure of the plants as a result of learning what Philocles teaches them.

But Theocles urges Philocles to go beyond knowledgeable appreciation of particular plants to something grander. What is of ultimate importance, according to Theocles, is appreciation of the "Order, Union, and Coherence of *the Whole*" (C 2.162). His "main Subject, insisted on" is that there is a beautiful harmony to all of nature. While Philocles has an astute understanding of "*Simples*," Theocles wants him to expand his focus to encompass the organization of nature as a whole.

> "O my ingenious Friend!" said he, "whose Reason, in other respects, must be allow'd so clear and happy; How is it possible that with such Insight, and accurate Judgment in *the Particulars* of natural Beings and Operations, you shou'd no better judg of the Structure of Things *in general*, and of the Order and Frame of NATURE? Who better than your-self can shew the Structure of each Plant and Animal-Body, declare the Office of every *Part* and *Organ*, and tell the Uses, Ends, and Advantages to which they serve? How therefore, shou'd you prove so ill *a Naturalist* in *this* WHOLE, and understand so little the Anatomy of *the World* and *Nature*, as not to discern the same Relation of Parts, the same Consistency and Uniformity in *the Universe!*" (C 2.159–160)

Philocles discerns order within all the "innumerable Parts of the Creation." He understands how the different elements of each thing are "united, and conspir[e] fitly within themselves." But he appreciates "neither Union nor Coherence" in "the Whole it-self." Philocles sees "the Correspondency or Union of each *part* of Nature" but has to learn to see "*intire* Nature *herself*." Philocles is missing the forest for the trees.

A key word for expressing what Theocles wants Philocles to see, a word Shaftesbury adverts to time and time again, is "system." Careful study of the natural world shows that small systems function as parts of bigger systems, that bigger systems function as parts of still bigger systems, that those bigger systems function as parts of even bigger systems, and so on. Study of the natural world eventually reveals that all these embedded systems function as parts of one entire system, a system of all things. As Theocles says in a passage with the marginal heading "System of the World," "All things in this World are *united*" (C 2.162). Consider the different parts of a leaf. See the beauty of how the entire thing works as a unit. The leaf, though, is just one part of the tree, which is a more complex yet no less systematic unit. Equally systematic but of even greater complexity is the system comprising the tree and the animals who feed on it and disperse its seeds. And so on, until we eventually realize that there is a "Universal System" (C 2.162). When we examine carefully, we see that everything is "fitted and join'd" together, each contributing to the "Order, Union, and Coherence of *the Whole*" (see also C 2.10–12).

Philocles hears what Theocles is saying. He understands that he's supposed to appreciate the systematic whole. But he doesn't think he's capable of such a "Mystical Love" (C 2.137). Shaftesbury had berated himself for the same failing. Theocles takes on the challenge of enabling Philocles to overcome his emotional limitation. He makes a deal with Philocles: meet me at sunrise tomorrow morning, walk with me through nature, and I will do my best to evoke in you love for the world as a whole. "I will endeavour to shew you," he says, "*that* Beauty which I count *the perfectest*, and *most deserving of* Love . . . [I]f you are content to wander with me in the Woods you see, we will pursue those *Loves* of ours, by favour of the Silvan Nymphs: and invoking first the *Genius of the Place*, we'll try to obtain at least some faint and distant View of *the sovereign Genius* and *first Beauty*" (C 2.138). Philocles agrees to the plan. The rest of the first day they spend in and near the house with the other visitors, speaking of matters more suitable to "Company." Then, just before dawn on the second day, Philocles wakes, rises quickly, and races to catch up with Theocles, who has already left the house. They meet "on the most beautiful part of the Hill" just as the sun "draws off the Curtain of Night, and shews us the open Scene of Nature in the plains below" (C 2.193).

Theocles is happy to have escaped his other guests and gotten out into nature. The "Fields and Woods," he says, are a welcome "Refuge from the toilsome World of Business," a "Retreat" for the contemplative soul who wishes to contemplate the "Cause of Things" (C 2.193). Theocles then launches into his attempt to evoke in Philocles theistic love.

Theocles begins with an examination of an oak tree. An oak tree, both characters unquestioningly assume, remains a single thing throughout its life. It has an identity. That identity cannot consist of the tree's outward form, for other things—such as "a Figure of Wax . . . cast in the exact

Shape and Colours of this Tree"—could have the same outward form and yet not be an oak tree (C 2.195). Nor can it consist of the physical stuff of which the oak tree is made, as the tree will remain "*One and the same*; even when by Vegetation and change of Substance, not one Particle in it remains *the same*" (C 2.196). What the tree's identity must consist of, rather, is the "Concurrence" of all its individual pieces "*in one common End*," the enduring organizational principle of which its different elements partake, the "*Sympathizing of* [its] *Parts*."

The same reasoning applies to the identity of a person. A person is a single thing, retaining an identity throughout the years. But that identity cannot consist of physical matter, as every particle of a person changes over time. The "*Stuff*... of which we are compos'd," says Theocles, "wears out in seven, or, at the longest, in twice seven Years, [as] the meanest Anatomist can tell us. Now where, I beseech you, will that same *One* be found at last, supposing it to lie in the *Stuff* it-self, or any part of it? For when that is wholly spent, and not one Particle of it left, we are *Our-selves* still as much as before" (C 2.196). Nor can a person's identity be based on any idea or emotion, as all of a person's ideas and emotions change as well. There's no single mental item that has the constant existence that would be needed to fund a person's identity. So since a person remains "*one and the* same, when neither *one* Atom of Body, *one* Passion, nor *one* Thought remains the same," his identity must be based on "a Sympathy of Parts." His identity must consist of an overall organization, of a "simple Principle" of which all the person's different aspects partake (C 2.197).

Theocles next sets out to show that the natural world as a whole is just as organized as a tree, and considerably more organized than most people. If Theocles can convince Philocles of that—if he can establish that there is "*a uniting Principle* in Nature" that brings all its aspects into "*Harmony* and *Order*"—then Philocles will have to embrace the idea that nature has an identity that is as robust as that of an oak tree, a "*Self*" that is no less real (even more real, actually) than Philocles's own (C 2.200–201).[64]

The case Theocles makes for the organization of nature is observational. He points to the "mutual Dependency" found at both the micro and macro levels of plant and animal biology (C 2.162). He explains the coordinating purposes of light, wind, water, fire, the harmonious movement of planets, stars, sun, moon (C 2.162–163 and C 2.207–209). He has us consider the continents. At the Poles we see the environmental benefits of extreme cold and snow (C 2.214–215). In India we witness the symbiosis between "Land-Creatures" and the Indus River (C 2.215). We come to understand the usefulness to myriad species of the flooding of the Nile, of the topology of the Himalayas, of the "Gums and Balsams" of Australia.

This systematic order of the natural world is the basis of Shaftesbury's argument for the existence of God. A classic version of the argument from design, the argument has three parts. The first is the set of empirical observations that establish the world's extensive order.

The second is the claim that there are only two possible explanations for the world's extensive order: random accident, or intelligent designing mind. So far as I can tell, Shaftesbury assumes this without argument. He takes it to be obvious that these are the only two choices. Writing at the turn of the eighteenth century, he doesn't betray any inkling of the possibility of the mindless but non-random processes that Darwin would later use to explain the organization of animals, plants, and ecosystems.

The third part of his argument from design is an inference to best explanation. The natural world manifests astounding systematicity. That an intelligent mind designed that system is a better explanation than that it arose randomly, by accident.

> Now having recogniz'd this uniform consistent Fabrick, and own'd the *Universal System*, we must of consequence acknowledg a *Universal* Mind ... For can it be suppos'd of any-one in the World, that being in some Desart far from Men, and hearing there a perfect Symphony of Musick, or seeing an exact Pile of regular Architecture arising gradually from the Earth in all its Orders and Proportions, he shou'd be persuaded that at the bottom there was no *Design* accompanying this, no secret Spring of *Thought*, no active *Mind*? Wou'd he, because he saw no Hand, deny the Handy-Work, and suppose that each of these compleat and perfect Systems were fram'd, and thus united in just Symmetry, and conspiring Order, either by the accidental blowing of the Winds, or rolling of the Sands? (C 2.164)

We would expect randomness to produce a "distracted Universe" (C 2.121). If everything originated in mindless accident, there would be "no Coherence in the World," "No Order, no Proportion," no evidence of a general "Project or Design." But observation reveals the natural world to be exactly the opposite—"a System compleat," all its components fitted to wondrously coherent design. The natural world bears the marks we would expect in the handiwork of a "supreme Intelligence."[65]

Shaftesbury presents this as a thoroughly rational conclusion. We thus see Theocles surveying the "Universal System" "from the minutest Ranks and Orders of Beings to the remotest Spheres" and then concluding that belief in God is "establish'd on abundant Proof, capable of convincing any fair and just Contemplator of the Works of Nature" (C 2.162). Shaftesbury intends to establish belief in God on a "rational and just Foundation."

Shaftesbury's argument from design relies on the findings of geology, botany, and biology.[66] He points to the minute phenomena revealed by the "mechanick Art" of microscopes (C 2.206), to the vast phenomena revealed by the "new philosophical Scene" of astronomy (C 2.196), and to all the different kinds of phenomena in between. "[T]o Minds, like yours, enrich'd with Sciences and Learning," says Theocles to Philocles, the "Order and Perfection" of everything in heaven and earth will become apparent (C 2.164). Theocles again: "The Contemplation of the Universe, its Laws and Government was, I aver'd, the only means which cou'd establish the *sound Belief* of a DEITY" (C 2.188). Just as one needs artistic knowledge of "*shades* and *masterly Strokes*" to judge accurately the beauty of paintings, so too one needs "Study, Science, or Learning" in order to judge the true beauty of nature (C 2.224). Shaftesbury disdains analytic exercises that do nothing to improve conduct or character, and he believes many thinkers of his day had become so enamored of their narrow empirical investigations that they forgot that the search for wisdom should be of the highest importance (C 1.127–180, 2.205). But he is no enemy of a rational understanding of nature, no enemy of science.[67]

His rational approach leads Shaftesbury to reject miracles. Many base their religious confidence on the occurrence of miracles. Shaftesbury, however, argues not merely that miracles are unnecessary for belief in a perfectly good god but that they are actually incompatible with such belief.

Here's how his anti-miracles argument goes. We can conclude the designer of the world is perfectly good when we see that the result of his design is perfectly "regular and orderly," when it runs entirely by "just and uniform" laws (C 2.188–190). But a miracle, by definition, is a violation of regular and orderly uniform laws. A miracle is "Breach of Laws, Variation and Unsteddiness of Order," a "mangling and disfigurement of *Nature*," "Irregularity and Discord," manifestation not of a "just and uniform" will but rather of "Caprice" (C 2.189–190). Far from proving the existence of a perfectly good god, the occurrence of miracles would imply that the universe is the result of imperfect creation, or chaos. As Philocles says to a miracle-touting character,

> For whilst you are labouring to unhinge Nature; whilst you are searching Heaven and Earth for Prodigys, and studying how to *miraculize* every thing; you bring Confusion on the World, you break its

Uniformity, and destroy that admirable Simplicity of Order, from whence the ONE infinite and perfect Principle is known. (C 2.189)

A master craftsman will design a machine that fulfills its purpose smoothly on its own, without the need for ad hoc alterations. It is a poor craftsman whose mechanism relies for its operation on jury-rigged, one-off interventions. But the occurrence of miracles would imply that the creator of our world is like the poor craftsman. Those who think belief in God requires miracles have things exactly backward. They contend, illogically, that atheism follows from realization of the world's "Harmony, Order, Concord," while theism follows from "Irregularity & Discord."[68] As Shaftesbury sardonically puts it, "The World is *Accident*, if it proceed in Course: but *Wisdome*, if it run Mad."[69]

Shaftesbury's commitment to rational understanding of nature and his resultant rejection of miracles is more thorough than that of other writers of his day with reputations for a rational approach to religion.[70]

Toland says some things in *Christianity not Mysterious* that on their own may suggest a rejection of miracles. He condemns the irrational reliance on miracles of "the *Papists*, the *Jews*, the *Bramins*, the *Mahometans*." He ridicules the silly credulousness of those who believe that "*Christ* was born without opening any Passage out of the *Virgin's* Body" or "that a Head spoke some Days after it was sever'd from the Body, and the tongue cut out."[71] It turns out, however, that Toland's objection is not that such people believe in miracles per se. The problem is that they believe in too many miracles, that a miracle can happen for too trivial a reason. "God is not so prodigal of *Miracles*" that he will deal them out them willy-nilly.[72] God only plays the miracle card when it's really important.

> The Order of Nature is not alter'd, stopp'd or forwarded unless for some weighty Design becoming the Divine Wisdom and Majesty. And, indeed, we learn from *Scripture* and *Reason*, that no *Miracle* is ever wrought without some special and important End.[73]

As we've seen, *Christianity not Mysterious* contends that the birth of Isaac was a miracle. It asserts that the curing of "the blind, the deaf, the lame, the diseas'd" by Jesus and the disciples was miraculous as well.[74]

Locke also argues that God doesn't work by miracles—unless it's really important. God can miraculously violate the laws of nature whenever he wants. But miracles are precious. Better to save them up for special occasions.

> For though it be as easie to Omnipotent Power to do all things by an immediate over-ruling Will; and so to make any Instruments work, even contrary to their Nature, in subserviency to his ends; Yet his Wisdom is not usually at the expence of Miracles (if I may so say) but only in cases that require them, for the evidencing of some Revelation or Mission to be from him. He does constantly (unless where the confirmation of some Truth requires it otherwise) bring about his purposes by means operating according to their Natures.[75]

If God were to perform too many of them, "Miracles would lose their name and force."[76] The rarity of miracles ensures that God will get the most bang for the buck for each one. Some examples Locke cites: Moses's staff becoming a snake and devouring the staff-snakes of the Pharaoh's magicians; Jesus's walking on water and feeding the five thousand; the disciples' curing the deaf, dumb, and blind. God's purpose in all these cases was to convince observers of the credentials of his messengers. The miracles were unassailable marks of authority, the seal God set on what Moses, Jesus, and the disciples had to say.

Ralph Cudworth, another one of Shaftesbury's predecessors who endorsed rational religion, argued that God executed His providence through "the Regular and Orderly Motion of Matter."[77] Cudworth was especially well-known for his idea of a "*Plastick Nature*," which explained phenomena that could not be accounted for by the movement of dumb matter or the conduct of conscious beings.[78] These ideas of Cudworth's helped lay the groundwork for the development of the modern view of scientific laws. Cudworth maintained, however, that "there is also besides this [i.e., besides the regular and orderly operations of plastic nature], a Higher Providence to be acknowledged, which presiding over it, doth often supply the Defects of it, and sometimes Overrule it."[79] The providential overruling of the regularly and orderly operations is the occurrence of miracles, which are sometimes necessary for God to achieve purposes the laws of nature cannot.[80]

Shaftesbury, in contrast, gives no quarter. He denies categorically that a truly good god would design a world in which the laws of regular and orderly motion would ever need to be circumvented. The design of a truly good god would be regular and orderly through and through. A truly good god would create a world that has all and only the beauty that science can reveal.[81]

Shaftesbury's uncompromising rationalism is also evident in his answer to an objection to his argument for a perfect creator of nature.

The objection is that certain natural occurrences don't make sense to us. We can see the logic of some of what goes on in nature, but we can't see it all. Some natural occurrences appear stubbornly mysterious, pointless, random. The conclusion that nature has been designed by a perfectly harmonious and ordered mind is supposed to be based on the harmony and order of the observable phenomena. But if we cannot discern harmony and order in some of those phenomena, it looks as though we are unwarranted in attributing them to a perfectly harmonious and ordered mind after all.

In response, Shaftesbury does not deny that some natural phenomena appear to us to be disorderly and inharmonious. He claims, however, that it's more rational to conclude that the recalcitrant phenomena are part of a harmony and order we have not yet discerned than that they are random or ill-designed (C 2.163–165, C 2.203–204). He argues for this claim by pointing to the perception a person entirely "ignorant of the Nature of the Sea or Waters" would have of a large sailing vessel anchored on a perfectly calm day (C 2.163–164; see also 2.203). If the person were on board and examined all the rooms below, he would appreciate how many different parts of the ship work together to perform complex functions. But because the ship would be still, he would not be able to see the purpose of the sails above. Nonetheless, it would be unwarranted for him to "pronounce the Masts and Cordage to be useless and cumbersom, and for this reason condemn the Frame, and despise *the Architect*." For since there are so many parts of the machine that he realizes work so well, the most rational conclusion for him to draw is that the sails are also well-designed, even if he is at the moment unable to see what that design is. Now compare this view of the ship to our perception of the world. There have been numerous features of the world whose purpose we have not initially understood. As a result of careful observation and scientific study, however, we have come to see that they do indeed serve a purpose. We have achieved the realization that what had initially seemed random or ill-designed in actuality perfectly fills a role in the system of which it is a part. But since we have had so many of these experiences in the past—of initially not understanding the purpose of a thing, and of then coming to realize that it does indeed serve a purpose—the rational conclusion to draw is that those things we do not now understand also fill a systematic role.

Imagine you are acquainted with someone brilliant. In the past she has done things you initially did not understand the rationale for. But you eventually came to see that those things were perfectly planned and executed. You now realize that they were exactly the right things to do, even though you hadn't been able to see it at the time. Now imagine that this person does something that you do not understand the rationale for. Your past experience gives you reasonable grounds for trusting that in fact she has full justification for what she is doing—that her actions really are part of a systematic plan, even if you currently cannot see the reasons for them. Our relationship to the natural world, according to Shaftesbury, is the same as your relationship to the plans of the brilliant person. We have had many experiences in the past of encountering natural phenomena we initially did not understand and then coming to see their role in the overall system. We have come to realize that the systematic workings of nature are more sophisticated than what we ourselves could have designed. It is thus reasonable to conclude that things we don't currently understand do indeed serve a purpose. The very brilliant person's track record gives you rational grounds to infer that even if you can't see the point of an action of hers right now, it does indeed have a point. Just so, nature's track record gives us rational grounds to infer that its occurrences follow a deep order even if we can't discern that order at the moment. This is a rational argument for concluding there's an underlying reason even for those things we can't see the reason for.

Some recent commentators have claimed that Shaftesbury believes religion outstretches rationality. According to Patrick Müller, Shaftesbury believes that rational thought alone cannot get us all the way to belief in a perfect God: "In contemplating the beauty of nature, fancy transcends the limits of the human mind . . . Theocles' sublime meditations do not attempt to produce logically sound arguments; they are allegorical verbal paintings of the deity's creation. The order of the divine cosmos, its inherent goodness [and] its '*Mysterious* Beauty' cannot be rationally *understood* by human beings."[82] As Müller sees it, belief in a perfect God is actually "anti-rational."[83] John McAteer says that Shaftesbury believes in "a kind of mystical vision of the natural world, a vision of things 'too wonderful' for human beings to understand,"[84] and that Shaftesbury believes it is "in vain" to "seek to rationally understand the basic principles of nature."[85] Yu Liu contends that Shaftesbury wants "to free himself from his own rational control or to lose himself in his admiration," and that as a result Shaftesburean beauty "is certainly not predicated" on "the ideas of order and regularity."[86]

Müller, McAteer, and Liu are mistaken to suggest that Shaftesbury bases his religion on anti-rational grounds. Shaftesbury's religion is based on the experience of the beauty of nature, and for Shaftesbury our experience of the beauty of a complex entity is downstream of our understanding of the entity's unity. It's true that Shaftesbury thought there are particular natural phenomena whose purpose we cannot understand. But Shaftesbury thought he had a rational argument for the conclusion that nature as a whole is beautiful nonetheless: we have observed enough things in nature that do make sense that it is rational to assume that there is a sensible purpose for even those particular processes we do not (yet) understand.

But Müller, McAteer, and Liu are right to stress the emotionally positive character of Shaftesbury's appreciation of the beauty of nature. Like the person who learned about the architecture of the black box building, Philocles does not merely come to a new understanding. He also develops a new love. Theocles's account of the world's unity produces in Philocles an experience of joy, not just an exercise of understanding. Says Philocles: "'Tis true, said I, (Theocles!) I own it. Your *Genius*, the *Genius* of the Place, and the GREAT GENIUS have at last prevail'd. I shall no longer resist the Passion growing in me for things of a *natural* kind" (C 2.220).[87] Philocles's positive emotional response is downstream of his rational understanding of the order of nature—just as a mathematician's delight in an elegant proof and a mechanic's satisfaction in an ingenious machine depend on their expert understanding. Philocles's response to nature is "cognitively rich"—inextricably linked to his understanding of the object.[88] But it's a truly emotional response nonetheless.

For Shaftesbury, knowledge of the natural world is an essential component of the proper identification and appreciation of the beauty of God's creation. The importance of such knowledge for appreciation of the world's beauty is something Philocles learns. He used to be like the many who form their judgments "freely on the first view" (C 2.225). But he now realizes that he must understand objects if he is to grasp their true beauty. Pretty-as-a-picture scenic views are "slight superficial Beautys." Their charms are "very shallow," they sit "upon the Surface." By acquiring scientific knowledge, Philocles comes to see a deeper beauty. Theocles compares this appreciation of the beauty of nature to the sophisticated responses of expert art critics.

> What difficulty to be in any degree knowing! How long ere a true *Taste* is gain'd! How many things shocking, how many offensive at first, which afterwards are known and acknowledg'd the highest *Beautys*! For 'tis not instantly we acquire the *Sense* by which these Beautys are discoverable. *Labour* and *Pains* are requir'd, and *Time* to cultivate a natural Genius. . . . In Painting there are *Shades* and *masterly Strokes*,

which the Vulgar understand not, but find fault with; in Architecture there is *the Rustick*; in Musick *the Chromatick* kind, and skillful Mixture of *Dissonancys*. And is there nothing which answer to this, in THE WHOLE? (C 2.224)

Training in the arts will uncover for us beauty in objects to which we previously gave no regard. Scientific learning is even more necessary for understanding the full extent of the "*Master-pieces* in NATURE."

Shaftesbury's rationally anchored conception of nature's beauty leads him to value exactly those things Burnet and Locke denigrated.[89] Theocles imaginatively transports Philocles to "the darkest and most imperfect Parts of our Map" (C 2.214), to places that initially appear "ghastly and hideous" (C 2.217). They scale massive, jagged mountains that fill them with "giddy Horror" (C 2.217). They tremble in the "faint and gloomy Light" of a deep forest of "lofty Pines" and "falling Trees which hang with their Roots upwards" (C 2.217–218). They consider "particular Animals [that] are deform'd even in their first Conception, when the Disease invades the Seats of Generation, and seminal Parts are injur'd and obstructed in their accurate Labours." And Theocles convinces Philocles that even these "seeming Blemishes cast upon Nature" are in fact part of its comprehensive beauty (C 2.123). "Things seemingly deform'd are amiable; Disorder becomes regular; Corruption wholesom; and Poisons (such as these we have seen) prove healing and beneficial" (C 2.217). "The Wildness pleases," says Theocles when considering "the scaly Serpents, the savage Beasts, and poisonous Insects" of the desert (C 2.217). Though these animals are in a sense "terrible" and "contrary to human Nature"—though they do not serve any Lockean human purposes—they "are beauteous in themselves" (C 2.217). The world's beauty includes things that look deformed and seem wasteful before we understand them. Once we come to "view [Nature] in her inmost Recesses," we will contemplate everything with "Delight" (C 2.217; see also 2.220 and 2.224–225).[90]

Shaftesbury's high estimation of nature's beauty is evident in his disdain for those who praise landscapes by saying that they're as pretty as a painting. "Ridiculouse!" he scoffs. That phrase gets things exactly backward. Rather, "when a real good Picture is to be commended; say of it, '*This is like perfect Nature & not like Paint.*'"[91]

Because the beauty of wild places is so exquisitely complex, human interference diminishes it. Theocles is a "bitter Enemy" of the environmental degradation mining causes (C 2.219). Of those who rifle the earth for precious minerals he says, "Not satisfy'd to turn and manure for their

Use the wholesom and beneficial Mould of this their EARTH, they dig yet deeper, and seeking out imaginary Wealth, they search its very Entrails" (C 2.210–211). Nor is it only such gross destruction of nature that Shaftesbury's characters contemn. They think that turning a wild place into a garden is also a falling away.[92]

Given *The Moralists*' identification of beauty with symmetry, proportion, and order, we might expect to find there a fondness for formal gardens: perfectly ordered plans of perfectly regular lawns, perfectly formed borders, and perfectly straight paths.[93] But Philocles and Theocles prefer "original Wilds" (C 2.217). Says Philocles,

> I shall no longer resist the Passion growing in me for Things of a *natural* kind; where neither *Art*, nor the *Conceit* or *Caprice* of Man has spoil'd their *genuine Order*, by breaking in upon that *primitive State*. Even the rude *Rocks*, the mossy *Caverns*, the irregular unwrought *Grotto's*, and broken *Falls* of Waters, with all the horrid Graces of the *Wilderness* it-self, as representing NATURE more, will be the more engaging, and appear with a Magnificence beyond the formal Mockery of princely Gardens. (C 2.220)

In comparison to the immense intricacies of any natural ecosystem, the surface symmetries of a formal garden are piffling, its man-made ordering a beauty merely skin deep. The "primitive State" has a "genuine Order" whose beauty no human plan can match (C 2.220).[94]

Formal gardens, as well, are static. The kind of beauty they possess can be captured in a single moment. The order of a wild place, in contrast, is temporally extended, the continuous unfolding of lawful processes. Theocles: "The temporary Beings quit their borrow'd Forms, and yield their elementary Substance to New-Comers. Call'd, in their several turns, to Life, they view the Light, and viewing pass; that others too may be Spectators of the goodly Scene, and greater numbers still enjoy the Privilege of NATURE" (C 2.205). The surface appearances of wild places constantly change. Yet those changes are determined by "sacred and inviolable *Laws*." The beauty of wild places consists of the elegance and lawfulness with which those changes occur.

As an example of this beautiful order-in-change, Theocles points to waste and corruption. "New Forms arise: and when the old dissolve, the Matter whence they were compos'd is not left useless, but wrought with equal Management and Art, even in *Corruption*, Nature's seeming Waste, and vile Abhorrence. The abject State appears merely as *the Way* or *Passage* to some better. But cou'd we nearly view it, and with Indifference, remote from the Antipathy of Sense; we then perhaps shou'd highest raise our Admiration: convinc'd that even *the Way it-self* was equal to the *End*" (C 2.205–206).

Our senses of sight, smell, and touch can produce in us an antipathy to waste and corruption. It can seem disgusting. But on learning the role these processes play in the larger natural systems—through an understanding of the science of it all—we come to appreciate the sublime organization of what had initially struck us as a "vile Abhorrence." We come to see that these too are among the "masterpieces in nature." To make his case for the beauty of nature, Theocles here points to neither a formal garden nor a landscape idyll nor any scene we'd typically feature as aesthetically pleasing. He directs us instead to the logic of decay.

Shaftesbury himself was a keen observer of the beauty of waste. His involvement in the management of his estate's farmland led him to make a careful study of the varying benefits of different kinds of manure. In a 1707 letter Shaftesbury articulated his fine-grained views on the subject, discoursing on the relative merits of ox dung, cow dung, sheep dung, the dung of different kinds of fowl, the dung of wild animals versus domesticated ones, and the dung of a mule versus the dung of each of its parents. At the end of what Voitle aptly calls a "two-thousand-word essay on manure," Shaftesbury described the worshipful attitude such farming experience can awaken.[95]

> Mean while I have this inexpressible Satisfaction in these sort of speculations; that with their help in this Country-Retirement I can converse more intimately with Nature; view the greatness of her Design and Execution, & in the simplicity and Uniformity of her operations descry that soveraign hand that guides & governs all, with infinite Wisdom and Bounty; so that a student of this sort can never fail not only to believe; but to be (if I may say so) even conscious of a God, & witness to his Divine Economy.[96]

As a result of careful study and investigation, Shaftesbury came to see in excrement the beauty of God (see also C 2.210–211).

Shaftesbury expresses a similar love of nature in his private notebooks. He reminds himself there that experiencing the great good of nature has nothing to do with owning "*a neat House: Garden: Seat*," nothing to do with the envy one might garner from conventionally impressive possessions.[97]

> He who truly studdyes Nature, & *lies with Nature*, needs not either a Garden, or Wood, or Sea, or Rocks, to contemplate, & admire. A

> Dunghill, or Heap of any seeming Vile & Horrid Matter, is equall nay Superior to any of those pretended orderly Structures of things forcd out of their natural State. He [that] sees not the Beauty of corruption; can see nothing in Generation or Growth: and he who has not allways before, & can kindly & benignly view the incessant & Eternall Chang & Conversion of things one into another, will in the midts of his Gardens & other Artifices, oftener arraign & disparage Nature, than applaud, & accompany Her.[98]

Shaftesbury sought to impress on himself the superiority of wild beauty to "pretended orderly Structures of things forcd out of their natural State." He wanted to appreciate not just forests and oceans but also dunghills and heaps of seemingly vile matter, in which one can witness "the Beauty of corruption," the beauty of the laws that convert one thing into another.

"Beauty of every kind," Shaftesbury says, "naturally captivates the Heart" (C 3.20). The grander the order of an object, the more captivating its beauty. But rational investigation reveals that the order of nature is very grand indeed. That's why a cognitively rich appreciation of natural beauty is so intensely uplifting, rapturous.

> In the meanest Subjects of the World, the Appearance of *Order* gains upon the Mind, and draws the Affection towards it. But if *the Order of the World it-self* appears just and beautiful; the Admiration and Esteem of Order must run higher, and the elegant Passion or Love of Beauty . . . must be the more improv'd by its Exercise in so ample and magnificent a Subject. For 'tis impossible that such a *Divine Order* shou'd be contemplated without Extasy and Rapture; since in the common Subjects of Science, and the liberal Arts, whatever is according to just Harmony and Proportion, is so transporting to those who have any Knowledg or Practice in the kind. (C 2.43)

The greater the beauty of an object, the greater the love it arouses. Through knowledge of the system of nature we come to see the stupendous beauty of the world as a whole. Correspondingly stupendous is the love appreciation of it will arouse.

This love of nature's beauty produces love of nature's author. Admiration for "whatever in Nature is beautiful" leads to admiration for the "Sovereign Genius" responsible for the natural order, for the "original and comprehensive One" (C 2.220–221). Since nature's beauty is surpassing, love for its author will be surpassing as well: ecstatic appreciation of the creator of cosmic unity. Theocles gladly calls this love "enthusiasm," but in the same breath he reminds Philocles that it is based on rational understanding. "All Nature's Wonders serve to excite and perfect this Idea of their *Author*. 'Tis here he suffers us to see, and even converse with him, in a manner sutable to our Frailty. How glorious is it to contemplate him, in this noblest of his Works apparent to us, The *System* of *the bigger World!*" (C 2.207). We appreciate nature's wonders through "Study, Science, or Learning" (C 2.224). The positive emotions of perfect theism grow out of appreciation of nature's wonders. Rationality transports us to love.[99]

The enkindling of this love in Philocles is the underlying narrative thread of *The Moralists*. About religious matters Philocles had previously been ironic, bemused, detached. He enjoyed philosophical give-and-take, and was good at it, but the activity was for him essentially a game, a kind of banter. He'd adopt positions others were opposing, for the fun of it, and was not especially displeased if his ingenious counter-arguments provoked shocked indignation. He'd advance skeptical arguments about God as fluently as non-skeptical ones. And as just one more position to be intellectually bandied about, belief in God did not elicit from him any real passion. It did not engage in any significant way with his emotions or motivations.[100] But after spending time in nature with Theocles, he is transformed. Surprisingly to his friend Palemon and even to himself, there has arisen within him an ardor that shatters his former detachment (even if he can't resist still sometimes engaging in a bit of skeptical needling of "over-serious" interlocutors). Theocles asks whether his "poetick Extasys" have led Philocles "into some deep View of *Nature*, and the *Sovereign* GENIUS" that would prove "the *Force of Divine* BEAUTY" (C 2.223). Philocles affirms that he has been won over. "You have indeed made good your part of the Condition, and may now claim me for *a Proselyte*" (C 2.223). "I had," he tells Palemon, "chang'd my Character" (C 2.123). He finds himself now animated by a "nobler Love" (C 2.120), an "extravagance" of "Admiration" that was "unknown to me before" (C 2.224) "PHILOCLES, the cold indifferent PHILOCLES, is become a Pursuer of the same *mysterious* BEAUTY," says Theocles with a "significant" smile (C 2.219–220).

Philocles's development embodies Shaftesbury's synthesis of deism and enthusiasm. The great virtue of deism is its rationality. Deism tells us to believe only that for which we have convincing evidence, that we should never deny reason within ourselves. But that is only part of the story. True religion also "affects the Temper" (C 2.42). It shapes the "Course of the Affections." For this emotional power, "divine Passion" is needed.

Enthusiasm is passionate in just that way. Enthusiasm is a spirit within that is moved by "an Opinion or Conceit of something majestick and divine" (C 3.20). Enthusiasm is dangerous when untethered from reason. But when it grows out of fully rational apprehension of the world—when the passion is a response to nature as it actually is—it completes religion within a person. The result is *"Philosophical Enthusiasm,"* "a fair and plausible Enthusiasm, a reasonable Extasy and Transport," an enthusiasm that is "agreeable" (C 2.119, 2.224). Other writers opposed enthusiastic states to calm philosophical reflections, contrasted reasonable frames of mind with transporting ecstasies. Shaftesbury unites them through the experience of beauty, an experience that starts with rational understanding of the natural world and ends with rapturous love for nature's creator.

Shaftesbury wanted his readers to feel what Philocles came to feel. He gave *The Moralists* a form he thought would accomplish that. It's a Bildungsroman, with Philocles's development of love for nature's creator the personal progress. Shaftesbury strengthens our identification with Philocles by having him tell the story in first-personal letters. Those letters are to a friend named Palemon, who is himself struggling to develop expansive love, which is another device to foster the reader's sympathetic identification. Also crucial is the character of Theocles, whom Shaftesbury portrays as the most appealing of characters, the most intelligent, the most delightful to be with, the most worthy of emulation. And then there are the florid landscape descriptions and paeans to nature's beauty, which bloom repeatedly during Philocles's and Theocles's walk through the wilds. The elevated rhetoric of these passages might seem, if you come to *The Moralists* seeking only discursive argumentation and find yourself trying to fillet the logical skeleton out of the lengthy (very lengthy) novelistic features (who has time to wade through all that fluff?), exasperating. But Shaftesbury has his characters explicitly comment on how highfalutin they themselves sound. There's a self-mocking humor to those passages that attempts at logico-philosophical filleting will miss (see C 2.109–111 and 2.210–211). And Theocles and Philocles always return to more flat-footed rational discourse. At the same time, Shaftesbury does sincerely want *The Moralists* to engage not only our reason but also our emotions, just as those with big ideas who choose to write philosophical novels have always done.[101] Toward that end, his characters' encounters out of doors, in "the free Air," are supposed to vivify a transformative experience the natural world can effect in even the most aloofly rational. Perhaps current expectations concerning philosophical argument and writing style are too far removed for Shaftesbury's approach to work well on us. But I hope we can still appreciate his attempt to spark in readers the cognitively rich emotional response he thought essential to true worship.[102]

Shaftesbury said that he originally intended the dialogue between Theocles and Philocles to be read by only a few friends. But either he was being disingenuous or he changed his mind. For he not only published versions of it on its own in 1704 and 1709, he also included it in *Characteristicks*.

One of the illustrations added to the 1714 edition of *Characteristicks* was a frontispiece portrait of the author. The engraver worked from a 1700–1701 portrait painting. The central figure of Shaftesbury is much the same in both images. But Shaftesbury instructed the engraver for the *Characteristicks* frontispiece to make significant changes to the setting of the earlier portrait.[103] In both pictures, Shaftesbury stands in a room next to an arched exterior doorway. But while in the earlier painting a servant stands in the doorway, blocking our view almost entirely, in the later frontispiece the servant is gone and we can see out.

Directly outside the doorway are rectangular lawns with straight paths. In the middle distance are a square wall and a straight row of trees trimmed to identical pyramid shapes. But where the picture draws the eye, what we're most powerfully attracted to, is the landscape beyond— through the house, out the door, past the manicured lawns, past the topiary trees—to distant rugged hills rising under dramatic skies. The room houses books of philosophical wisdom. The garden and arbor look pleasant enough. But what the composition frames is a yearning to light out for the hilly wilds.

## 6. What Happens When Shaftesbury Meets Darwin?

Between Shaftesbury's time and ours, there's been a momentous scientific development that would seem to throw Shaftesbury's view of nature into doubt: the evolutionary account of the origin of species. When Shaftesbury looked at the amazing biological order of plants and animals, he considered only two explanations: randomness or intelligent design. When we look, we see the results of evolution. What happens when Shaftesbury's view of nature's beauty encounters Darwin?

On one way of looking at things, Shaftesbury's view can embrace the evolutionary explanation without any trouble at all. Nature is beautiful, according to Shaftesbury, because it operates by invariable laws. We admire nature's creator not because he miraculously alters the regular course of events but because he has created a system that produces marvels of order as a matter of regular course. The theory of evolution just adds to our understanding of the laws of nature—adds to our understanding of the beautiful system God has created. Reading Darwin would thus have deepened Philocles's and Theocles's appreciation of the author of nature. They would have seen how the evolutionary processes God created produce things of great beauty.

On another way of looking at things, however, Shaftesbury's view crumbles. Shaftesbury believed that the appropriate response to nature's beauty is appreciation for the mind that designed it. Nature is an artifact; religion, love for the artificer. But evolutionary theory undermines the idea that nature is an artifact. Evolutionary theory shows that the ordered organisms that so impressed Philocles and Theocles have been spit out by forces that are mindless. The intentions of a conscious mind add exactly nothing to our explanation of the phenomena. Nature is a "realm of contingency," its denizens the "accidental result of an unplanned process."[104] It is no longer appropriate to respond to nature with love for a designer because, within our best natural explanations, there is no longer any role for a designer to play.

Even so—even if evolution undermines *The Moralists*' attempt to lead us from a cognitively rich, emotionally transporting appreciation of nature to love for a conscious designing God—its account of a cognitively rich, emotionally transporting appreciation of nature would remain. It would still give us a vivid picture of the valuing of wildness—of how scientific understanding can lead one to think of pristine nature as sacred.

As well, the first version of *The Moralists* (called *The Sociable Enthusiast* and published anonymously in 1704) contains a glimmer of the notion that viewing nature as sacred does not necessarily require a distinct designing mind, even if Shaftesbury edited it out in later versions. In the later versions, on the morning of the second day Theocles looks around and says: "O mighty *Nature!* Wise Substitute of *Providence!* impower'd *Creatress!* Or Thou impowering DEITY, supreme Creator!" (C 2.194). Here the mind that has created nature is distinct from nature. Nature is a "substitute" of providence. Nature is an "impower'd creatress." But the "impowering Deity"—the "supreme Creator"—is something else.

In the 1704 version, however, Theocles says this: "O mighty *Nature!* Wise in thy Designs, powerful in thy Operations, and bounteous in thy distributions and Providence O Divine and Universal Spirit! or rather thou divinity it self, Supreme and Sovereign."[105] Here nature itself is apotheosized. Theocles isn't praising a mind that has created nature and is distinct from it. He is praising the natural operations directly. Nature is "divinity it self." This is not merely a natural religion. This is a religion of nature.

Even in the final version of *The Moralists*, Shaftesbury did not hide entirely the distance between what he worshipped and the religion of his day. The other guests at Theocles's estate are conventional Christians. At one point during dinner they begin talking about the strength of their Christian faith. But, Philocles says, theirs "was not a Face of *Religion* I was like to be enamour'd with . . . If ever I became so, I found it wou'd rather be after Theocles's manner. The *Monuments* and *Church-yards* were not such powerful Scenes with me, as the *Mountains*, the *Plains*, the solemn *Woods* and *Groves*; of whose Inhabitants I chose much rather to hear, than of the other" (C 2.182). True religion for Shaftesbury is not to be found in the church. It is to be found in the beauty of the science of mountains, plains, woods, and groves. It is to be found where Philocles first meets Theocles: "roving in the Fields" (C 2.126).

CHAPTER TWO

# Virtue

IN HIS EARLY NOTEBOOKS Shaftesbury anguished over not feeling the love he thought he should feel for God. He also anguished over not feeling the love he thought he should feel for other people.

Shaftesbury believed that human beings are designed to be social, that we are built to live in harmony with other humans. As evidence of our natural sociability, he points to the conspicuous presence in human psychology of familial ties, "Love of Fellowship and Company, Compassion, mutual Succour, and the rest of this kind" (C 2.45). Sociability is the essence of human nature. To be true to one's nature is to be in concord with other humans (C 2.9, 2.77, 2.210–213).

But when Shaftesbury looked within he saw unsociable—even anti-social—tendencies. He had a few lifelong friends for whom he felt deep affection. But toward people in general, toward many in his social circle, and even toward his own family, his overriding emotion was often antipathy. So many of them seemed to him so often to be petty, foolish, perverse.

This misanthropy is evident in Shaftesbury's *Inquiry*. Humans, he writes there, are guilty of the "greatest Corruptions and Degeneracys" in all of creation (C 2.96). Unlike any other species, humans exhibit cruelty and "perverse Inclinations" (C 2.82). Humans and humans alone violate "Proportionableness, Constancy and Regularity in all their Passions and Affections" (C 2.96). To follow unspoiled human nature is good, but it's desperately "hard to find a Man who lives NATURALLY, and as a Man" (C 2.56).

Shaftesbury found socializing hellish. He had "to smile, frown, pitty, applaud" not in accord with his "reall Character" but "as is prescrib'd" by company.[1] People expected him to speak when he preferred to be silent, to be silent when he preferred to speak. All of it made him feel (like a character out of Sartre) "nauseouse."[2]

Shaftesbury blamed other people for his sense of alienation. But he also blamed himself. He admonished himself for not developing "a more enlarg'd Mind," "a more generouse Heart."[3] He strove to "Love Men,"[4] to be "truly philanthropic," to make his "Affection be as it ought to be."[5] "But," he lamented, "which way is this possible?"[6] Between himself and the rest of humanity was a yawning "Gulph."[7] He was "singular."[8] Even people who disagreed with each other about the most fundamental things were more in "harmony & agreement with one another, in respect of what they are towards *me*."[9] He had to hide his true self, lest he "appear horrid & affrighting."[10]

His sense of alienation led Shaftesbury to call himself an "Idiot," a "Fool!," a "Monster with respect to" others. His most common self-epithet, one he used at least a dozen times, was "Wretch!"[11] He often wrote the word in a hard-pressed hand that reveals an emotional intensity the printed quotation doesn't convey.

The venom and self-flagellation of Shaftesbury's private notebooks are largely absent from *Characteristicks*. The tone he publicly projects is calm, self-assured—bemused rather than tortured. In *The Moralists*, nonetheless, we can see Shaftesbury raising the same issue of how to love humanity with which he wrestled in private.

The first character we meet in *The Moralists* is a young nobleman named Palemon. The first words out of Palemon's mouth are: "O wretched State of Mankind!—Hapless Nature, thus to have err'd in thy chief Workmanship!" (C 2.109). Palemon wishes he could love humanity, but—"O what Treacherys! what Disorders! And how corrupt is all!"—their conduct repels him (C 2.112). People who in public appear as friends craftily plot each other's ruin less than an hour later. Many would gladly sacrifice the "the State it-self" to satisfy their own ambitions (C 2.113). In company there is "much Folly and Perverseness ... and strange Appetites" (C 2.114–115). "Licentiousness," "Villanys and Corruptions" abound (C 2.111, 2.116).

Philocles, the narrator of *The Moralists*, initially has "*Man-hater*" tendencies similar to Palemon's (C 2.112). "[W]iser Heads" may think universal love is "heroick," Philocles says. "But for my part, I see so very little Worth in *Mankind*, and have so indifferent an Opinion of *the Publick*, that I can propose little Satisfaction to my-self in loving *either*" (C 2.136).

We saw in the last chapter that Shaftesbury sought to instill in himself love for God by coming to appreciate the beauty of nature. In this chapter we'll see how Shaftesbury sought to remedy his negative feelings toward humanity by cultivating moral beauty.

## 1. Moral Sense

Shaftesbury didn't start out with the idea of moral beauty. He started out, in the 1699 version of the *Inquiry*, with the idea of moral sense. We'll look first at his early version of moral sense. We'll then look at how in *The Moralists* he developed the idea of moral beauty, and retrofitted the *Inquiry*'s moral sense to cohere with it.[12]

In the *Inquiry*, Shaftesbury situates his view of virtue within his larger teleological view of goodness. Something is good, according to this teleological view, if it contributes to the "Existence or Well-being" of the system of which it is a part (C 2.10). Every animal is a part of its species. A particular animal, say a tiger, is a good member of its species—it is a good tiger—if it contributes to the well-being of the tiger species as a whole. There is also "a System of all Animals," which consists of the "*Animal-Order*" or "*OEconomy*" of all animal species (C 2.11). A good animal is one that contributes to the well-being of "animal Affairs" in general (C 2.11). The system of all animals, moreover, works with the system "of Vegetables, and all other things in this inferior World" to constitute "*one System* of a Globe or Earth*"* (C 2.11). Something is a good earthly thing if it contributes to the existence of earthly things in general. And the system of this earth is itself part of a "*Universal System*" or "a *System of all Things*" (C 2.11). To be "*wholly* and *really*" good, a thing must contribute to the good of the universe as a whole (C 2.11). This progression of ever-larger systems is a bit dazzling, and we might wonder how we can know (or even make sense of) whether something is contributing to the well-being of the universe as a whole. Shaftesbury avoids this problem by discussing in detail only that which makes "a sensible Creature" a good member of its species—by focusing on whether an individual animal is promoting the well-being of its conspecifics (C 2.12). Shaftesbury seems to believe that an animal that contributes to the well-being of its species will also always contribute to the well-being of the universe as a whole, which ensures that a good member of a species will also be wholly and really good.

Goodness is within the reach of all sensible creatures, not only humans but also non-human animals. A creature is good if its affections promote the well-being of the system of which it is a part. Non-human animals are just as capable of possessing this type of affection as humans.[13] "VIRTUE or MERIT," on the other hand, is within the reach of "*Man* only" (C 2.16). That's because virtue is tied to a special kind of affection that only humans possess. This special kind of affection is a second-order affection, one that has as its object other affections. All animals feel positively toward certain things (what appears to be good to eat, for instance) and negatively toward other things (what appears to want to eat them). But non-human animals lack the reflective capacity for (second-order) affections about their own (first-order) affections. A lion doesn't feel good or bad about wanting to eat the gazelle. It just wants to eat it. Humans are different. We can be conscious of our own passions. We not only feel desires and aversions. We also have the reflective capacity to become aware that we are feeling desires or aversions. And when we reflect on our own passions, we develop feelings about them. Say you feel malice toward a competitor who has bested you in a fair competition. Then you become aware you're feeling that. You may now feel negatively toward your own malice. Or you feel compassion toward someone in distress and then become aware you are feeling that: you may now feel positively toward your own compassion. This second-order sentiment about first-order motives is the basis of moral judgment (C 2.18). If you judge that you morally ought to do something, it's because you have a positive (second-order) sentiment toward your (first-order) inclination to do it. If you judge that you morally ought not to do something, it's because you have a negative (second-order) sentiment toward your (first-order) inclination to do it. The same holds for your judgments of other humans. If you judge me to be virtuous (or vicious), it's because you have a positive (or negative) affective response toward what you perceive to be the affection motivating me. These are the phenomena Shaftesbury has in mind when he says that "the *Affections* of Pity, Kindness, Gratitude, and their Contrarys, being brought into the Mind by Reflection, become Objects. So that, by means of this reflected Sense, there arises another kind of Affection towards those very Affections themselves, which have been already felt, and are now become the Subject of a new Liking or Dislike" (C 2.16). Humans alone make moral judgments because humans alone have the reflective capacity for the crucial second-order "Sentiment or Judgment."

Shaftesbury calls this capacity to feel (second-order) sentiments about (first-order) inclinations "a Sense of Right and Wrong" or "*moral Sense*" (C 2.23–27, 2.29–31, 2.35).[14] When our sense of right and wrong is operating properly—when it's fulfilling its teleological purpose—it produces positive feelings toward affections in accord with the well-being of humanity and negative feelings toward affections in conflict with the well-being of humanity. People are virtuous to the extent that these second-order feelings guide their conduct (C 2.16–18).

That's the early version of moral sense. Now on to moral beauty.

## 2. Moral Beauty

Shaftesbury develops the idea of moral beauty on the second day of the *Moralists* dialogue between Theocles and Philocles. Most of the second day consists of Theocles convincing Philocles that nature as a whole is beautiful. Nature is unified. When we perceive its unity, we feel profound joy and admiration.

Toward the end of the second day—in a section with the marginal heading "Beauty moral"—Theocles asks Philocles if he can discern another category of beauty, one that "relates to us" more directly than the beauty of nature, architecture, and sculpture (C 2.238, Philocles says he can't think of anything.

Theocles urges him to "Think, think again."

Sorry, says Philocles, don't know what you mean. If you want to continue with this, you're going to have to give me a hint.

The other category of beauty, Theocles says, is of those things of which you are most directly conscious, things that are most "immediately *your own*" and "solely in, and from *your-self*."

"You mean my *Sentiments*?" Philocles asks (C 2.228).

Yes, says Theocles, "your *Sentiments, Principles, Determinations, Actions*," and whatever else flows from your "*Will*" and "is ingender'd in your *Heart*" (C 2.228). Those things, your "*mental* Children," can be beautiful just as physical objects can be (C 2.229). "[T]here is in certain *Figures* a natural Beauty, which the Eye finds as soon as the Object is presented to it" (C 2.231). And there is as natural a beauty "of Actions."

> No sooner the Eye opens upon *Figures*, the Ear to *Sounds*, than straight *the Beautiful* results, and *Grace* and *Harmony* are known and acknowledg'd. No sooner are ACTIONS view'd, no sooner the *human Affections* and *Passions* discern'd (. . .) than straight *an inward* Eye distinguishes, and sees *the Fair* and *Shapely, the Amiable* and *Admirable*, apart from *the Deform'd*, the *Foul, the Odious*, or *the Despicable*. (C 2.231)[15]

We distinguish between the beauty and ugliness of human affections just as we distinguish between the beauty and ugliness of figures and sounds. We recognize "moral Beauty and Deformity." We recognize "Beauty of Soul" (C 2.234, 2.231).

Philocles says he gets it. We have positive responses to the beauty of art and nature. We can have the same positive responses to the non-physical aspects of human beings. A person's character can be beautiful just as art and nature can be.

The dialogic to-ing and fro-ing highlights that Shaftesbury is putting forward something new. Philocles has acknowledged that there is a beauty of architecture, of sculpture, of nature. He is then led to the realization that minds can be beautiful too. The distinction between beauty and deformity that he recognizes in other arenas also applies to character.

After writing the *Moralists*, Shaftesbury returned to the *Inquiry*, adding to it several passages that turned the approvals of the moral sense into positive responses to moral beauty. Here's one of the passages that does the job; its marginal heading, "Moral Beauty and Deformity," matches the corresponding part of *The Moralists*.

> The Mind, which is Spectator or Auditor of, cannot be without its *Eye* and *Ear*; so as to discern Proportion, distinguish Sound, and scan each Sentiment or Thought which comes before it. It can let nothing escape its Censure. It feels the Soft and Harsh, the Agreeable and Disagreeable, in the Affections; and finds a *Foul* and *Fair*, a *Harmonious* and a *Dissonant*, as really and truly here, as in any musical Numbers, or in the outward Forms or Representations of sensible Things. (C 2.17)

We respond positively to the harmonious and negatively to the dissonant, positively to the proportional and negatively to the lopsided. So too, we respond positively to certain human characters and negatively to others. When we consider the conduct of different people, our feelings do not "remain neutral" any more than they remain neutral when we look at beautiful and ugly bodies (C 2.17). Our heart "constantly takes part one way or other." We distinguish between the "Beauty, and Comeliness" of "one *Turn of Affection*, one *Behaviour*, one *Sentiment* and another." There is "*moral* and *intellectual*" beauty just as there is beauty of "Bodys, Colours, and Sounds." We recognize "a Beauty and a Deformity as well in Actions, Minds, and Tempers, as in Figures, Sounds, or Colours" (C 2.25). This moral beauty is what virtue consists of.

The "likings" of our moral sense have now become a subset of our responses to beauty.

## 3. The Moral Beauty of Socrates

One way of classifying moral philosophers is by distinguishing between those whose fundamental concept is a positive to try to attain, and those whose fundamental concept is a negative to try to avoid. Plato belongs in the positive camp, his philosophy an urging upward to the great positive of the form of the good. Aristotle belongs there too, with eudaimonia the positive goal toward which his moral philosophy aims.

Hobbes belongs in the negative camp. At the heart of Hobbes's thought is something very bad, the war of all against all. His moral philosophy is a set of rules for escaping and staying away from that dreadfulness. Equally negative is seventeenth-century Calvinism, which begins from belief in the sinfulness of human nature and goes on to tell us what we must do given our ineluctably wretched condition.

Shaftesbury's first account of the moral sense did not give conceptual priority to the positive or the negative. The early *Inquiry*'s moral sense approved of virtue and disapproved of vice, but there was no reason to think that one or the other was primary. With the development of moral beauty, however, Shaftesbury makes the positive fundamental, aligning himself decisively with the positivity of Plato and Aristotle and against the negativity of Calvin and Hobbes.

The positivity of Shaftesbury's view stands out in contrast to a description Santayana gives of the difference between morality and aesthetics. Santayana writes, "while aesthetic judgments are mainly positive, that is perceptions of good, moral judgments are mainly and fundamentally negative, or perceptions of evil."[16] Santayana's thought is that the paradigmatic aesthetic experience is of being attracted to something, while the paradigmatic moral experience is of being opposed. Shaftesbury rejects that characterization of moral experience. For Shaftesbury, what is fundamental is beauty, which can belong to nature, to artworks, to bodies—and to minds (C 3.111–114). Virtue is a kind of beauty, and, as a kind of beauty, it attracts.

A crucial inspiration for Shaftesbury's idea of moral beauty is the character of Socrates, especially as portrayed by Xenophon and Plato in their respective versions of the *Symposium*. In Xenophon's *Symposium*, one of the characters, Critoboulus, contends that being good-looking has more value than the entire "King's empire."[17] For good-looking people others will do anything: give away all their money, allow themselves to become enslaved, go through fire. Of the object of his own affection Critoboulus says, "I gaze at Cleinias with more pleasure than at all the other things that are beautiful among human beings; I would accept being blind to all the rest before I would accept being blind only to Cleinias. I am burdened by the night and by sleep because I don't see him then, and I know the greatest gratitude to the day and to the sun because they reveal Cleinias to me."[18] Critoboulus and his friends are not talking about the merely handsome, the kind of good looks you'd typically expect to see in any random group of people. They're talking about the extraordinarily attractive, the absolutely stunning—about beauty that stops you in your tracks.

Socrates was not one of the good-looking people. Socrates was famously ugly. He had bug eyes that stuck out like a crab's, a pug nose with nostrils that opened high and wide, lips that were thick like a donkey's. People likened his appearance to a grotesque, to a satyr. Yet Socrates had an attractive effect on others that was no less mesmerizing than that of the fantastically beautiful. His conversation cast a spell. It left his interlocutors "transported, completely possessed."[19] They fell in love with him. For Socrates they'd go through fire.

One character in Plato's *Symposium*, the beautiful Alcibiades, is confounded by these feelings. Despite Socrates's bug-eyed, pug-nosed, donkey-lipped appearance, Alcibiades is completely in his thrall. "[T]he moment he starts to speak," Alcibiades says, "I am besides myself: my heart starts leaping in my chest, the tears come streaming down my face."[20] Alcibiades eventually comes to realize that Socrates does possess great beauty, but it's beauty of a non-physical sort. Within Socrates's soul are things "so godlike—so bright and beautiful, so utterly amazing—that I no longer had a choice—I just had to do whatever he told me."[21] Alcibiades sees in Socrates "a beauty that is really beyond description and makes" Alcibiades's own physical beauty "pale in comparison."[22] In Plato's *Phaedo* and *Crito*, other characters express (albeit in a different key from Alcibiades) a similarly profound love for Socrates. The beauty of Socrates's soul fills them with admiration and affection.

There's a jokey episode in Xenophon's *Symposium* in which Socrates and Critoboulus engage in a kind of beauty contest. Socrates loses; everyone votes for Critoboulus.[23] There's a sense, though, in which Socrates really is the most beautiful. He has a quality of soul with the greatest attractive power. As much as we may enjoy physical beauty, mental beauty is the "most engaging" of all. "Nothing affects the Heart like ... *the Beauty of Sentiments, the Grace of Actions, the Turn of Characters*, and *the Proportions and Features of a human Mind*" (C 1.136). This idea of mental beauty is the centerpiece of Shaftesbury's moral philosophy.

## 4. What Moral Beauty Consists Of and How We Judge It

Shaftesbury develops a view of what moral beauty consists of, and of how we judge whether someone possesses it.

As we've seen, beauty in general consists of "Unity of Design" (C 1.89, 1.150, 2.161, 2.164, 3.214). Anything that has multiple parts that can be in unity with each other can be beautiful. An artwork can be beautiful, a machine can be beautiful, a natural object can be beautiful, nature as a whole can be beautiful. A human character can be beautiful as well.

Shaftesbury uses various words for the property of beauty: "harmony" when describing the beauty of music; "proportion" when describing the beauty of architecture; "regularity," "order," "balance," and "symmetry" at other times. We saw in the last chapter that Shaftesbury uses cognates of "integrity" when describing the beauty of nature. He also uses that word when describing beauty of character (C 1.55, 2.45, 2.49, 2.64, 2.65, 2.100, 3.135).

Integrity is the property of being one, of wholeness. Something has integrity when it constitutes a single coherent entity, when each part harmonizes with every other. We generally use the word "integrity" nowadays to signify internal harmony, the state of being in agreement with oneself. To have this kind of integrity is to act in accord with one's own principles, all of one's psychological aspects cohering with each other. To lack this integrity is to be in conflict with oneself, to harbor incompatible affections. Shaftesbury affirms the importance of this internal integrity, contending that it is something the virtuous possesses and the vicious does not. The virtuous person has "*A Mind or Reason well compos'd, quiet, easy within it-self, and such as can freely bear its own Inspection and Review*" (C 2.66). The virtuous person finds "Converse *with himself*" pleasurable (C 2.66). He experiences the "*mental Pleasures*," his psychological harmony providing him "*the chief Means and Power of Self-enjoyment*" (C 2.73). Within the vicious person, in contrast, there is conflict. The vicious person's motivational principles are in "Contradiction" (C 2.71), his psyche riven by "Contrariety and Disturbance" (C 2.66). "*Knavery* is mere *Dissonance* and *Disproportion*" (C 1.129).

But internal harmony is not the only aspect of integrity essential to moral beauty. To have the integrity of which moral beauty consists is also to be in harmony with the rest of humanity. A person has this kind of integrity when "all his Inclinations and Affections, his Dispositions of Mind and Temper [are] sutable, and agreeing with the Good of his *Kind*, or of that *System* in which he is included, and of which he constitutes a PART" (C 2.45). "To love the Publick, to study universal Good, and to promote the Interest of the whole World, as far as lies within our power, is surely the Height of Goodness" (C 1.23). Shaftesbury develops this point by drawing an extended contrast between "PARTIAL AFFECTION" and "INTIRE AFFECTION (from whence *Integrity* has its name)" (C 1.64). The former is a regard for "some *one* Part of Society" while the latter is "an *intire, sincere* and *truly moral*" regard for "Society *it-self*" (C 2.63–64). "INTIRE AFFECTION or INTEGRITY" is "Consciousness of just Behaviour towards Mankind in general" (C 2.64–65). It is not "social Love *in part*" but rather love for "compleat Society" (C 2.64). This is the love of humanity that in his notebooks Shaftesbury excoriated himself for lacking, that Palemon and Philocles find themselves bereft of at the beginning of *The Moralists*.

So there are two aspects of the integrity that is moral beauty: within the virtuous person, and between the virtuous person and the rest of humanity. All the parts of the morally beautiful person harmonize with each other, and the morally beautiful person harmonizes with everyone else. "[T]o have one's Affections *right* and *intire*, not only in respect of one's self, but of Society and the Publick: This is *Rectitude, Integrity*, or VIRTUE" (C 2.45). Shaftesbury often makes this point in terms of a system. Something is a system when all its elements fit together perfectly, each working with every other toward a unitary purpose. The internal aspects of a morally beautiful person constitute a perfect "*Self-system*" or "private System" (C 1.46, 1.56, 1.60). And the morally beautiful person is a perfect cog in the "*System of the Kind*," in the public system of humanity of which each of us is a part (C 2.46). This public or humanity-wide aspect brings the unity of beauty into accord with the teleology of the *Inquiry*, according to which a creature is good when its motives promote the good of the species of which it is a part.

That's what moral beauty consists of. How do we judge it?

According to Shaftesbury, we judge moral beauty the same way we judge the beauty of other things, by the experience of a positive affection. We experience a positive "internal Sensation" not only when we hear musical harmonies, not only when we observe a proportionate building, not only when we appreciate the balance of nature, but also when we witness fully integrated characters. "Nor can [one's mind] with-hold its *Admiration* and *Extasy*, its *Aversion* and *Scorn*, any more in what relates to one than to the other of these Subjects" (C 2.17). We have a "taste" for some characters over others. As we've seen, Shaftesbury retrofits the moral sense of the first version of the *Inquiry* so that it becomes the capacity to experience these positive feelings for integrated characters. Our "liking" of affections that align with our teleological purpose (the second-order affection of the moral sense) becomes an aspect of a general emotional sensibility tuned to the standard of order, regularity, and balance. This epistemological retrofitting is made easier by the consistently central role that affection plays: in both the earlier moral sense account and the later moral beauty account, our moral judgments are based on our affective responses to affective features of human character.

Why does Shaftesbury put affection in the driver's seat? Because he believes that to be virtuous is to have certain kinds of motives, and because he believes that affections alone can motivate. Shaftesbury never states outright what Hume would explicitly argue for: that reason on its own is motivationally inert.[24] But the Humean claim is implied by what Shaftesbury does say. Throughout the first version of the *Inquiry*, he attributes every instance of motivation to affection. He does assert that reason is necessary "to secure a right application of the Affections," but there he is granting to reason merely the instrumental role of discovering what will best benefit the species (C 2.20). Affection remains that which motivates us to pursue that benefit. Shaftesbury says as well that the motivational force of an affection can be directly opposed only by the motivational force of "*contrary* Affections" (C 2.23).[25] If one has a motivating affection, one will "necessarily act according to it" unless it is opposed by some other affection (C 2.30). "[T]here is no speculative Opinion, Persuasion or Belief, which is capable *immediately* or *directly* to exclude or destroy" a natural affection (C 2.25). "[N]othing beside contrary Affection, by frequent check and control, can operate upon it, so as either to diminish it in part, or destroy it in the whole" (C 2.26). Shaftesbury acknowledges that beliefs can cause alterations in the affections, and that the altered affections can lead us in directions opposite to those we'd been motivated to follow before. If I come to believe a particularly charismatic person is a great benefactor to humanity, I may then become motivated to emulate behavior of hers to which I would otherwise have been opposed. If I come to believe that a particular group of people is trying to destroy humanity, I may become motivated to attack them in ways that would previously have offended my sense of right and wrong. But belief's role in motivation is once again instrumental. It operates on my motivation only "indirectly, by the intervention of opposite or of favourable Affections causally excited by any such Belief" (C 2.26). Affection is the source of all motivational force. Belief on its own mounts no motivational pushback.

A question we might have for Shaftesbury is whether his view of what moral beauty consists of is conceptually prior to his view of how we judge moral beauty, or vice versa. That is to say, in a world in which our moral sense was built to approve of disintegrated characters, would we all be wrong about what characters were morally beautiful (consistence claim prior), or would disintegrated characters be in fact morally beautiful (judgment claim prior)?

There is certainly evidence that Shaftesbury wanted the consistence claim to be prior. He wanted to be a "*Realist* in MORALITY," where that realism involved "immutable" and "*eternal Measures*" of morality that are independent of any mind (C 2.151, 2.21, 1.184, 1.208). On this view, the sense of moral beauty is special because, as Schneewind explains, "through it we become aware of an objective order."[26] Shaftesburean moral sentiments, as Irwin puts it, have "an indicative (or detective) role" in that they inform us whether or not motives accord with mind-independent moral measures.[27] Such mind-independent moral measures were necessary for Shaftesbury's refutation of what he took to be the pernicious subjectivism of Hobbes and the despicable voluntarism of the Calvinists. Here's a passage in which he makes an emphatic statement of the mind-independence of beauty in general and of moral beauty in particular.

> HARMONY is Harmony *by Nature*, let Men judg ever so ridiculously of Musick. So is *Symmetry* and *Proportion* founded still *in Nature*, let Mens Fancy prove ever so barbarous, or their Fashions ever so *Gothick* in their Architecture, Sculpture, or whatever other designing Art. 'Tis the same case, where *Life* and MANNERS are concern'd. *Virtue* has the same fix'd Standard. The same *Numbers*, *Harmony*, and *Proportion* will have place in MORALS; and are discoverable in the *Characters* and *Affections* of Mankind; in which are laid the just Foundations of an Art and Science, superior to every other of human Practice and Comprehension. (C 1.217–218; see also 1.207)

Shaftesbury bases his claim of the mind-independence of morality on a comparison to aesthetics. This is opposite to what most people today would expect. Most people today would expect a comparison between morals and aesthetics to support a claim of the subjectivity or mind-dependence of morals. That's because most people today believe that aesthetics is subjective or mind-dependent. But Shaftesbury is an objectivist about beauty. He believes the standards of beauty have an existence that is independent of human responses, distinct from any "human Practice and Comprehension." Even if we responded totally differently, the same sounds would be beautifully harmonious, the same structures would be beautifully symmetrical. And the same characters would still be beautifully integrated. To Shaftesbury, the assimilation of morals to aesthetics advances the case for a mind-independent moral standard.

There's a problem, however, with this way of getting to the mind-independence of morals. Shaftesbury says that harmony would be harmony, and symmetry would be symmetry, regardless of how humans respond. That claim is supposed to help convince us that virtue would be virtue regardless of how humans respond. But this line of thought involves an illicit slide between non-normative and normative interpretations of the key terms. It may be uncontroversial to grant that there are non-normative properties of harmony and symmetry that have a mind-independent existence—that some sounds would be harmonious and some objects would be symmetrical regardless of human responses. But to say those sounds and objects are beautiful is to invoke normativity. It is to imply that the harmonious and the symmetrical are more valuable, are in some sense *better* than the dissonant and the lopsided. And Shaftesbury has given us no reason to accept that harmony and symmetry would continue to be normatively superior even if human minds were constructed to respond negatively to them and positively to dissonance and lopsidedness. By the same token, it may be relatively uncontroversial that there would be a non-normative difference between integrated and non-integrated human minds regardless of how we respond to them. But that's not what Shaftesbury needs to establish the mind-independence of morals as something normative. What he needs is that an integrated mind would be more valuable, would be *better*, even if our sensibility was constructed to respond positively to the disintegrated. The comparison with the non-normative properties of harmony and symmetry doesn't help with that.[28]

To complicate matters, Shaftesbury also says some things that suggest that the normative aspect of morals is dependent on our responses. Here's one such passage.

> For let us carry *Scepticism* ever so far, let us doubt, if we can, of every thing about us; we cannot doubt of what passes *within our-selves*. Our Passions and Affections are known to us. *They* are certain, whatever the *Objects* may be, on which they are employ'd. Nor is it of any concern to our Argument, how these exterior Objects stand; whether they are Realitys, or mere Illusions; whether we wake or dream. For *ill Dreams* will be equally disturbing. And a good *Dream*, if Life be nothing else, will be easily and happily pass'd. In this Dream of Life, therefore,

our Demonstrations have the same force; our *Balance* and *OEconomy* hold good, and our Obligation to VIRTUE is in every respect the same. (C 2.99; see also 2.25)

Shaftesbury is saying here that our obligation to virtue will remain the same even if we are wrong about everything else about the world (even if we're brains in vats). That's because our obligation to virtue is based on our "Passions and Affections." And so long as our passions and affections remain the same, our obligation to virtue will remain the same, no matter how the world happens to be. But this implies that our obligation to virtue will change if our passions and affections change, even if the world stays the same. Shaftesbury wants to establish that our obligation to virtue is based on what we care about, and that as a result our obligation to virtue isn't endangered by even Cartesian skepticism, since even Cartesian skepticism can't raise doubt about what we care about. But that point also implies that our obligation to virtue is untethered from our being right about anything outside our own minds.

I don't think Shaftesbury would have been at all happy with the mind-dependent implication I've just attributed to him. I think he very much wanted to be a "*Realist* in MORALITY," where that realism involved a mind-independent standard that defeated Hobbesian subjectivism and Calvinist voluntarism (C 2.151). But there are times when his ardor to convince us of why virtue should matter to us pushes him, unwittingly, in the mind-dependent direction.

## 5. Two Obstacles to Moral Beauty: Egoism and Partiality

Essential to moral beauty is impartial care for the "publick Interest" (C 2.18), an "equal, just and universal Friendship" with all humankind (C 2.137). Virtuous people will love the public, study universal good, and promote the interests of the whole world as far as lies within their power (C 1.23). Some of Shaftesbury's most astute and influential psychological insights come in his discussion of the obstacles to the development of this aspect of moral beauty. Two obstacles he explores in depth are selfish egoism and partiality.

Shaftesbury takes Hobbes to be representative of selfish egoism. As Shaftesbury interprets him, Hobbes believes that the ultimate motive behind every human action is self-preservation. There is "only one Master-Passion, Fear, which has, in effect, devour'd all the rest."[29] The real goal of everything we do—the only thing we care about for its own sake—is warding off our own destruction.

If this egoist view is correct, then achieving moral beauty is impossible. Moral beauty involves genuine friendship, a direct concern for the welfare of others. It involves caring about others for their own sakes, not simply as means to one's own preservation. But Hobbesian egoism implies that one's own preservation is the only thing one ever cares about for its own sake.

Shaftesbury argues that such egoism is simply bad psychology. The human mind is "too complex a kind, to fall under one simple View, or be explain'd thus briefly in a word or two. The Studiers of this *Mechanism* must have a very partial Eye, to overlook all other Motions besides those of the lowest and narrowest compass" (C 1.72–73). As examples of the "thousand other Springs" of human action, Shaftesbury points to the plethora of motives that lead people to act "counter to *Self-interest*," such as passion, humor, caprice, vengeance, and vindictiveness (C 1.72–73). Shaftesbury's most significant attack on egoism, however, comes in his discussion of the "*herding* Principle" (C 1.70).

The herding principle is the innate desire of a creature to associate with members of its own species (C 1.69–72, 2.45–47, 2.178–181, 3.134). The strength of the herding principle in species varies, depending on the extent to which cooperation among conspecifics contributes to the thriving of the species as a whole. No species (Shaftesbury thought) can thrive if its parents do not care at all for their young. So nature has implanted in all animals at least some degree of concern for offspring. But certain animals can thrive with very limited parental concern and nothing more. Nature has implanted in members of those species little concern for conspecifics beyond that for newborns. As an example of a non-sociable species, Shaftesbury cites the elephant. This may not be totally off base as a description of adult males (who live on their own or in only loose association with other males), but it's a drastic mischaracterization of female elephants and their young. Perhaps Shaftesbury would have done better to cite the anti-social octopus, or maybe the giant panda, which spends almost the entirety of its adult life munching alone in bamboo forests. Other species, in contrast, can thrive only if their members engage in intensive cooperation for subsistence and safety. In those species nature has implanted a powerful concern not merely for offspring but for other conspecifics as well. As examples of sociable species Shaftesbury cites beavers, wolves, ants, and bees.

What about the human species? Are we more like pandas or beavers? Shaftesbury's answer: beavers, emphatically. We're "Creatures whose

OEconomy is according to a *joint-Stock* and *publick-Weal*" (C 3.136). We belong in the category of *"thorowly associating* and *confederate-Animals"* (C 3.134). Conspicuous features of human life make this clear. Human childhood is "long and helpless" (C 2.179). Even after grown to adulthood, a human being is relatively "feeble and defenseless . . . more fitted to be a Prey himself, than live by Prey on others." But while other animals unfit for predation can subsist by "grazing," a human "must have better Provision and choicer Food than the raw Herbage." While other animals can survive without housing or clothing, humans require "a better Couch and Covering than the bare Earth or open Sky."

Yet humans thrive despite their "Weakness" and "necessitous State" (C 2.179). They thrive because they excel at helping each other. And they excel at helping each other because they are implanted with strong mutual concern, a powerful herding principle. It starts with child-rearing. Human children can survive only if their parents expend prolonged, concentrated effort to raise them. If parents didn't have great love for their children for a very extended period of time—if they didn't care tremendously about their children's long-term welfare—they wouldn't have the motivation such an immense task requires. And it doesn't stop with parental affection. Siblings and other relatives are also bound by affection that leads them to help each other. So too are members of the same settlement. Circles of mutual concern radiate outward.

> If there be any thing of Nature in that Affection which is between the Sexes, the Affection is certainly as natural towards the consequent Offspring; and so again between the Offspring themselves, as Kindred and Companions, bred under the same Discipline and Oeconomy. And thus *a Clan* or *Tribe* is gradually form'd; *a Publick* is recogniz'd: and besides the Pleasure found in social Entertainment, Language, and Discourse, there is so apparent a Necessity for continuing this good Correspondency and Union, that to have no Sense or Feeling of this kind, no Love of *Country*, *Community*, or any thing *in common*, wou'd be the same as to be insensible even of the plainest Means of *Self-Preservation*, and most necessary Condition of *Self-Enjoyment*. (C 1.70)

Individual humans cannot "subsist" without "Society and Community." That humans do subsist—that they thrive—is testimony to the intense "Sense of Fellowship" they have with each other. It is as natural for us to care for others—to exhibit true kindness, compassion, and mutual succor—as it is for "the Stomach to digest, the Lungs to breathe, the Glands to separate Juices, or other Intrails to perform their several Offices" (C 2.45).

Shaftesbury is not doing conjectural history here. He's not considering an "imaginary *State of Nature*" (C 2.179), nor drawing implications about a hypothetical contract. He means to describe what in fact leads humans to engage in sociable cooperation. He's arguing that egoism is simply wrong as a description of human psychology.[30]

Shaftesbury intends his account to be continuous with scientific investigation of other parts of the natural world. Beavers, ants, and bees all cooperate in the "Arts of Storing, Building, and other Oeconomy" (C 2.179). Many beasts of prey are "very kind and loving" toward each other. Wolves, for instance, "strictly *join* in the Care and Nurture of the Young; and this *Union* is continu'd still between 'em. They houl to one another, to bring Company; whether to hunt, or invade their Prey, or assemble on the discovery of a good Carcase" (C 2.180; see also C 3.132–133). This care that non-human animals exhibit toward each other shows that egoism is false of them. Corresponding human phenomena show that it's false of humans as well.

The continuity Shaftesbury draws between humans and other animals sets him apart from rationalist and Christian thinkers who began with the assumption that the leading feature of human beings—exalted reason, immaterial soul—removes them to a realm distinct from the zoological. Shaftesbury differs from empirical examiners of our day in thinking of Nature as a purposive agent, as something to capitalize. But the nuts and bolts of his explanation of sociability—that humans have been endowed with powerfully altruistic traits that enable the species to thrive even though its individuals are weak and needy—can be straightforwardly translated into non-capitalized parlance. This explanation is a clear antecedent of the naturalistic examinations of human nature in Hume and Smith, a precursor to the new "science of man."

Shaftesbury uses this picture of human nature to attack Hobbes's social contract theory. He takes that theory to begin with the claim that humans originally existed in a state of nature that was an unsociable war of all against all. Such a picture is flatly contradicted by the facts of human nature as Shaftesbury understands them. Our innate constitution compels us toward society. Our inborn "Facultys" move us directly toward "Fellowship or Community" (C 2.178). Sociability is as natural to humans—as inextricably built into human nature—as self-interest (C 2.179).

Shaftesbury also argues that there is an incoherence in Hobbes's combination of the claims that it is not wrong to kill or maim other humans in the state of nature and that the original compact justifies allegiance to government:

> 'Tis ridiculous to say, there is any Obligation on Man to act sociably, or honestly, in a form'd Government; and not in that which is commonly call'd *the State of Nature*. For, to speak in the fashionable Language of our modern Philosophy: "Society being founded on a Compact; the Surrender made of every Man's private unlimited Right, into the hands of the Majority, or such as the Majority shou'd appoint, was of free Choice, and by a Promise." Now *the Promise* it-self was made in the *State of Nature*: And that which cou'd make *a Promise* obligatory in the State of Nature, must make *all* other Acts of Humanity as much our real Duty, and natural Part. Thus *Faith, Justice, Honesty*, and *Virtue*, must have been as early as the State of Nature, or they cou'd never have been *at all*. The Civil Union, or Confederacy, cou'd never make *Right* or *Wrong*; if they subsisted not before. He who was free to any Villany before his Contract, will, and ought to make as free with his Contract, when he thinks fit. The *Natural Knave* has the same reason to be *a Civil one*; and may dispense with his politick Capacity as oft as he sees occasion: 'Tis only *his Word* stands in his way—A Man is oblig'd *to keep his Word*. Why? Because *he has given his Word to keep it*.—Is not this a notable Account of the Original of moral Justice, and the Rise of Civil Government and Allegiance! (C 1.68–69; see also C 1.103–111, 1.72–76, 2.310–321)

Shaftesbury's argument is in the form of a dilemma. Either promises in the state of nature have obligatory force, or they do not. If promises in the state of nature do have obligatory force, then Hobbes can account for our obligation to obey government but only by abandoning his story about a state of nature in which violence toward others is not wrong. That's because someone who acknowledges that promises are naturally obligatory will have no grounds for denying that other things are naturally obligatory as well: "If in original and pure Nature, it be *wrong* to break a Promise, or be treacherous; 'tis as truly *wrong* to be in any respect in human, or any way wanting in our natural part towards human Kind" (C 1.69). If, on the other hand, Hobbes claims that promises do not have obligatory force in the state of nature, then he has to abandon his account of our obligation to obey government. For if a promise in the state of nature has no obligatory force, and if the only difference between a knave in the state of nature and a knave in the commonwealth is that the latter made a promise in the state of nature, then the commonwealth-knave is no more in violation of his obligations than the nature-knave.

Egoism falsely describes human nature. But Shaftesbury thinks it is a dangerous view nonetheless, one that it is crucial to defeat. For propagating the belief that it is impossible to have real concern for others will diminish individuals' drive to cultivate their benevolent tendencies. The Hobbesian view is self-fulfilling "Poyson" that induces people to act more selfishly. As Shaftesbury puts it in his 1698 preface to Whichcote's sermons, Hobbes "made War (if I may say so) even on Vertue it self" by "explod[ing] the Principle of Good-nature" and denying any "Enjoyment or Satisfaction in Acts of Kindness and Love."[31] In *Sensus Communis*, Shaftesbury makes a similar objection to religious versions of egoism, arguing that justifications of morality based on the afterlife are counterproductive because their emphasis on external rewards weakens people's commitment to virtue for its own sake.

> I have known a Building, which by the Officiousness of the Workmen has been so *shor'd*, and *screw'd up*, on the side where they pretended it had a Leaning, that it has at last been turn'd the contrary way, and overthrown. There has something, perhaps, of this kind happen'd in *Morals*. Men have not been contented to shew the natural Advantages of Honesty and Virtue. They have rather lessen'd these, the better, as they thought, to advance another Foundation. They have made *Virtue* so mercenary a thing, and have talk'd so much of its *Rewards*, that one can hardly tell what there is in it, after all, which can be worth rewarding. (C 1.61)

Focusing extensively on the external rewards of virtue can increase mercenary motivations so much that other kinds of motivation will be crowded out. Someone who has been "brib'd only, or terrify'd into an honest Practice" may cease to find the practice intrinsically valuable (C 1.61). Shaftesbury is making the same point as the "overjustification hypothesis" of recent experimental psychology, which holds that

> a person's intrinsic interest in an activity may be undermined by inducing him to engage in that activity as an explicit means to some extrinsic goal. If the external justification provided to induce a person to engage in an activity is unnecessarily high and psychologically "oversufficient," the person might come to infer that his actions were basically motivated by the external contingencies of the situation, rather than by any intrinsic interest in the activity itself. In short, a person induced to undertake an inherently desirable activity as a means to some ulterior end should cease to see the activity as an end in itself.[32]

If a child who loves reading for its own sake is told repeatedly that she will be given external rewards for finishing a certain number of books, she may lose her intrinsic love of reading and become less likely to read when no external rewards are promised. In the same way educators can undermine love of reading, egoists who try to justify morality by pointing to external rewards can corrode the love of real virtue. The intention behind the construction of an egoistic social contract theory is admirable enough. Social contract theorists believe that to describe the state of nature as a pleasant place is "to render it inviting" (C 2.180). So they go in the opposite direction, painting the state of nature in the darkest colors imaginable in order to motivate people to cherish and promote our social structures. They make the state of nature out to be by "many degrees worse than the worst Government in being. The greater Dread we have of *Anarchy*, the better *Country-men* we shall prove, and value more the *Laws* and *Constitution* under which we live" (C 1.180). But while the social contract theorist's imaginary story might be well-intentioned, the overjustification hypothesis explains how it can backfire. Better to encourage the innate sociability humans share than induce mercenary motives that can crush it.

The existence in human nature of the herding principle shows that self-interest isn't an insurmountable obstacle to the impartial love that is essential to virtue. But the herding principle does not lead inevitably to virtue. In fact, an uncultivated herding principle is the very cause of the second obstacle to moral beauty.

Morally beautiful people love humanity. They have the drive "to promote the Interest of the whole World" (C 1.23), an "equal, just and universal Friendship" (C 2.137). They're characterized not by "PARTIAL AFFECTION," which is a regard for "some *one* Part of Society," but by "INTIRE AFFECTION," which is "an *intire, sincere* and *truly moral*" regard for "Society *it-self*" (C 2.63–64). A fully virtuous person is one who works for the good of all. Essential to virtue is impartiality.

But the herding principle produces partiality. The problem here is not (as the egoist claims) that individuals don't sincerely care about other people. They truly do. The problem is that the herding principle can lead them to care sincerely about only some people, to the detriment of others. This obstacle to virtue is our innate disposition to tribalism.[33]

We are emotionally disposed to feel great concern for those with whom we are "intimately conversant and acquainted," for people in our "narrower Sphere of Activity" whose companionship we can "see" and "enjoy" and "taste" (C 1.70, 1.172). The trials and tribulations of distant folk tend to leave us cold. The bond that exists within the "contracted Publick" of those "sensible" to us does not "find Exercise for it-self in so remote a Sphere as that of the Body Politick at large" (C 1.70).

In *The Moralists*, Shaftesbury draws clearly this distinction between concern for people one knows "by sight" and concern for the masses of humanity one knows only "*in Idea*" (C 1.71). Philocles thinks himself fully capable of loving a companion. But, he says, the "*complex universal*" love for all of humanity is "beyond my reach. I cou'd love the Individual, but not the Species. This was too mysterious; too metaphysical an Object for me" (C 2.137). The narrator of *Sensus Communis* makes the same point: "Universal Good, or the Interest of *the World in general*, is a kind of remote philosophical Object. That *greater Community* falls not easily under the Eye. Nor is a National Interest, or that of a whole People, or Body Politick, so readily apprehended" (C 1.70). We have no direct acquaintance with the millions of people who make up the "Body Politick at large" (C 1.70). We are psychologically built to care about those with whom we have sensible interaction in a way we are not built to feel for people of whom we have merely a "Notion," an abstract idea (C 1.71).

But the problem is worse than a mere lack of concern. The herding principle leads us not only to love those in our narrow circle but also to hate those outside it. We cherish connection with those we're close to. We adore being in concord with them. And it turns out that one of the best ways of strengthening that connection—one of the most effective means of bolstering fellowship within the group—is to set ourselves in opposition to those outside. Empathy for friends and family can be intimately connected to antipathy to strangers.[34]

Shaftesbury describes this problem in terms of the great "force of the *confederating Charm*" (C 1.71). People crave "combining" with those with whom they have "*close Sympathy*" (C 1.71). The resulting desire "to move in Concert" leads subsets of society to conceive of their collective good as being in conflict with the rest of society. The power of fellowship is fueled by a shared hostility toward non-fellows. "[T]he *associating Genius* of Man is never better prov'd, than in those very Societys, which are form'd in opposition to the general one of Mankind, and to the real Interest of the State" (C 1.72). Because there is such a great delight to incorporating—and because small groups have such a potent psychological advantage over large groups—human beings are deeply susceptible to "Subdivision by *Cabal*" (C 1.71). "To *cantonize* is natural; when the Society grows vast and bulky" (C 1.71). Our emotional limitations facilitate this tendency. A sincere, non-selfish love for those in our small society can thus all-too-easily morph into a zeal that is destructive to society as a whole. "[B]y a small mis-guidance of the Affection, a Lover of Mankind becomes a Ravager: A

Hero and Deliverer becomes an Oppressor and Destroyer" (C 1.71). "[T]he social Aim is disturb'd, for want of certain Scope."

Consider the word "conspire." Its etymology of breathing together is morally neutral. And the word's base meaning of combine or unite can carry positive connotations as easily as negative ones. Indeed, Shaftesbury's characters in *The Moralists* rhapsodize about how multitudinous physical elements "conspire" to produce wonders of the natural world—about the "peaceful Concord, and conspiring Beauty of the ever-flourishing Creation" (C 2.209). But when we say that human beings are "conspiring," negative connotations are almost inevitable. We instinctively distrust people whispering to each other. We assume that individuals who are excluding others by breathing together are scheming with those on the inside at the expense of those on the outs. The *"conspiring Virtue"* (C 1.71) seems inseparable from purposes nefarious.

Francis Hutcheson addressed the phenomena of partiality as well. He too wanted to explain the tendency not only to promote the interests of our own group but also to oppose the interests of others. Hutcheson's explanation begins from the idea that humans are innately disposed to universal benevolence. He thinks we are endowed with moral and public senses whose default settings favor that which benefits all of humanity. He thinks as well that real disinterested malice does not exist. No one truly wishes for others' misery. Because of this deep-seated benevolence, we will oppose people whose aims we believe to be harmful to humanity. Unfortunately, we may become so accustomed to opposing those people that eventually we develop toward them a standing hostility that can look like malice. Imagine you oppose a political party because you sincerely believe its policies are harmful to society. If your belief in the harm of those policies is particularly powerful, that opposition may become so entrenched in your psyche that you end up harboring negative feelings toward anything you associate with the party, even if some of those things aren't actually harmful in themselves. This Hutchesonian explanation of partiality is fundamentally flattering to humanity. What we really care about is the good of everyone. The problem is just that our benevolent tendencies can be misdirected by mental associations we've accidentally formed. By consciously reflecting on the non-veridicality of those associations, Hutcheson believes, we can free ourselves of those misleading thoughts. And once we are free of those misleading thoughts, we will recover the impartial benevolence that is original to human nature.[35]

Shaftesbury's account is not as flattering. There's a sense in which he believes it's natural for us to care about humanity as a whole, but (as we will see in chapter 5) it's an aspirational sense. Love for all is a goal we have to work hard to achieve. It's not a matter simply of clearing our minds of a few adventitious associations and then letting our underlying benevolence shine through. To reach the goal of impartiality, we have to overcome powerful drives of partial sociability.

Joshua Greene puts this point in terms of two moral problems. One is "the problem of Me versus Us: selfishness versus concern for others."[36] The other is the problem of "Us versus Them: our interests and values versus theirs." According to Greene, long-ago evolutionary pressures from when humans lived in small groups solved the first problem by wiring the brain for emotions beneficial to kith and kin, such as love, guilt, honor, and loyalty. That same wiring, however, produced hostility toward those outside one's group, which gave rise to the partiality that is the root of the second problem. "Our brains are wired for tribalism. We intuitively divide the world into Us and Them, and favor Us over Them."[37] Greene's first problem—the problem of individual selfishness—dominated much of the moral theorizing of Shaftesbury's time. Hobbesian egoism was the great bugbear. Among Shaftesbury's most important predecessors, the Cambridge Platonists emphatically denounced Hobbes himself and devoted great effort to defeating his philosophy. Among Shaftesbury's most important successors, Hutcheson gave top priority to refuting the updated version of Hobbesian egoism that Mandeville advanced in his *Fable of the Bees*. Shaftesbury's early work falls squarely within that anti-egoist tradition, in both tone and content. The first book he published (in 1698) was an edition of sermons by the Cambridge Platonist Benjamin Whichcote, and in his preface Shaftesbury highlighted the moral importance of Whichcote's attack on Hobbes. His second published work (in 1699) was *An Inquiry concerning Virtue*, the entire second half of which is devoted to showing that we are built to be sociable with our fellows and are not selfish in the way Hobbes describes.

Shaftesbury never backed away from those anti-egoist claims. But he seemed to come around to thinking that Hobbesian egoism was not the gravest civic threat. The selfishness and corrupting greed of political leaders can certainly cause societal damage. But narrowly selfish private citizens generally pose minimal danger to the public weal. "[O]f all Characters, the thorow-selfish one is the least forward in *taking Party*. The Men of this sort are, in this respect, true *Men of Moderation*. They are secure of their Temper; and possess themselves too well, to be in danger of entering warmly into any Cause, or engaging deeply with any Side or Faction" (C 1.72). Thoroughly selfish individuals chart a moderate course. They are not swept by passion toward violent hostility. Much more dangerous are partisan zealots, those whose excessive attachment to a cause pulls them toward destructive hatred of others. It's not selfishness that drives the zealot. The zealot is motivated by "sociableness." But it's a sociableness that is misdirected to one part of society at the expense of others. The "very Spirit of *Faction*, for the greatest part, seems to be no other than the Abuse or Irregularity of . . . *social Love*, and *common Affection*" (C 1.72). It's Greene's second problem—"Us versus Them (not Me versus Us)"—that Shaftesbury came to see as politically the most pressing.

Shaftesbury's attitude toward Thomas Hobbes softened as a result. It was standard practice to label Hobbes a monster, to assail him as a loathsome standard bearer of immorality and damnation. Shaftesbury's early work has that tone. But by 1709, Shaftesbury seemed to think that although Hobbes's philosophical position was incorrect, his heart was in the right place. Hobbes was no partisan. He was in fact an "anti-Zealot." He really did care about the good of society as a whole.

> [T]he good sociable Man, as savage and unsociable as he wou'd make himself and all Mankind appear by his Philosophy, expos'd himself during his Life, and took the utmost pains, that after his Death we might be deliver'd from the occasion of these Terrors [the terrors, that is, of the English Civil War's "Spirit of Massacre" and "Ravage of Enthusiasm"]. He did his utmost to shew us, "That both in Religion and Morals we were impos'd on by our Governors; that there was nothing which by Nature inclin'd us either way; nothing which naturally drew us to the Love of what was without, or beyond *our-selves*": Tho the Love of such great Truths and sovereign Maxims as he imagin'd these to be, made him the most laborious of all Men in composing Systems of this kind for our Use; and forc'd him, notwithstanding his natural Fear, to run continually the highest risk of being a MARTYR for our Deliverance . . . Whatever *Savages* [people like Hobbes] may appear in Philosophy, they are in their common Capacity as *Civil* Persons, as one can wish. Their free communicating of their Principles may witness for them. 'Tis the height of Sociableness to be thus friendly and communicative. (C 1.57. See also C 1.58–60)

Hobbes's espousal of egoism is self-defeating, since the very making of that espousal contradicts his own interests. If Hobbes really cared only about himself, he would have publicly avowed anything but his selfish theory. But by publishing these views rather than taking the prudential course of keeping them secret, Hobbes created the opportunity for the sort of rational discussion of political institutions from which all stood to benefit. The dire picture Hobbes painted is itself a proof of his "Humanity," of his "love for Mankind." There was a time when I read this ad hominem as biting sarcasm. But it now seems to me to be gentle raillery. I think Shaftesbury really did admire Hobbes. He understood Hobbes's reaction to the political and religious violence of his time. He believed Hobbes had a sincere, non-partisan commitment to try to make things better.

At the same time, Shaftesbury continued to criticize divisive partiality. In the voice of the Miscellanarian of the third volume of *Characteristicks*, Shaftesbury castigates the authors of "Controversial Writings" (C 3.8; see also 1.42). Shaftesbury is, obviously enough, not opposed to philosophical refutation and defense. But he disdains contemporary authors' zeal for attack and counterattack. He understands the temptation to such "Feuds." They're "not so wholly unprofitable" (C 3.11). A work of "highest Eloquence and profoundest Erudition" might not draw many readers (C 3.9). But if the author attacks a *"living Antagonist,"* the public is more likely to take notice. If the antagonist responds in kind, and the author launches yet another counter, the spectacle may draw an even bigger crowd. People love to watch a fight. "[W]hen Issue is well join'd, the Repartees grown smart, and the Contention vigorous between the learned Partys, *a Ring* is made, and *Readers* gather in abundance." The more adversarial a performance, the easier it is to attract attention and money. Of this booksellers are well aware, which is why they constantly urge authors to these contentious back-and-forths. Shaftesbury tells the story of an unscrupulous glazier who gives a football to local youths and encourages them to play in a street, where they end up breaking many windows. The glazier profits from the "ruins of Glass cover[ing] the stony Pavements," even while the football itself becomes fatally deflated (C 3.11). Just so: booksellers profit from the kind of iterated fray that can be counted on to eventually drain the discussion of any meaningful content.

Most of these *"polemick* Writings" vanish without a trace in a year or two, all the *"Defenses,* the *Answers, Rejoinders,* and *Replications"* in the end little more than fuel for the fires of *"Pastry-cooks"* (C 3.10-11; see also 1.164-165). But the adversarial bickering does lasting damage along the way. It reduces public philosophy to mere amusement, to malicious diversion. It turns worthwhile intellectual debate into "a kind of *Amphitheatrical* Entertainment exhibited to the Multitude, by these *Gladiatorian* Pen-men" (C 3.9). Readers no longer engage meaningfully with ideas. Like sports fans, they simply root for their favorites to "maul" and "kill" the opposition. "Every one *takes party,* and encourages his *own* Side."

Controversial writing of this sort fosters a factionalism that rends society, an ugly partiality that is the gravest obstacle to moral beauty.

## 6. Self-Improving Artists

In the introduction to his *Treatise of Human Nature,* Hume credits "my Lord Shaftesbury" as one of the "philosophers in *England,* who have begun to put the science of man on a new footing."[38] Hume was right to give Shaftesbury that credit. Shaftesbury developed a new kind of astute attention to sentiments and motives, pioneering a moral psychological approach that would become extraordinarily fruitful for Hutcheson, Hume, and Smith.

Hutcheson, Hume, and Smith all followed Shaftesbury in his development of the moral sense, and in his connection of virtue to beauty. The theories of moral sense and beauty that Hutcheson, Hume, and Smith developed were all different in certain respects from Shaftesbury, as well as from each other. But the basic framework that would become so distinctive of the moral philosophy of the Scottish Enlightenment was set by Shaftesbury.[39]

I want to turn, however, to a difference between Hutcheson and Hume, on the one hand, and Shaftesbury, on the other. The difference is that Hutcheson and Hume placed more emphasis on third-personal moral evaluation, while Shaftesbury placed more emphasis on first-personal efforts to improve one's character.

In Hutcheson and Hume, sentiments that have moral content belong, for the most part, to observers. The Hutchesonian moral sense produces sentiments of approval that are the basis of moral evaluations of other people but are not typically motivating themselves.[40] The sentiments that underlie Humean moral judgments are not in the business of motivating naturally virtuous actions; the motives of naturally virtuous action are distinct passions without explicit moral content.[41] Hutcheson's and Hume's main focus is on how someone who is observing others comes to form judgments of their virtue or vice. Their model is an observer looking at something that already exists and assessing whether or not it is beautiful.

Shaftesbury's model is an artist trying to make something beautiful. He is concerned first and foremost not with judgments of other people but with what it is like for a person to be an *"Architect* of *his own Life"* (C 2.38). The important point for Shaftesbury is that a person should become a "self-improving Artist." One should become an artist whose medium is not "Stone or Marble" but one's own character. His philosophy is an exhortation to treat one's self as a work of art.

It's worth emphasizing the perspective Shaftesbury is urging when he tells us to become self-improving artists—to become artists whose medium is the self. It's a perspective of self-reflection, of critically examining oneself with the goal of alteration and improvement. This perspective is a defining feature of Shaftesbury's thought as a whole. His private notebooks constitute a years-long engagement with this perspective, an extended series of exercises in self-reflective criticism and revision. The moral sense emerges from this perspective; it's the capacity to judge one's own affections and sentiments, a second-order view of one's own first-order motives. As we'll see in chapter 4, the subject of *The Judgment of Hercules* is the moment a person steps back from first-order desires and inclinations and makes a conscious decision about which of them to follow and which to eschew. As we'll see in chapter 5, the essence of *Soliloquy's* "advice to an author" is to become "a strong *Self-Examiner*," to hold a mirror up to one's own ideas so that one can "play the Critick thorowly upon" oneself (C 1.105–106).[42]

This perspective is evoked by Shaftesbury's diction itself. The *Oxford English Dictionary* draws on Shaftesbury's writing for examples of usage over six hundred times. The largest category consists of noun adjuncts that begin with "self." Here's a partial list of Shaftesbury's words: self-abasement, self-advising, self-command, self-control, self-destructive, self-dislike, self-enjoyment (in the sense of possessing a self at all), self-entertainment, self-examiner, self-formation, self-governed (when applied to one thing rather than a state), self-ill, self-improving, self-injury, self-inspection, self-oppressor, self-neglectful, self-study, self-valuation, self-worth. Shaftesbury's writing is one of the earliest examples of usage in most of these entries, and he's the first or second for: self-command, self-control, self-dislike, self-entertainment, self-examiner, self-formation, self-governed, self-ill, self-improving, self-injury, self-inspection, self-neglectful, self-oppressor, and self-valuation. In an unpublished note, he urges himself to be a "Self-Legislatour."[43] The word "autonomy" as applied to individuals rather than political states did not appear in English until a 1798 translation of Kant. But Shaftesbury's urging us to think of our selves as works of art—and the "self" noun adjuncts he uses to articulate that perspective—show that he placed self-governance at the center of his moral philosophy a hundred years before. Standing back and critically reflecting on one's own motives is the essence of moral agency for Shaftesbury no less than it would be for Kant.

But Shaftesbury differs from Kant in a crucial respect. Kant believes that our ability to shape our affections is very limited.[44] He holds, for instance, that there cannot be any obligation to feel affectionate love for humanity since it's impossible to make oneself feel such a thing.[45] Ought implies can: since it is not the case that we can make ourselves feel love for all, it cannot be the case that we ought to feel it. On Kant's view, we must steel ourselves to do the right thing regardless of—and often despite—our sentiments. Calvinists and Hobbesians also take the fundamental shape of our affections to be largely fixed. Calvinists think we are fated to deal with ineluctably corrupt motives. Hobbes thinks we need to alter external circumstances to achieve acceptable results because our fundamental selfish motivations are fixed.

Shaftesbury's self-improving artists, in contrast, aim to improve their entire characters.[46] They seek to make themselves harmonious, not just to have one side of themselves prevail in internal conflict. To illustrate this goal, Shaftesbury tells a story of two brothers. The elder brother uses his greater strength to unfair advantage in their games of "Foot-Ball" (C 1.116). At first the younger brother tries to fight for the ball, but it is "to little purpose" (C 1.117). Then the younger brother arrives at a different strategy. He decides to ignore the ball and "lay about his elder Brother. 'Tis then that the Scene changes. For the elder, like an arrant Coward, upon this Treatment, presently grows civil, and affords the younger as fair Play afterwards as he can desire" (C 1.117). The conflict between people's unruly affections and their reasonable motives is like the battle between the two brothers. People may take their unruly affections to be givens and resign themselves to battling against them again and again. But that's the wrong strategy. What one ought to do is work to transform the unruly affections into "handsom and noble" sentiments (C 2.238). Having ugly internal aspects but producing correct behavior from fear of punishment, from desire for reward, or from brute psychological force exerted over regrettable appetites: none of those constitutes true self-improvement. Truly self-improving artists transform all their internal aspects into something beautiful.[47]

The philosopher nowadays most closely associated with this idea that we ought to treat our selves as works of art is Nietzsche.[48] Shaftesbury's and Nietzsche's conceptions of self-as-a-work-of-art are similar in certain respects. Both believe the perspective artists take on their creations aptly models the critical and reflective distance we ought to take in order to fashion our selves into something worthwhile. Both affirm the importance of unity of character. There is, however, a fundamental respect in which Shaftesbury and Nietzsche differ.

In Nietzsche, the comparison to a work of art can seem to be a paean to subjectivity, or at least an affirmation of the difference between the great artist and those who came before. When Nietzsche glorifies "real artists of life,"[49] when he praises becoming "poets of our life,"[50] he is trumpeting originality, individuality, the breaking of molds. Uniqueness is praiseworthy. Nietzschean artists create out of the peculiar strengths and weaknesses of their soul something that is *theirs* and no one else's, something "all their own."[51] It's their difference from predecessors—their "great liberation"[52]—that distinguishes the Nietzschean artists. They want to become "human beings who are new, unique, incomparable, who give themselves laws, who create themselves."[53] To be a Nietzschean artist is to be a "free spirit," an "immoralist," someone who breaks values in order to remake them, one's life an exercise in "*mak[ing]* something that is not yet there."[54] Nietzschean artists are members of the "cult of the untrue."[55]

Shaftesbury's understanding of life as a work of art has opposite implications. Shaftesbury's "thorow *Artist[s]*" never violate the "known Rules" of their art (C 1.162). They "abhor any Transgression" (C 1.162). They hew religiously to "the *Justness* and *Truth of Work*" (C 2.162). This difference from Nietzsche is embedded in Shaftesbury's use of the word "artist" itself (see also C 1.145).

When we post-Nietzscheans hear of a true artist, we are likely to think of a free-spirited painter, musician, or poet, a Beethoven or Rimbaud or Picasso, an innovator in the fine arts. When Shaftesbury was writing at the turn of the eighteenth century, "artist" was used differently: to designate someone skilled at accomplishing a practical task, "a craftsperson, an artisan," a "Mechanic" or "Artificer."[56] A wheelwright is this type of artist, as is a cobbler, a cooper, or any other adept workman. Distinctive of such an artist is the ability to achieve a tangible goal, the possession of a practical skill. Shaftesbury has this meaning in mind when he speaks of the "Artists" of old Egypt who engaged in manufacture and trade (C 1.27–28). Hume and Burnet use "artist" for someone who can fix the springs and pendulum of a watch.[57] The same meaning is present when Shaftesbury says that a magistrate is an "Artist" who has the practical goal of calming the unruly fears of citizens (C 1.11).

By the middle of the eighteenth century, however, "artist" had also come to be used to refer to painters, musicians, and poets. Shaftesbury uses the word that way too. In this passage his artists are sculptors: "Thus the best Artists are said to have been indefatigable in studying the best Statues: as esteeming them a better Rule, than the perfectest human Bodys cou'd afford' (C 1.90–91; see also 1.128). Here his artists are painters: "According to this Rule of the *Unity of Time*, . . . one shou'd ask an Artist, who had painted this History of *The Judgment of* HERCULES,

"Which of these four Periods or Dates of Time above propos'd he intended in his Picture to represent"' (C 3.219; see also 3.218, 3.247, 1.89, 1.126–28, 1.139–140). Elsewhere Shaftesbury's artists are orators (C 1.147), writers (C 1.203, 1.207), and musicians (C 1.85). In the index he compiled for *Characteristicks*, under the heading "Artists *rejoice in Criticism*," Shaftesbury writes, "*See* Poet, Painter, Architect" (C 3.255).

So there's an older definition of "artist": one skilled in practical tasks, such as a cobbler or cooper, an *artisan*. And there's a newer definition: one who practices the fine arts, such as a painter or musician, a *fine artist*. We might think there are important differences between them. Fine artists engage in aesthetic activities that are not useful, or at least are not primarily useful, not valued chiefly for their usefulness. Artisans produce works whose raison d'être is precisely their usefulness. Painters and musicians are lauded for their originality, for their capacity to create something novel. Cobblers and coopers may be esteemed for the ability to make exactly what was expected, to succeed at an established craft.

What's notable about Shaftesbury's usage is that his "artist" seamlessly covers artisans and fine artists. Both types cohabit the word when he writes, "[W]ithout *a Publick Voice*, knowingly guided and directed, there is nothing which can raise a true Ambition in the Artist; nothing which can exalt the Genius of the Workman" (C 3.247). He compares "our Writing-Artists, to the *Manufacturers* in *Stuff* or *Silk*" (C 3.5), placing writers and fabric-makers in the same category. Perhaps most representative of Shaftesbury's non-distinction between the artisan and the fine artist is the following:

> There is nothing more certain, than that a real *Genius*, and thorow *Artist*, in whatever kind, can never, without the greatest unwillingness and shame, be induc'd to act below his Character, and for mere Interest be prevail'd with to prostitute his *Art* or *Science*, by performing contrary to its known Rules. Whoever has heard any thing of the Lives of famous *Statuarys*, *Architects*, or *Painters*, will call to mind many Instances of this nature. Or whoever has made any acquaintance with the better sort of *Mechanicks*, such as are real Lovers of their Art and *Masters* in it, must have observ'd their natural Fidelity in this respect. (C 1.162)

Here we find "mechanicks" rubbing shoulders with "statuaries, architects [and] painters." Shaftesburean artists are both old-fashioned artisans and avant-garde artistes. To be an artist, for Shaftesbury, is to make things—to fashion out of raw materials a finished product. And that's the job of both the painter and the cooper.

What makes someone successful at that job? According to Shaftesbury, successful artists are those committed to "the *Justness* and *Truth* of *Work*," to "*Truth*, and *the Perfection of their Art*" (C 1.162–163). He claims, famously, that "all *Beauty is* Truth" (C 1.89).[58]

Some might balk at Shaftesbury's making truth the measure of artistic success. Strictly speaking, some might object, truth is a property of propositions that describe correctly states of affairs. But the bits of music and machinery that artists produce are not in the propositional business of describing states of affairs. True and false claims may be made *about* them. But the music or machine itself just *is*. Every bit of music or machinery that exists, equally exists. There is no sense in which one can be any more or less true than any other.

Such a dismissal of Shaftesbury's notion of the "truth of work" would betray a constricted conception of truth. *True* can be used to designate representational accuracy between a proposition's content and the state of affairs the proposition purports to describe. But that is not the word's only—nor its earliest, nor its most literal—meaning. *True* is also commonly used "of a person," such as when we speak of a true friend, of those who act true to form, of someone whose heart remains true.[59] In such cases, to be true is to be "faithful" or "loyal, constant, steadfast." *True* can be used to describe "linear objects," to signify that they are straight or level. An 1875 book on carpentry and joinery gives instructions on how a "strip [can] be cut and planed up perfectly true and even on its sides and ends." *True* can be used of music or a singer's voice, in the sense of being "correct in pitch" or "exactly in tune." *True* can be used of mechanical things, in the sense of being "accurately formed" and "correctly calibrated." An 1885 instructional manual for harness-makers and carriage-builders gives the following instruction: "To find if the axle is true in the line of the arms, get the height from the ground to the middle of the axle cap." The other day I took my bicycle to the shop for a tune-up and the mechanic told me that as part of the service he would "true the wheels." The answer to a crossword puzzle clue of "set straight" is "trued."

All these senses of "true" involve agreement or matching. Representational accuracy—agreement between a proposition and a state of affairs the proposition purports to describe—is one type of match. But it is only one type. There can also be an agreement or match between an object and a standard against which it is compared: between a friend's conduct and an expectation of loyalty, between a road and a criterion of straightness, between voiced notes and musical pitches, between car parts and a model of mechanical precision, between a bicycle wheel and a circle.

When Shaftesbury tells us that true artists are those committed fully and above all else to the "truth of work"—that "all beauty is truth"—he means that true artists are committed to making things in accord with the standard of beauty. And this reveals clearly the difference between Shaftesbury's and Nietzsche's exhortation to treat one's self as a work of art. The Nietzschean artist is a member of the "cult of the untrue" in that he refuses to abide by pre-existing standard. The Nietzschean "breaks values." The Shaftesburean artist hews religiously to the "the truth of work." An exemplar for Nietzsche could be Picasso breaking the rules of three-dimensional perspective. An exemplar for Shaftesbury could be a master craftsman refining a clock.

To be a self-improving artist, for Shaftesbury, is to aim to impart unity to one's character. Nietzsche too makes unity a goal. But Shaftesbury's notion of the unity that is beauty is pre-established and restricted in a way that Nietzsche's is not.[60] Rather than create new values "that had not been there before" (Nietzsche's words), Shaftesbury's artist of life hews to objective models "of *Order*, *Peace*, and *Concord*" (C 2.238). Shaftesbury's artist of life aims for the harmony within oneself and with humanity as a whole that is the teleological end of human nature.[61]

Consider an ancient Athenian's attitude toward the perfect body. He accepts a standard of what that body is like, believes in established proportions of muscle, sinew, and girth that define bodily beauty. Perhaps he has never met a person who has achieved that standard exactly. But he's seen it in sculpture and painting, and he knows of people who have approached it. As he puts in the effort to form his own body, he has the standard in mind. Shaftesbury's conception of making one's character into a thing of beauty is akin to that. There's an objective model of characterological perfection, an established standard of elegance for affections and desires and motives. It's the work of a lifetime to try to match it. Perhaps no one ever totally succeeds. But the closer to it one draws, the more virtuous one becomes: the more in line—the truer—one becomes to the beauty of God's creation.

The difference between Nietzsche's and Shaftesbury's artists of life is mirrored by the difference between Goethe and Shaftesbury on the myth of Prometheus.[62] Goethe takes Prometheus to symbolize an artist's independence from God. On Goethe's view, what's important about Prometheus is his revolt against Zeus, his rebellion. Goethe's Prometheus mocks Zeus, claiming that time is the master of them both, rather than Zeus his master. Goethe's poem ends with Prometheus boasting to Zeus that he will create a race of humans in *his image*, and that they will "ignore you, as I do!" Prometheus's creativity is a God-like power. In exercising his creative power, Prometheus becomes a rival to the gods. The lesson of Goethe's Prometheus is that the true artist frees himself from prior constraints, creating as he chooses rather than being restricted by God.

The passage in *Soliloquy* in which Shaftesbury discusses Prometheus is often cited as a key inspiration for Goethe. But the message Goethe takes from the myth could hardly have been more different from what Shaftesbury intends. Here's the passage.

> I must confess there is hardly any where to be found a more insipid Race of Mortals, than those whom we Moderns are contented to call *Poets*, for having attain'd the chiming Faculty of a Language, with an injudicious random use of Wit and Fancy. But for the Man, who truly and in a just sense deserves the Name of *Poet*, and who as a real Master, or Architect in the kind, can describe both *Men* and *Manners*, and give to an *Action* its just Body and Proportions; he will be found, if I mistake not, a very different Creature. Such a *Poet* is indeed a second *Maker*; a just PROMETHEUS, under JOVE. Like that Sovereign Artist or universal Plastick Nature, he forms *a Whole*, coherent and proportion'd in it-self, with due Subjection and Subordinacy of constituent Parts. He notes the Boundarys of the Passions, and knows their exact *Tones* and *Measures*; by which he justly represents them, marks *the Sublime* of Sentiments and Action, and distinguishes *the Beautiful* from *the Deform'd*, *the Amiable* from *the Odious*. The moral Artist, who can thus imitate the Creator, and is thus knowing in the inward Form and Structure of his Fellow-Creature, will hardly, I presume, be found unknowing in *Himself*, or at a loss in those Numbers which make the Harmony of a Mind. (C 1.128–129)

Goethe takes the crucial aspect of the Prometheus myth to be the conflict between Prometheus and Zeus, the contrast between artistic creation and following God. But Shaftesbury's contrast is between bad poets, who care only about vulgar rhyme and ridiculous displays of wit, and true poets, who work to represent accurately the nature of virtue. Shaftesbury's true poet is a *just* Prometheus *under* Jove, not a rebel fighting against Jove. His "moral artist" admires God, emulates God as far as he can. Shaftesbury's artists are glorious not to the extent that they separate from God, as Goethe would have it, but to the extent that their creations accord with—are true to—the beauty of God's design.[63]

## 7. Why Be Moral?

Why should we care about virtue? Why should we put in all that work to impart beauty to our character?

Shaftesbury's thinking about this question evolved. He never explicitly repudiated his earlier views. But by changing emphases and adding new elements, he did in the end affirm something different from what he started with. I'll group his thoughts into three answers. The first is the answer he gave in the 1699 *Inquiry*; the second, the answer he initially developed in *The Moralists*; the third, an answer that has its origins in *The Moralists* but is developed further in *Sensus Communis* and *Soliloquy*.[64]

### "VIRTUE IS *THE GOOD*, AND VICE *THE ILL* OF EVERY-ONE"

Here's how Shaftesbury begins Book 2 of the 1699 *Inquiry*: "We have already consider'd what Virtue is, who may be allow'd in any degree virtuous. It remains now to shew, what Obligation there is to Virtue, and how any one may have reason to embrace Virtue, and shun Vice."[65] What Shaftesbury goes on to say reveals that he intends this to be a question about the relationship between morality and happiness. Will the virtuous person be the most happy and the vicious person most miserable? Or might virtue be "*the Ill*, and depravity *the Good* of every Creature"?[66]

Shaftesbury initially gives voice to the worry that virtue and happiness are in conflict. Virtue involves promoting the welfare of others. But some may think that promoting the welfare of others "must often contradict and go against" the welfare of self. Indeed, some may think "that there is a perfect opposition between" promoting "the *common Interest*" and "the attainment of *privat Good*"—that virtue requires "self-denial, and, as it were, self-desertion."[67]

By the final section of Book 2 of the *Inquiry*, Shaftesbury claims to have demonstrated that the worry is groundless. Virtue not only promotes the general good of humanity but also the particular good of the virtuous person. Virtue is "a Happiness and a Blessing to each Creature in *particular* possessing it, and is *that* by which alone Man can be happy, and without which he can never but be miserable."[68] "Rectitude or Virtue must be the advantage, and Vice the injury and disadvantage of every Creature."[69] "[T]o yield or consent to any thing ill or immoral, is a breach of *Interest*, and leads to the greatest Ills," and, "on the other side, *Every thing that* is an improvement of Virtue, and that is establishing to right Affection and Integrity, is an advancement of Interest, and leads to the greatest and most solid happiness and enjoyment of Life."[70] Every character trait that is "good to all Society, and to Mankind *in general*" is "equally a Happiness and a Blessing" for the person who possesses it.[71] Virtue is "is *that* by which alone Man can be happy, and without which he can never but be miserable."[72] To be virtuous is to be happy. To be vicious is to be miserable. As Shaftesbury puts it in the final sentence of the book: "And thus Virtue is the Good, and Vice the Ill of every One."[73]

What comes between the question that opens Book 2 (Will virtue make us happy and vice make us miserable?), and the answer (Yes!) that closes it? A series of arguments that Shaftesbury calls his *"Moral Arithmetic."*[74] This is an enumeration of the advantages and disadvantages of virtue and vice, a computation "by way of Addition or Subtraction" of the effects of virtue and vice on a person's "Interest or Happiness in Life." When we do this summing up, Shaftesbury argues, we see that virtue comes out resoundingly ahead. Shaftesbury unleashes a battery of arguments to make the point.

First, he argues that sociable affections are intrinsically preferable to unsociable affections. Sociable affections are pleasurable.[75] To feel kindness, love, friendship, or gratitude is to be in a state of mind that is enjoyable. To have a "mild condescending Temper" that does "not easily take offence, and easily forgives" conduces to "Health and Contentment." Positive affection toward others promotes "easy and pleasant Living." On the other side, unsociable affections of malice, hatred, resentment are unpleasant. They are brooding and rancorous, a "plague and torment" to the person experiencing them.[76] "[T]o hate, to be envious, to be enrag'd, to carry Bitterness and Malice, is to *suffer*."[77] In a passage with an intensity that makes you wonder whether he had anyone particular in mind, Shaftesbury writes: "[W]hoever hates, whoever is angry, or feels rancor, is wounded, distress'd, agrriev'd; this cannot be otherwise in its own nature. So that whoever has ill will, and is carried to the injury, harm or sufferance of others, suffers within himself, and carries a wound within: and where the Passions of his horrid kind are deeply infixt, there the Heart is ulcerated, the Wound kept open and not cured; and the horridest of Tortures are thus made perpetual."[78] One's negative feelings toward others end up tormenting oneself.

Second, sociable affections have beneficial communicative effects that unsociable affections do not. When we care about others, we delight in what they delight in. We *"Participate in the Joy, Pleasure, or Prosperity of whom we love or kindly affect.*"[79] We transmit to each other our "Happinesses" and "Joys."[80]

> Now the Pleasures of *sharing Good with others*; of receiving it in fellowship and company; of gathering it from the pleased and happy States of those around us . . . ; the Pleasures or Delights of this sort are so infinitely spreading diffusive through our whole lives, that there is hardly such a thing as Pleasure or Contentment, of which this is not a part, and which, if this were taken away, would not totally sink and be corrupted, or at the least lose its chiefest vigor, that which made its refinement, and without which it would be dross.[81]

Nothing compares to the pleasure of communicative joys. Think of two friends laughing more uncontrollably at something because each of them understands perfectly why the other finds it so funny, or of one partner being more aroused by the realization that the other is aroused.[82] The mutuality of shared pleasure—the reflecting of it back and forth between people—amplifies delight.

Unsociable individuals may gain some of these communicative pleasures because there may be some other people they share joys with. Even a "destroyer or ravager" who openly violates the "Laws of Society" will feel the need for some "Friends, with whom he shares his Good, in whose Welfare he delights, and whose Joy he makes *his* Joy."[83] But the more people you are in affective harmony with, the more communicative joys you will experience. A person who cares about humanity impartially thus "enjoys a satisfaction vastly above what is receiv'd from that limited, entangled, and much corrupted pleasure of imperfect, *partial*, and *unintire* Affection."[84] When writing the first version of the *Inquiry*, Shaftesbury also thought that there is a psychic cost to distinguishing between a small group of people whose joys you can share and a larger group of people toward whom you feel hostility. Undergoing "the changeable successions of alternate Hatred and Love, Aversion and Inclination towards the same Object"—i.e., toward humanity—will diminish one's enjoyment of the good of even those within one's charmed circle. There's "an inconsistency and contradiction" to such a mindset. It produces "continual disturbance within, unquietness, disgust."[85]

Third, if we are sociable we will be able to bear our own survey. And being able to bear our own survey is the single most important ingredient to happiness. It is almost unavoidable, according to Shaftesbury, that human beings will reflect on their own conduct. Each of us "is forc'd to receive reflections back into his Mind of that which passes in it self, of the actions of his Will, and of his foregoing Behavior in the common course of his natural Temper towards his fellow Creatures, as well as in all occasions besides."[86] Each of us "is forc'd of necessity to endure the *review* of his own Mind and Actions, and to have representations of himself and his own Affairs constantly before him, obvious to him, and passing in his Mind."[87] Even "giddy and heedless people" whom we think of as unreflective cannot help but ruminate on their past deeds. All of us will judge ourselves, whether we want to or not.[88] When sociable people review their own conduct, they'll like what they see. Knowing that they've treated others well, and that they merit others' love and esteem, will produce happiness or peace within. Such a person will have "*a Mind or Reason in good order, reconcilable to it self, such as creates it self no unpleasant views, nor is of ill reflection.*"[89] On the other side, unsociable people will be tormented by their own review. There is nothing more "horridly offensive and agrieving" than to recall having done something "odious" and "of ill merit."[90] This is the sting of "natural Conscience," a pain that has nothing to do with externally bestowed punishment.[91] It's the knowledge of having acted badly itself that stings.[92] Shaftesbury uses numerous words for this state of mind: "self-contradiction," "self-disapprobation," "self-dissatisfaction," "self-accusation."[93] People who realize they've not been true to humanity are plagued from within by "*harshness, distast, sowerness, turbulence.*"[94]

If a vicious person's character becomes known, she will incur the "aversion," "contemt and hatred of mankind."[95] But the harms of self-disapprobation will afflict her even if other people don't know about it. And the effort of concealing her character from others brings its own special harms. By affecting the "subtilty and feignedness of carriage" concealment requires, she forfeits the "candor and ingenuity" essential for "ease and freedom" of mind.[96] She will invariably view other people as threats who might discover what she really is and reveal it to the world. As a result, "all trust and confidence in others, familiarity, inwardness, and heartiness with others must be in a manner lost," to be replaced by "suspicions, jealousies, hatred and enmity."[97] Most egregious of all, such a person will never be in real communion with others. Unable to share her true self, she will be relegated to a kind of permanent psychological exile, completely alone with what she really is, utterly alienated. Her internal state will be tantamount to "banishment or expulsion from human Commerce."[98] Were we to "form a Hell in our Imaginations," we could fashion nothing worse than to be "estranged from Mankind, and to be after this manner in a Desert, and in the horridest of Solitudes, even when in the midst of Society; and to live with Mankind as with a foren Species."[99] The inner life of such a person "becomes a Wilderness where all is laid waste, every thing fair and goodly remov'd, and nothing extant but what is dismal and horrid."[100]

Shaftesbury does consider the possibility of a human without a conscience, someone who is not at all disturbed by the thought of having treated others badly. He seems to have in mind what we would call a psychopath, a person lacking totally in human empathy. This mental condition, Shaftesbury contends, is the worst of all—"the horridest state of Savageness, Immanity [Inhumanity] and unnatural Passion."[101] "[N]ot to be sensible to the odiousness or mere deformity of Crime and Injustice (. . .) and to be so far without conscience, is to be most of all miserable in Life."[102]

A fourth argument Shaftesbury gives is based on the (interestingly odd) claim that the human mind tends toward "vexation."[103] If there's no mental force to oppose it, a person's vexatious tendency will grow into a strong habit. It will make a person liable to the "highest impatience,"[104] producing a temper in which "the slightest thing diseases and provokes, where displeasure and offence are always ready to arise . . . where bitterness and choler in a manner swim at the top and over all, and where something of a forward and malignant kind is ever stirring and active."[105] Left to our own devices, we are likely to become sullen, irritable, discontent, depressed. In this state, the mental pleasures "can be but very rarely experienced, must be faint, and of small continuance."[106] But getting out of oneself and engaging with other people will "allay and turn those Motions."[107] Friendship and society will check our natural tendency to vexation.

But the selfish unsociable person may still have plenty of physical pleasure, yes? Well, actually, no. This is Shaftesbury's fifth argument. Even "the *pleasures* of the *Body*, and the satisfactions belonging to Sense" pale in solitude. Without companions and fellowship, the "highest voluptuousness in eating or drinking" is hardly more enjoyable than the plainest sustenance.[108] Even the most depraved sensualist will find meager relish out of indulging himself alone. "The very notion of a *Debauch* (. . .) carries with it an apprehension of reference to Society, or to a Gang, or something of Fellowship."[109] To make anything "*truly pleasant*," a sensualist must find some way of "communicating his Joy, and sharing it at least with some *one* single person."[110] Not only the pleasures of mind but also the pleasures of body depend on sociability.

Underlying all these arguments is Shaftesbury's belief that human souls crave company as lungs crave oxygen. Humans of all creatures "can least bear Solitude or an intermission of social Enjoyment."[111] Even "ununiform and inconsistent livers" find "solitude and desertion" a torment.[112] Deprived of human commerce, a human "is hardly able to endure his Being." His life grows "heavy," he is condemned to "sadness, dejection and melancholy."[113]

The 1699 *Inquiry* is a remarkable performance. It's hard to imagine a stronger expression of sociability's importance for happiness, or the miseries of its lack. It's all the more striking coming from someone who in his private notebooks was excoriating himself for being a "monster" with respect to others, who was lamenting that even people who disagreed with each other about the most fundamental things were more in "harmony & agreement with one another" than they were with him, who was experiencing between himself and the other people an unbridgeable "gulf."

### "*BEAUTY* AND *GOOD* ARE STILL THE SAME"

One of the most famous aspects of *The Moralists*, and indeed of Shaftesbury's entire corpus, is the claim that "BEAUTY" and "Good" are "*one and the same*" (C 2.223, 2.232, 2.235).[114] Rivers says the claim is "one of the most important features of Shaftesbury's philosophy."[115] Fowler says that it "pervades Shaftesbury's entire system."[116]

At the same time, the beauty-good claim has long been the object of scathing criticism. In 1732, Berkeley ridiculed Shaftesbury's notion of "the beauty of virtue" as being entrenched "within the general and indefinite."[117] In 1751, Brown accused Shaftesbury and his followers of being "so *enamoured*" of their rhetoric "that they seem utterly to have forgot they are *talking in Metaphor*."[118] Martineau concludes his 1886 discussion of Shaftesbury by remarking that "we can only say" that the beautiful and the good "were blended in his idea of the right; and that their precise relations to each other are left undetermined."[119] In 1916, Albee suggested that while there may be some kind of relationship between "the Beautiful and the Good," Shaftesbury himself fails "to establish the true nature of that relationship, in any really philosophical sense."[120] Tiffany wrote in 1923 that the comparison of beauty and goodness contributed an "aspect of flimsiness and the air of diletanteism" to Shaftesbury's work.[121] Filonowicz maintained in 2008 that Shaftesbury's "celebrated identification of the Good and the Beautiful has almost always been found unconvincing. It surely enhanced his renown in the eighteenth century; probably many a salon intellectual was impressed to learn that [the beautiful was the good]. Most thoughtful philosophers, though, were quick to denounce this equation as pretentious nonsense."[122] The "whole thing is incoherent," Filonowicz concludes. "I say: give the whole thing up."

Even commentators generally sympathetic to Shaftesbury worry that his beauty-good claim is half-baked. Stolnitz develops a construal of the claim that he takes to be philosophically important while also suggesting that Shaftesbury's own writing does not clearly rule out less favorable readings. The claim is "less rigorous than it ought to be," Stolnitz writes.[123] It runs the risk of being interpreted as a "category-mistake," or as being "pieced together by ignoring (or failing to understand) the distinction between the 'is' of predication and the 'is' of identity."[124] Rivers thinks Shaftesbury's claim slides between different meanings: "In some places it seems that he is drawing an analogy purely for rhetorical purposes between art and morals, in others that he really means that the beautiful is the good."[125] Bernstein defends Shaftesbury for the most part but nonetheless concludes: "The various meanings of Shaftesbury's celebrated equation point to values which are sometimes in contradiction with one another and, more often, in comparative disharmony... some scholars have wondered whether Shaftesbury's identification of the good with the beautiful means much of anything. The real problem is that this equation means too much, and combines... ideas which... had better be kept distinct. Shaftesbury's celebrated equation was central to his lofty role as a prophet of a humanity at one with itself. It was also central to the confusions of his thought."[126]

The opprobrium directed at the beauty-good claim is misguided. The claim is Shaftesbury's way of summarizing a straightforward conclusion. It's the same conclusion Shaftesbury argued for in Book 2 of the *Inquiry*—that virtue will make a person most happy—modulated to the *Moralists'* equating of virtue to moral beauty.

The two-day dialogue of *The Moralists* has the same arc as Book 2 of the *Inquiry*. The dialogue opens with a question similar to the one at the beginning of Book 2 of the *Inquiry*. Book 2 of the *Inquiry* begins with the question of whether virtue or vice will make a person most happy. *The Moralists* begins with Theocles and Philocles asking how we should engage in the "pursuit of *Happiness* and *Good*" (C 2.127). If we want to have the best life, both works start by asking, what should we take to be most "valuable and worth the cherishing" (C 2.129)? It's the same question Socrates poses in the *Republic* when he asks how we ought to live.

Some people believe "that our real *Good* is PLEASURE" (C 2.128). Philocles contends that as an answer to their question, pleasure is either meaninglessly tautologous or obviously false (C 2.128–129).[127] Other people believe their real good consists of wealth or fame or flashy things, but all answers of that sort are failures too (C 2.239–241). Philocles also rejects the idea that our real good consists of satisfying whatever passions we happen to find ourselves with. Philocles himself, however, does not know what the right answer is (C 2.130).

Theocles thinks he knows. But rather than "tell you at once the Nature of this which I call GOOD" (C 2.135), Theocles decides to unfold his answer slowly, over the course of an extended conversation.

On the second day, toward the end of the dialogue, Philocles sums up what he takes Theocles's answer to be: "So that BEAUTY, said I, and GOOD with you, THEOCLES, I perceive, are still *one and the same*" (C 2.223).[128] Shaftesbury goes out of his way to make sure we are aware that this is Theocles's answer to the earlier question of what "our real *Good*" is by footnoting the earlier passage and having Theocles respond, "'Tis so . . . And thus are we return'd again to the Subject of our Yesterday's Morning-Conversation. Whether I have made good my Promise to you, in shewing the true *Good*, I know not." Philocles assures Theocles that he has succeeded in meeting "the terms in which you engaged me that morning. . . . You have indeed made good your part of the Condition, and may now claim me for *a Proselyte*" (C 2.223).

A little while later Theocles says that while many people chase all kinds of questionable things (pleasure, wealth, fame) because they think that it will make them happy, "with us, PHILOCLES! 'tis better settled; since for our parts, we have already decreed, 'That *Beauty* and *Good* are still the same'" (C 2.232). At the end of that sentence is another footnote referring to the passage from the earlier day when the question about what will truly make us happy was first raised. A short time after that, Philocles once again affirms Theocles's answer: "I am ready enough to yield there is no real *Good* beside *the Enjoyment of Beauty*" (C 2.235).

The beauty-good claim is, then, a response to the question of what our real good is, of how one can achieve the best life, of how one ought to live. Theocles's answer is that beauty is our real good, that beauty should be our ultimate end, that a life pursuing beauty and the good life are one and the same.

At the end of the *Inquiry*, Shaftesbury claimed that people will be most happy if they are virtuous and most miserable if they are vicious—that the highest good for every person is virtue. At the end of *The Moralists*, Shaftesbury has Theocles claim that the highest good for every person is moral beauty, which is how he conceives of virtue. One's "Good," in Shaftesbury's terminology, is what will make one happiest (see C 1.126–127 and

1.190–196). The *Inquiry* concludes that "Virtue is the Good, and Vice the Ill of every-one." *The Moralists* concludes that beauty and good are "one and the same."[129] As Shaftesbury puts it toward the end of *The Moralists*, we are happiest when "we are reconcil'd to the goodly *Order* of the Universe [so] that we harmonize with *Nature*; and live in Friendship both with God and Man" (C 2.242).

We can question the specificity of Shaftesbury's views. But the basic idea of the beauty-good claim is clear enough. Beauty is harmony. Moral beauty is harmony of one's internal principles and harmony between oneself and humanity. We will have the best life if we value moral beauty. The good life and a life that values moral beauty are one and the same. This view does not seem to be obviously any more vague, incoherent, or confused than the prescriptions for how to live delivered by, say, Socrates or Epictetus.

That's not to say the beauty-good claim is obvious. Shaftesbury still owes us reasons to believe that humans will be happiest by pursuing moral beauty. We can group what he says about this in *The Moralists* into two main arguments.

The first *Moralists* argument for the happiness of a life of moral beauty is based on moral beauty's being constant and in our control.[130] When Theocles and Philocles first pose the question of what our real good is, they set a condition any successful candidate must meet. If something is our real good, it must "constantly" make us happy: "*Nothing can be good but what is constant*" (C 2.128).[131]

Philocles worries that nothing will meet this condition, that everything that provides enjoyment at one point will "nauseate and grow weary" at another (C 2.242). Theocles responds to Philocles's worry by arguing that the condition is met by moral beauty. Moral beauty will "afford Contentment and Satisfaction always alike, without variation or diminution" (C 2.134). Indeed, the more proficient you become at morally beautiful conduct, the greater your enjoyment of it will become. As well, the enjoyment of moral beauty is entirely within your own control. The joys people receive from "movable *Goods*" such as "*Plate, Jewels,* [or] *Apartments*" are "uncertain," depending as they do on "Fortune, Age, Circumstances, and Humour" (C 2.242). Riches and fame are no less fickle. Those who place ultimate value on such things inevitably suffer dissatisfaction and misery. But "if instead of placing Worth or Excellence in these *outward* Subjects, we place it . . . in the *Affections* or *Sentiments*, in the *governing Part* and *inward Character*; we have then the full Enjoyment of it within our power" (C 3.121). If we make our highest joy the beautifying of our own affections—if we realize that "Consistency of Life and Manners" and "Harmony of Affections" are our greatest good—then our *"Content and Happiness"* will be entirely within our own control, insulated from fortune (C 2.242; 2.63). Nothing can impose loss or disappointment at our core. We will have no reason to be anything but grateful to providence for having "plac'd our Happiness and Good in things *We* can bestow upon *ourselves"* (C 2.243).

The second *Moralists* argument for the happiness of a life of moral beauty is based on moral beauty's naturalness. There are three steps to this argument. The first step is that observation of living things in general reveals that every creature is happiest when it acts naturally and miserable when it acts unnaturally (C 3.129-137). For members of every species, there is nothing "more desirable than *to follow"* nature (C 2.242). A life in conflict with natural affection is "wretched" (C 1.76).

The second step is that it is natural for humans to value beauty over deformity. The evidence for this claim is that humans value beauty over deformity at every age and in every culture. That there is a difference between beauty and deformity and that beauty is preferable is something "no-one goes about to *teach*: nor is it *learnt* by any; but [is] *confess'd* by All" (C 2.232). The drawing of this distinction is apparent even in the behavior of infants, who are pleased by ordered, proportional shapes and prefer them to disordered, irregular ones. People disagree about which things are beautiful and which are not, but about whether there is such a distinction all are "universally agreed" (C 2.232). Indeed, it is precisely because people agree that there is such a normative distinction that they end up arguing with each other about which things are beautiful.[132] Shaftesbury's claim here is not that humans have innate propositional knowledge about the nature of the beautiful, nor that humans invariably identify correctly which things are really beautiful. He thinks people misperceive the extent to which things are harmonious and ordered, and as a result how people respond can fail to track what is truly beautiful (C 1.217-218). His claim is that humans have an innate sensibility to favor what they perceive (or misperceive) to be harmonious and ordered, to be beautiful.[133]

The third step is that it is natural to apply the normative distinction between beauty and deformity to conduct and character. All humans take "Beauty of Soul [to be] as real, and necessarily moving" as beauty of figures, colors, and sounds (C 2.231). There is *"a natural Prevention*, or *Prepossession* of the Mind, in favour of this moral Distinction" (C 2.25). We naturally distinguish *"the Fair* and *Shapely, the Amiable* and *Admirable,* apart from *the Deform'd, the Foul, the Odious,* or *the Despicable"* in "*human Affections* and *Passions*" as well as in physical objects (C 2.231). There is "a natural Beauty of *Figures*" and "as natural one of Actions" (C 2.231; see also 2.232).

We do not distinguish the beautiful from the deformed in conduct and character at as early an age as we distinguish it in simple shapes. We must become cognitively sophisticated enough to understand how behaviors result from affections and passions, for it is affections and passions that we find beautiful or deformed, not bare behavior itself. But once we do develop an understanding of internal motivations—once we develop the "Capacity of seeing and admiring in this new way" (C 2.25)—we distinguish between them and prefer some to others as invariably as we do in the case of figures, colors, and sounds. We naturally respond to "a *Foul* and *Fair*, a *Harmonious* and a *Dissonant*" in conduct no less than in music and painting (C 2.17). We are just as naturally disposed to feel positively toward "Beauty and Comeliness" in character as we are to feel it toward features of physical bodies (C 2.17). It is as innate or instinctive for us to distinguish harmonious minds from disharmonious minds, and to prefer the former, as it is for us to do so with figures, colors, and sounds. This does not mean our moral judgments are always correct. Just as we can make mistakes about the beauty of an object, so too can we make mistakes about beauty of conduct and character. But drawing the normative distinction between moral beauty and deformity is natural to us, even if we often fail to do so correctly.[134]

In the negative views to which Shaftesbury was reacting, morality consisted of commands. Our reason to obey the commands was to avoid punishment. According to the negative view of Hobbes, our duty is to obey the commands of a sovereign with the power to destroy those who disobey. According to the negative view of the Calvinists, our duty is to obey the commands of a God with the power to condemn us to eternal torment. For Shaftesbury, morality is not a matter of obeying commands. It doesn't require resisting natural tendencies. It's not a yoke to bear. We'll be happiest if we pursue moral beauty, because that's what we are naturally fitted for. To be virtuous is to go with the flow. As health is to the body, virtue is to the psyche. Moral beauty is our good.

Before discussing the third answer to the "why be moral?" question, we need to address an interpretive issue. Shaftesbury's first two answers were versions of the idea that virtuous character makes for the happiest life. How does that square with Shaftesbury's criticism of self-interested views of morality?

Shaftesbury is very clear that if you benefit others only because you think it will promote your own welfare, then you will lack virtue even if you do the right thing.

> Whatsoever therefore is done which happens to be advantageous to the Species, thro' an Affection merely towards Self-good, does not imply any more Goodness in the Creature than as the Affection it-self is good. Let him, in any particular, act ever so well; if at the bottom, it be that selfish Affection alone which moves him; he is in himself still vitious. Nor can any Creature be consider'd otherwise, when the Passion towards Self-good, tho ever so moderate, is his real Motive in the doing that, to which a natural Affection for his Kind ought by right to have inclin'd him. (C 2.14; see also 2.61–62)

You will be virtuous if you benefit others because you care about their welfare, not if your only goal is to promote your own interests. But given that Shaftesbury thinks the motive of promoting your own interests is incompatible with true virtue, why does he spend so much time arguing that acting virtuously will make you happy? Isn't that like a teacher who tells students that they will achieve real learning only by focusing on the intellectual merits of the material and not by merely regurgitating lectures on the exams—and then spends half the semester stressing to students that they need to say such-and-such on the final exam in order to get an A? As Hutcheson says of his own attempt to defend this type of view, "It may perhaps seem strange, that when in this *Treatise* Virtue is supposed *disinterested*; yet so much Pains is taken, by a *Comparison* of our several *Pleasures*, to prove the *Pleasures of Virtue* to be the greatest we are capable of, and that consequently it is truest *Interest* to be *virtuous*."[135]

Numerous commentators have addressed this interpretive issue. Some have come to the exasperated conclusion that Shaftesbury is inconsistent.[136] Others have tried to show that despite his seeming denigration of self-interested motives, Shaftesbury is an egoist after all, someone who thinks that the justification for all conduct is ultimately one's own pleasure.[137]

I think the more accurate interpretation is that Shaftesbury's views on the relation between virtue and happiness are in line with what Den Uyl calls "classical virtue ethics"—the eudaimonism of Plato, Aristotle, and the Stoics.[138] These eudaimonistic thinkers do affirm that virtue benefits its possessor. Nonetheless, they deny that people who possess virtue do the right thing because they think it will make them happy. To possess virtue is to be committed to certain values, and it's those values that motivate the virtuous person, not the self-interested benefits that may result. For the virtuous person, virtuous conduct is intrinsically choice-worthy. Caring about other people is not merely a means to some distinct pleasurable experience.[139] Caring about other people for their own sakes is itself essential to, is constitutive of, the experience of living well. This is not akin to a teacher who tells students what to say on the exam in order to get an A. This is akin to a teacher who tries to impress on students that it will profoundly enrich their lives to engage fully with the material for its own sake, not because of a grade.

But it's also the case the Shaftesbury's thinking evolved from the early versions of the *Inquiry* and *The Moralists*. In *Sensus Communis* and *Soliloquy*, he explores new aspects of the non-egoist view of moral motivation. The resulting position constitutes one of Shaftesbury's most profound and underappreciated moral insights. We turn to that position now.

## "THE *HONEST MAN* . . . CAN'T DELIBERATE IN THE CASE OF A PLAIN VILLANY"

Shaftesbury distinguishes between, on the one hand, valuing something instrumentally, and, on the other hand, valuing something for its own sake, because it is beautiful (C 2.221–222). A merchant who gains pleasure by calculating the profit he can make by shipping goods across the ocean values the ocean instrumentally. A shepherd who gains pleasure by standing on a cliff contemplating the ocean's beauty (and perhaps losing track of his sheep as a result) values the ocean for its own sake. The shepherd is responding to the beauty of the ocean, not to its instrumental capacity to satisfy desire.

Once he has established this idea of valuing beauty for its own sake, Shaftesbury makes two moves. The first is to pivot from the third-person observer perspective of the shepherd to the first-person creator perspective of the artist. In the same way the shepherd delights in the ocean's beauty even though he stands to gain nothing from it, artists can be motivated to create things of beauty independent of any beneficial consequences their creations may have for them.

The second move is to apply this motive to the work of the self-improving artist. Just as an artist of physical objects can have a motive to create things of beauty independent of any consequences, so too self-improving artists can have a motive to make of themselves something beautiful independent of any consequences. A sculptor has a non-negotiable commitment to the beauty of her sculpture. Self-improving artists have a non-negotiable commitment to the beauty of their selves.

Thorough artists care about beauty in a manner that makes them willing to sacrifice any other benefit to achieve their goals. If you ask why creating beauty matters so much to them, you're not likely to get much of an answer. That's because for thorough artists, making something beautiful will be an ultimate end, where answers to the "why" questions run out. Their motive to create beauty is as independent of other results as is the shepherd's joy in the beauty of the ocean.

Shaftesbury thinks we have all heard stories of sculptors and painters willing to suffer great hardship for their art. We can find the same commitment in "the better sort of *Mechanicks*" (C 1.162). No matter how "dissolute, or debauch'd" they may be in other aspects of their lives, they "wou'd chuse to lose Customers and starve, rather than by a base Compliance with the World, to act contrary to what they call the *Justness* and *Truth of Work*" (C 1.162). Shaftesbury describes a poor mechanic who refuses to produce shoddy work even though a rich customer promises to pay handsomely for it. "'Sir' (says a poor Fellow of this kind, to his rich Customer), 'you are mistaken in coming to me, for such a piece of Workmanship. Let who will make it for you, as you fansy; I know it to be *wrong*. Whatever I have made hitherto, has been *true Work*. And neither for your sake or any body's else, shall I put my hand to any other'" (C 1.162–163). Sculptors, painters, and mechanics such as this are "real Lovers of their Art" (C 1.162). Like the shepherd gazing at the sea, they care about beauty for its own sake, not as a means to anything else. Beauty is for them ultimately valuable. It trumps every other consideration.

The truly virtuous person cares about moral beauty in the same nonnegotiable way true artists care about the beauty of their creations. "This is VIRTUE!," Shaftesbury says of the mechanic's commitment to doing things the right way regardless of the consequences, *"real Virtue*, and Love of *Truth*; independent of *Opinion*, and above the WORLD. This Disposition transfer'd to the whole of *Life*, perfects a Character. . . . For is there not a *Workmanship* and *a Truth* in ACTIONS?" (C 1.163). True artists' love of beauty underlies both their appreciation of beautiful works that already exist and their drive to create beautiful works themselves. In the same way, one's love of moral beauty can underlie appreciation of the virtue of others and the motivation to be virtuous oneself.

This motivation can have ultimate practical authority. If certain conduct is in accord with moral beauty, we may take that to be a reason for action that overrides any other consideration. The end of moral beauty may be for us of absolute value, not subject to calculative weighing, something that trumps everything else. Shaftesbury makes this point in his rejection of the view that to determine how to act is invariably to weigh "the Number and Exquisiteness of *the pleasing Sensations*" of each option and then to choose the option that maximizes those sensations (C 1.77). This is the view that holds that all practical reasons are to be reduced to the "same Coin" of fungible pleasures, what we would today call hedonistic Benthamite consequentialism (C 1.78). According to Shaftesbury, a person who makes decisions by thinking in this hedonistic consequentialist way doesn't actually have a true grasp on morality at all. To think in this way is to take whether to act virtuously to be an open question—a question that will be answered by a comparison of the pleasures produced by the virtuous and the vicious actions. But someone with a truly moral character "is incapable of doing a rude or brutal Action. He never *deliberates* in this case, or considers of the matter by prudential Rules of Self-Interest and Advantage. He acts from his Nature, in a manner necessarily, and without Reflection" (C 1.81). Those with true moral character do not weigh the results of virtue against the results of vice. They do not assign to virtue a comparative value based on the fungible states of pleasure it may produce. If acting in a certain way is virtuous, then those with moral character never even consider acting any other way. Of a "vile Action" they "wou'd not be guilty . . . for the whole World" (C 1.83).

Shaftesbury expands on his criticism of hedonistic consequentialism in his discussion of someone with "the Countenance of a Gentleman" who asks why he should "avoid being *nasty*, when nobody was present" (C 1.78). Shaftesbury's narrator answers the gentleman by pointing out that it would be unpleasant to smell one's own nastiness. The gentleman responds by stipulating that he is not able to smell himself because he has a cold. The narrator says that it would still be unpleasant to see oneself in a nasty condition. The gentleman stipulates that he cannot see anything because it is dark. The narrator says that he himself would not want to be nasty regardless of any olfactory or visual sensations, because being clean is what he owes himself, what becomes him as a human creature. "[T]ho I had neither Nose, nor Eyes, my *Sense* of the matter wou'd still be the same; my Nature wou'd rise at the Thought of what was sordid" (C 1.78). That is how anyone who truly cares about cleanliness will feel. The very asking of the question reveals that the asker does not properly appreciate the value of cleanliness. The narrator says that he would be "fully satisfy'd that he himself was a very nasty Gentleman who cou'd ask this Question; and that it wou'd be a hard matter for me to make him ever conceive what *true Cleanliness* was" (C 1.78). The mere fact that he asks for a reason not to be nasty reveals that he does not value cleanliness in the right way. The narrator then maintains that the case is exactly the same with regard to the question of why one should *"be honest in the dark"* (C 1.78). By asking such a question, a person reveals that he does not truly value virtue. A person who truly values honesty and other aspects of virtue, like a person who truly values workmanship and cleanliness, does not think of them as producers of separable, fungible pleasures that are to be weighed against others. A truly honest person "can't deliberate in the Case of a plain Villany" (C 1.81).[140]

Shaftesbury's perspective of the self-improving artist thus leads him to embrace an ethical commitment that is in some ways more similar to that of traditional deontology than to any kind of consequentialism. Like traditional deontologists, Shaftesbury thinks moral reasons have non-negotiable, overriding practical authority. Just as a true artist never considers producing bad art, a truly honest person "never deliberates" about whether to be honest. Like traditional deontologists, Shaftesbury thinks that when something is the right thing to do, the virtuous person will do it regardless of the consequences. Like traditional deontologists, Shaftesbury thinks the practical authority of moral reasons is intrinsic to them, not the result of their being commanded or of their being instrumental to any other end.

At the same time, Shaftesbury differs from traditional deontologists in two respects. First, central to traditional deontology is the notion of duty. "Duty" originates in something's being due, the payment of a debt that is owed. This is a fundamentally negative concept, a concept in which the negative is prior: you perform the action that is due because it would be wrong if you didn't, because if you didn't you would be in moral arrears. Central to Shaftesbury's view, in contrast, is the positive concept of creating moral beauty. Shaftesbury agrees with traditional deontologists that moral reasons are intrinsically normatively compelling. But in Shaftesbury, the model isn't being compelled to pay a debt. The model is feeling compelled to make something beautiful.

Second, Shaftesbury differs from traditional deontologists in his view of sentiment. Traditional deontologists believe that rationality alone grounds morality's authority. They deny that sentiment can give rise to the non-negotiable commitment morality demands. Shaftesbury, in contrast, describes a non-negotiable commitment that is based in the sentiment.

As we saw above (section 4), the role of sentiment is clear in Shaftesbury's account of the sense of right and wrong in the *Inquiry*. He acknowledges that the sense of right and wrong requires the reflective capacity to conceptualize motives. A creature who "cannot reflect on what he himself does" cannot have a sense of right and wrong (C 2.18). For this reason Shaftesbury says that human morality is based on *"rational Affections"* (C 2.21). But it is still affections that human morality is based on. Shaftesbury writes, "So that, by means of this reflected Sense, there arises another kind of Affection towards those very Affections themselves, which have been already felt, and are now become the Subject of a new Liking or Dislike" (C 2.16). Reflection paves the way for the feeling of moral sentiment. But the sentiment—the "Liking or Dislike," the "Exercise of the Heart"—is essential (C 2.16, 2.18). The role of sentiment is also clear in *The Moralists*. That work opens with Palemon bemoaning his failure to feel the love that a truly moral person will feel, lamenting that he lacks the kind of "human Heart" he thinks he should have (C 2.112). Philocles initially expresses the same emotional failing. Theocles then sets out to awaken in Philocles the appropriate "Sentiment" of love for humanity (C 2.136). The role of sentiment is clear as well in Shaftesbury's *Soliloquy*, in the contrast between the honest artisan and the nasty gentleman. What is right with the mechanic and wrong with the nasty gentleman is not a matter of reasoning. The mechanic's refusal to accede to a lucrative request to make something shoddy is not the result of intellect. He "has no other *Philosophy*, than what *Nature* and his *Trade* have taught him" (C 1.163). His refusal to make something shoddy—his surliness at even being asked—reflects his sensibility. It reflects his love of *"true Work,"* which he cares about above all opinion and worldly goods. And the nasty gentleman of the *Sensus Communis* seems like a clever enough fellow. There's nothing wrong with his reasoning process. Because he's not making any rational mistake, there may be no way to argue him into appreciating cleanliness.[141] The problem is that he lacks the sensibility that would make him averse to sordidness. There's something wrong with his "heart" (C 1.81).

In historiographies of modern moral philosophy, the field can sometimes seem to be exhausted by rationalist deontology (e.g., Clarke and Kant) and sentimentalist utilitarianism (e.g., Bentham and Mill). It can seem as though a non-negotiable commitment to rightness requires a purely rational foundation, while a sentimental foundation inevitably leads to consequentialist maximizing. At the turn of the twenty-first century, thinkers armed with new moral psychological insights began to explore the fruitful third alternative of sentimentalist deontology.[142] Shaftesbury could have saved us a lot of time. At the turn of the eighteenth century, he developed the picture of an impassioned and dedicated artist that models a commitment to doing what's right that is based in sentiment but is nonetheless categorical.

## 8. Literal or Metaphorical?

One of the most long-standing criticisms of Shaftesbury is that his view of moral beauty confuses the metaphorical with the literal. I'm not sure I have a firm grip on how to distinguish the metaphorical from the literal in moral philosophy. But it seems to me that Shaftesbury's view can be read as a literal claim of questionable plausibility, or as a salutary metaphor.

Shaftesbury says that virtue is a kind of beauty. We can construe this claim literally by holding that what makes every beautiful thing beautiful is its possession of the property of unity, proportion, balance. A building can be unified, proportionate, and balanced; as can a painting; as can a piece of music. A human character can be unified, proportionate, and balanced as well. When a person is virtuous—when a person's character is internally harmonious and in harmony with humanity as a whole—the person instantiates the same property of unity, proportion, and balance possessed by beautiful buildings, paintings, and music.

This literal reading of Shaftesbury's claim is coherent. But if it requires that there are necessary and sufficient conditions that all beautiful things meet, then it's not very plausible. It seems unlikely that we are responding to a single substantive property for which necessary and sufficient conditions can be given whenever we respond positively to all the things Shaftesbury thinks can be beautiful (a building, a painting, a piece of music, a person, an ecosystem). As we've seen, Shaftesbury uses a number of different words for the property of beauty: unity, proportion, balance, harmony, regularity, order, symmetry, integrity. The length of the list may itself be an indication that what is at play cannot be captured by a clean set of necessary and sufficient conditions.

Perhaps we can construe the claim as asserting a family resemblance between all the things to which Shaftesbury ascribes beauty, with the various words (unity, proportion, balance, etc.) suggesting the various related traits. This construal of the claim is more plausible than the necessary and sufficient construal, although how much more plausible, I'm not sure. I'm also not sure whether Shaftesbury would take the family resemblance construal to be a friendly or hostile suggestion. (Nor am I clear about whether the family resemblance construal makes the claim less literal.)

The other reading takes the notion of moral beauty to be a vivid way of comparing the creation of a beautiful work of art to the cultivation of a virtuous character—as a kind of metaphor. Does that metaphorical comparison serve a worthwhile purpose?

Metaphorical comparisons in moral philosophy serve a worthwhile purpose when they use our settled understanding of one thing to vivify a way of conceiving something else. We have a clear sense of the importance of keeping our end of a fair contract. Social contract theories direct our attention to the similarity between keeping our end of a fair contract and civic obligation. We have a clear sense of the importance of certain kinds of practice for becoming skilled at brick-laying or piano-playing. The virtue-as-skill analogy directs our attention to the similarities between becoming skilled at those tasks and developing the virtues. We have a clear sense of the importance of a state's being able to make its own laws rather than being forced to obey the dictates of a foreign power. Autonomy-based moral views direct our attention to the similarity between a state's making laws for itself and our duties being based on what we prescribe to ourselves rather than on what is externally imposed on us.

We have a clear sense of the difference between beauty and ugliness—between art and dreck, between quality craftsmanship and shoddiness, between politeness and vulgarity, between cleanliness and nastiness, between good writing and bad. Shaftesbury seeks to convince us that the distinction between virtue and vice is as compelling as, but even more important than, those other distinctions. The very reason we have to care about landing on the right side of those other pairs is of exceedingly greater power when it comes to virtue and vice (C 1.84–89, 3.185).

The comparison of virtue to beauty advances Shaftesbury's goal of replacing the then-dominant commandment-based concept of duty with a view of virtue as delightful and attractive. Shaftesbury can now model morality on the pursuit of something wonderful rather than on obedience to a law. The comparison conveys the idea that just as artistic refinement requires learning and examination, moral judgment can require careful conscious thought. It conveys the idea that to fashion a virtuous character is to bring all the various parts of a complex entity into one integrated whole. The phenomenology of an artist or writer who cares passionately about the beauty of work—who has an unshakable drive to *get it right*—enables Shaftesbury's endorsement of a non-negotiable deontological-like commitment to virtuous conduct.

Most fundamentally, Shaftesbury's comparison of virtue to beauty can activate the notion that the shape of your character is something that matters and that you can improve—that you can put your mind to making yourself a better person, and you will be happier for doing so.[143]

To contemporary academic philosophers who spend lots of time thinking about morality, that self-improvement message may sound banal. But

Shaftesbury wasn't writing for them. He was writing for readers who believed they should be virtuous but who worried that it might be difficult or unpleasant. Such people, Shaftesbury wrote in a letter to Locke, did not need any of the "new Discoverys" of philosophers such as Descartes and Hobbes. They needed only to "live up to what they know."[144] The comparison to beauty could fortify such readers against moral reluctance and discouragement.

Shaftesbury was also writing for readers who cared about literature, architecture, art, and manners—but who were heedless or dismissive of the shape of their characters, perhaps because they associated such matters with unbelievable religion or tedious moralism. The idea of moral beauty was Shaftesbury's attempt to reach these people and through a kind of literary legerdemain shift their perspective to the importance of the cultivation of virtue. It was his attempt to transmute a love of beautiful objects into enthusiasm for making of one's self a beautiful work of art.

CHAPTER THREE

# Art

THE SHAFTESBURY FAMILY motto was "Love, Serve." To place great stress on the motto as an explanation of Shaftesbury's conduct, as though he often had it foremost in mind and would have acted otherwise if the motto had been different, seems rather facile. But because it is such an apt and pithy description of Shaftesbury's aspirations, it's tempting to drape exposition around it. And maybe it's not entirely facile. The motto was associated with Shaftesbury's maligned grandfather, who was driven by powerful public-oriented aspirations that he sought to imbue in his grandson. Perhaps it's reasonable to say the motto is a fair encapsulation of a family ethos Shaftesbury internalized, as well as a symbol of a grandfather he strove to vindicate.[1]

"Love, serve." We've seen how Shaftesbury did rigorous philosophical work on himself to cultivate love, for God and humanity. Central to his notion of love for God was appreciation of the entire world—learning to see the beauty of everything in nature, from the most grand and sublime to the nittiest and grittiest. He wanted to inculcate in himself the sense that everything made by God is beautiful.

The love for humanity he tried to cultivate in himself was equally comprehensive. For just that reason, it may strike us as oddly impersonal. It was less like the intense affection we associate with close personal relationships and more like a serene paternalism. At least in certain reflective moments, Shaftesbury wanted to love humanity from a vantage beyond everyone else, far above the fray.[2] I'm not sure how pleasing we'd find this species of philanthropy in a companion. It might be inspiring to be around someone who can see in natural processes of waste and decay the same beauty he sees in mountains and oceans. To be around someone who feels the same toward every human might be less appealing. But Shaftesbury's exquisite estrangement from other people drew him to this impersonal ideal—even if the affection he had for several lifelong friends suggests a different picture.

Shaftesbury was equally committed to service. A clear indication of this commitment is his preference for Xenophon's representation of Socrates over Plato's. According to Shaftesbury, Xenophon's Socrates was a person actively involved in the life of his society, while Plato's Socrates retreated to contemplation. In Xenophon, "the Substance of the genuine socratick Philosophy was Action & Capacity, how to be useful in the World, a good Patriot, a good Friend, a good Economist & towards a Family etc."[3] In Plato, Socrates is consumed by abstract "metiphysicall & Theoclogical Notions." Xenophon's is the true Socratic philosophy. In Shaftesbury's frontispiece portrait of *Characteristicks*, the Xenophon volume stands upright atop the Plato volume, which is laid on its side.

Shaftesbury tried to hold himself to Xenophon's active ideal of service to family and country. But he didn't find it easy. Both arenas caused him immense frustration.

Shaftesbury was conscientious about his familial duties. He followed his parents' wishes as best he could. He put a great deal of effort into the agriculture and economics of his estate, into the management of his staff and tenants. He was diligent about facilitating marriages and providing dowries for his sisters. When engaged in these activities, however, he seemed driven less by care, warmth, or concern and more by a grim resolve to fulfill his obligations. When he was 18, Shaftesbury laid out a plan to remedy what he perceived to be his younger brother's poor education and lack of preparation for a career. When it looked like his plan might be disregarded, he wrote a letter to his father in which he complained that his offer of help was not being taken up. "I have acquitted myself entirely of my whole duty both as to God and Man in this case and to justifie my selfe to any rationall part of Mankind," he wrote.[4] He went on to say that with regard to the family he might "cease to act" in any way beyond that which he was obliged to do by his duty as a son. In a letter he wrote when he was 20, he said that his most heartfelt desire was for "perfect retirement" and to shun all worldly business, and that he engaged in public service not "voluntarily" but only because he was obliged "by birth" and a "principle of duty and necessity."[5] Five years later, he tried to adjudicate a disagreement between his parents. His efforts incurred his mother's hostility. In a letter back to her, he responded bitterly: "I thank [God] that He has been soe mercifull as to make me sensible what it is to bee a Son, and what I am to doe as such. I trust in him that Hee may one day also give you the Heart of a Mother."[6]

Even Shaftesbury's decision to start a family of his own seemed to have been based in duty. There are numerous indications that he had no desire to marry, and that he did so, after failed attempts to pressure his brother into marrying, only because of his obligation to further the Shaftesbury line.[7] As it happened, that decision turned out surprisingly well. Shaftesbury loved his wife and delighted in the infancy of his child, even if he died too early to have a full life with them.

Shaftesbury also sought to serve his country. A 1701 letter he wrote about his efforts in the recent election captures well his belief at the time that the best way to serve his country was to support King William and the Whig Party. "I had the strongest Obligation on Earth upon me to act with vigour as I have done since the Opportunity the King has most happily given us."[8] He goes on to exalt in the electoral success of his Whigs at the expense of "inveterate Toreyes." For his efforts, Shaftesbury notes, the "King himself... yesterday gave me most *hearty Thanks for my Zeal & Good Services* on this Occasion, and this before much Company." But Shaftesbury eventually felt betrayed by William, writing in 1704 that he had developed a "Diffidence of Courts, after having been deceiv'd so much in one I so early lov'd."[9] He also became repulsed by the conniving of politicians, both Whig and Tory. In a 1704 letter explaining why he could not urge his brother to run for Parliament, he wrote, "I know the difficulty there is in engageing a Man of strict Honesty in a Kind of Ambitiouse Service of the Publick, where Courtship and Application is become a necessary part."[10] In a 1705 letter he noted that his brother-in-law was discouraged from running for Parliament because of "his former Repulse and the Severe opposition & usage He mett with from the Whigg Interest," which seems to express his own attitude as well.[11] In the 1705 letter he laments being "disclaim'd" by a Whig politician he had helped elect. Even from the beginning of his career, when he was most closely associated with the Whig Party, Shaftesbury fell out of step with the partisan positions of his fellows, leading them to be exasperated with him, and he with them.[12]

All of these frustrations contributed to Shaftesbury's desire to withdraw—to remove himself from the messy goings-on in England, to immerse himself in reading and writing. It's hard to say to what extent he would have given in to this desire if he had been completely healthy. But as it turned out, he suffered from lifelong health problems that made extended periods away a virtual necessity. He retreated to Rotterdam twice, the first time in 1698–1699, the second in 1703–1704. In 1711, when he was very sick indeed, he retired to Naples, with its promise of a more salutary climate. He died there in 1714, never becoming healthy enough to return to England.

This retreating created a problem. Shaftesbury was committed to Xenophon's "genuine socratick Philosophy" of "Action & Capacity" that mandated being "useful in the World, a good Patriot, a good Friend, a good Economist & towards a Family etc." But how could he serve humanity when he was psychologically and physically ill-equipped to engage with the world? How could he reconcile his powerful motives to withdraw with the imperative "to be active again in affaires of the Publick & Friends"?[13] This problem shows through in a 1699 letter the family steward, Thomas Stringer, wrote to Shaftesbury upon hearing that Shaftesbury would be returning to England from his first retreat to Rotterdam:

> It being the happiest news to me that hath these many years reached my eares. And though some persons talk that you intend suddenly to returne into Westphalia whether several are already gone & others goeing, with whom you are to spend your time in a Platonick & retir'd life, confining virtue only with the Shades of the Chestnut Groves. Yet I hope better things from the Grandson of one of the greatest & wisest, as well as the best of men. It is impossible for me to believe that a person of such early ripenesse & worthy Principles who hath already set his hand to the plow & perform'd such eminent services for his Country, should not turn back or sink soe low in dispaire as wholly to desert his duty unto it. And, like Poeticall Lovers, delight in nothing but Shades & Woods at a time when his partes & abilities is most wanted to serve the publick.[14]

This is someone else writing to Shaftesbury, but it undoubtedly struck chords with Shaftesbury himself. *The Moralists*' fulsome description of Theocles's and Philocles's walk through the woods and their philosophical dialogue strongly suggests that there were elements of Shaftesbury's conduct that gave Stringer good reason to be worried about the rumors of Shaftesbury's retiring to a Platonic life in the groves.[15] Stringer must have also known that nothing would be more effective at inducing Shaftesbury to return to family and country than mentioning the first Earl and his principle of service. That was in 1699, when Shaftesbury still had the ability to return to a life of family management and political activity. How was he to confront the problem later on, when his abilities had diminished?

The answer was to write philosophy (see C 3.244). Whatever other successes people may have, if they make wrong decisions about what will make them happy, they'll be unhappy. And philosophy teaches what will make us truly happy, what our real good is and what our real ill (C 2.247). Philosophy is "the *Study of Happiness*" (C 2.244). Imparting philosophical truths is the most direct, the purest method of improving people's lives. Nothing can be of greater service to humanity than true philosophy.

And writing philosophy was something Shaftesbury was singularly equipped to do. It played to his strengths, circumvented his weaknesses. The difficulties he had with familial relations, societal expectations, and political machinations did not impede him—when in his study, pen in hand—from deploying his prodigious intellectual gifts and penetrating psychological insight. Nor was illness an insuperable obstacle. Even during periods when the active life was impossible, he was still capable of reading and thinking and writing, at least up until his final few months. Philosophy allowed Shaftesbury to square the circle: to retreat *and* to serve humanity.

But it would work only if his philosophical writing was effective. He needed to engage his readers, to reach people in a way that could facilitate their improving their lives. His philosophical ideas would be of no service to humanity if they were inaccessible.

The result of this conception of philosophy's aim was Shaftesbury's use of all the elaborate stylistic features that make *Characteristicks* so different from most canonical modern European philosophical texts. Many, from the eighteenth century on, have questioned Shaftesbury's judgment on this matter. Many have thought that the main effect of Shaftsbury stylistic choices was philosophical obstruction. But the elaborate style was strategic, a conscious decision born of Shaftesbury's deepest convictions about his underlying purpose. Beauty dominated his thinking about not only the content of his philosophy but also its form.

We turn now to how Shaftesbury thought about the beauty of art.

## 1. Art's Role in the Best Human Life

What role should artistic beauty play in a human life? Can appreciating beautiful art make someone a better person? Will it make someone happier?

There were those in the seventeenth century who attacked the arts, maintaining that they inevitably led a person astray. They thought theater was the cause of debauchery, immorality, and profaneness.[16] Church painting was idolatrous.[17] Fine architecture, equipage, and fashion made one "Deformed and Ridiculous both in Mind and Body."[18]

Shaftesbury defended the arts. He argued that appreciating artistic beauty can play a role in the quest for virtue and happiness. Not always clear, however, is how Shaftesbury conceived of that role.

Sometimes he seemed to believe that art could serve only an instrumental purpose. Appreciation of artistic beauty, on this view, can be useful in spurring people to live as they ought. But it should be thought of as merely a means, and ultimately dispensable. It has no role in the best human life, and those who remain focused on it will as a result fail to ascend to the highest level. A person who achieves the pinnacle of virtue and wisdom will disregard artistic beauty. The exemplar of this view is Epictetus.[19] According to legend, Epictetus had one fine possession, an iron lamp, but when it was stolen and he had to use a plain earthenware one instead, he literally couldn't have cared less.

Other times, Shaftesbury seemed to believe that artistic beauty was something to value for its own sake. On this view, appreciating artistic beauty is not merely a dispensable spur to something better. It is itself a fundamental aspect of the best life—a non-instrumental or final good for human beings.[20]

In this chapter I elucidate these views of Shaftesbury's on artistic beauty. I doubt that everything he says can be brought into coherence.[21] I will close, though, by offering Shaftesbury a position that, I hope, can resolve at least some of the tensions in his valuation of artistic beauty.

## 2. *Virtuosoship and the Promotion of Virtue*

Let's start with an uncontroversial point: Shaftesbury believes that appreciation of artistic beauty can serve a morally instrumental purpose.

Shaftesbury's belief in the morally instrumental value of the arts is evident in the index he wrote for *Characteristicks*. "Virtuosoship" is Shaftesbury's word for skill, knowledge, special interest, or accomplishment in the arts. And under that heading in the index, he contends that "Virtuosoship [is] *a step towards Virtue*" (C 3.291). In the texts the index refers to, he touts appreciation of the arts as being useful in promoting the cause of virtue (C 1.208, 3.99). Virtuosoship, he says, can be a "step towards the becoming a Man of Virtue and good Sense" (C 1.205).

Shaftesbury acknowledges that in claiming that virtuosoship can be a step toward virtue, he is opposing the seventeenth-century tendency to see the arts as morally pernicious. He realizes that many moralists will deny there is anything morally worthwhile in the activities of painters, sculptors, and "the rest of the *Virtuoso*-Tribe" (C 1.205). But he is convinced that in affirming the moral value of the arts he has "Reason on my side," even though the prevalent custom of opposing the arts and virtue "be ever so strong against me" (C 1.205).

More controversial is *how* Shaftesbury thinks appreciation of artistic beauty can be a step toward virtue. Some commentators have held that Shaftesbury believes the transition from artistic appreciation to virtue is inevitable and spontaneous, something that happens automatically. On this view, observing artistic beauty promotes virtue the way sunbathing produces a tan. As one commentator puts it, Shaftesbury suggests "the absurd dogma that beauty effected a kind of moral magic."[22] There are a couple of sentences that taken in isolation appear to give credence to this interpretation.

> Who can admire the *outward* Beautys, and not recur instantly to the *inward*, which are the most real and essential, the most naturally affecting, and of the highest Pleasure, as well as Profit and Advantage? (C 3.114)

> This too is certain; That the Admiration and Love of Order, Harmony and Proportion, in whatever kind, is naturally improving to the Temper, advantageous to social Affection, and highly assistant to *Virtue*. (C 2.43)

These sentences seem to say that admiration of the physical beauty of even the lowest objects "instantly" or "naturally" produces love of virtue—that even lower forms of beauty effect a kind of moral magic.

But that's not actually Shaftesbury's position. Shaftesbury is clearly aware that love of physical beauty doesn't always lead to virtue. There is a large cast of characters whom he rebukes because they value beautiful things without taking the step up to virtue. It includes "an airy Spark who dotes on the beauty of his horse, hound, and hawk but "neglect[s] . . . and forget[s] what is *decent, handsom,* or *becoming* in human Affairs." It includes "a Man of Breeding and Politeness" who exerts great effort to refine his taste in architecture, statues, paintings, and music, but who doesn't realize that he should put effort into refining his moral taste. It includes a "Youth" who cares only about beautiful human bodies rather than beautiful human minds (C 1.84, 3.112, 1.208).

The cast also includes a clique he dubs *"the Gentlemen of Fashion"* (C 1.84). These are individuals with impeccable "Judgment in Proportions of all kinds," people with excellent taste in art, music, gardens, and ornament (C 1.84). The gentlemen of fashion adhere to strict aesthetic standards. "They condemn *this* manner; they praise *the other*. 'So far was *right*; further, *wrong*'" (C 1.88). They exert every effort to achieve *this*. They wouldn't be caught dead wearing *that*. At the same time, these "airy Wits" mock moral standards (C 1.84). They flaunt their disregard for rules of virtue. They ridicule "the *solemn* Reprovers of Vice" (C 1.84). They're often "irregular in their Morals" (C 1.84). They take great care to avoid "*a False Taste*" in one area—to develop accurate judgment about some non-moral subject—but they fail to have the "same regard to *a right* Taste in Life and Manners" (C 1.208). Virtuosoship can be a step toward virtue. But it's a step many virtuosos do not take.

To ascend to virtue, a person must engage in the hard intellectual and characterological work of discovering the nature of mental beauty and cultivating an appreciation of it. Appreciating artistic beauty can be a step up in that ascent, but it's only a first step:

> Where then is this BEAUTY or *Harmony* [of mind] to be found? How is this SYMMETRY to be discover'd and apply'd? Is it any other *Art* than that of PHILOSOPHY, or *the Study of inward Numbers and Proportions*, which can exhibit this in Life? If no other; Who, then, can possibly have a TASTE of this kind, without being beholden to PHILOSOPHY? Who can admire the *outward* Beautys, and not recur instantly to the *inward*, which are the most real and essential, the most naturally affecting, and of the highest Pleasure, as well as Profit and Advantage? In so short a compass does that Learning and Knowledge lie, on which *Manners* and *Life* depend. 'Tis *We our-selves* create and form our TASTE. If we resolve to have it *just*; 'tis in our power. (C 3.112–114)

This paragraph contains one of the sentences I quoted above that, in isolation, appear to imply that beauty effects a kind of moral magic. In context, however, we see that Shaftesbury is not saying that appreciation of physical beauty magically summons virtue. Appreciation of artistic beauty can be a helpful start. But to continue on to a love of moral beauty, one must put in the conscious self-work of true philosophy. It's in our power to do this, but it's something that takes effort.[23]

The other sentence that in isolation appears to imply the absurd dogma also looks different in context. That sentence is part of a passage Shaftesbury added to later versions of the *Inquiry*. It appears in the section that argues that perfect theism—belief in a perfectly good creator-god—promotes virtue. In the first version of the *Inquiry*, Shaftesbury explained how belief in a perfectly virtuous creator both stabilizes our judgments of right and wrong and strengthens our moral resolve in the face of difficulty and temptation. Then, in the later editions, he added the following:

> [T]he Admiration and Love of Order, Harmony and Proportion, in whatever kind, is naturally improving to the Temper, advantageous to social Affection, and highly assistant to *Virtue*; which is it-self no other than the Love of Order and Beauty in Society. In the meanest Subjects of the World, the Appearance of *Order* gains upon the Mind, and draws the Affection towards it. But if *the Order of the World it-self* appears just and beautiful; the Admiration and Esteem of *Order* must run higher, and the elegant Passion or Love of Beauty, which is so advantageous to Virtue, must be the more improv'd by its Exercise in so ample and magnificent a Subject. For 'tis impossible that such *a Divine Order* shou'd be contemplated without Extasy and Rapture; since in the common Subjects of Science, and the liberal Arts, whatever is according to just Harmony and Proportion, is so transporting to those who have any Knowledg or Practice in the kind. (C 2.43)[24]

What Shaftesbury is saying here is similar to a point Kant makes about the importance of appreciating "beautiful crystal formations," "the indescribable beauty of plants," and the rest of "what is *beautiful* in inanimate nature."[25] Cultivating appreciation of the beauty of nature is worthwhile, Kant believes, because it can strengthen one's disposition to love something in an entirely selfless manner, and selfless valuing is essential to morality. Along the same lines, Shaftesbury thinks that sensitivity to beauty in one arena can carry over to sensitivity to beauty in another. Appreciation of order of any kind, even of "the meanest subjects," can be "assistant to virtue," since virtue is itself a kind of beauty. But the beauty of the world as a whole is more "ample and magnificent" than anything else. Appreciation of the beauty of the world can thus heighten to the greatest extent possible one's sensitivity to beauty in general. Since virtue is a kind of beauty, the heightened sensitivity to beauty that appreciation of the world produces can be exceedingly "advantageous to virtue."[26]

When describing the "Extasy and Rapture" that comes from contemplating the beauty of the world, Shaftesbury adds a footnote referring to the *Moralists*' second day. That makes sense. This *Inquiry* passage reads like a precis of Philocles's development of enthusiastic appreciation. Recall, though, that the process by which Philocles came to this appreciation was far from simple, spontaneous, automatic. He started out *The Moralists* as a lover of beautiful things, but also as a moral and religious skeptic (C 2.135; 2.224–225). And it's not as if he walked out the door, saw some pretty flowers, watched a nice sunset, and was magically transformed. His moral and religious epiphany was the result of considerable intellectual and emotional effort—plentiful "*Labour* and *Pains*" of "*Examination* and *Search*" (C 2.224, 3.166). His step up to virtue was a deliberate accomplishment, one that started from his appreciation of artistic beauty but did not end there.

Essential to Philocles's transformation was the inspired teaching of Theocles. Such teaching is what Shaftesbury intends *Characteristicks* to provide its readers. Its connecting of virtue to the beauty of things is not a straightforward causal claim. It's not an assertion that artistic appreciation produces moral improvement as stimulus produces response. Like Theocles with Philocles, Shaftesbury aims to lead his artistically attuned readers to an appreciation of something new: the very thing they love about beautiful objects is present in even higher form in virtue. He is attempting to convince virtuosos that by their own lights they ought to put forth the effort of moral self-improvement. His connecting of the beauty of things to virtue is hortatory rather than descriptive.[27]

Shaftesbury's belief that appreciation of beauty can be morally advantageous stands out clearly when we look at what he says about those who lack such appreciation. In two letters from 1709, he identifies as one such person his "old tutor and governor," John Locke. Locke had the reputation of being completely indifferent to the arts, utterly unmoved by what we call aesthetics, blind to beauty.[28] Locke recognized, of course, that people preferred the appearance of certain things to the appearance of other things. But because Locke himself (according to Shaftesbury) did not appreciate beauty, the only explanation he could conceive of for such preferences was the simplistic egoist one. If individuals preferred one painting to another, it must have been because they thought it would be instrumentally more effective at garnering for them personal wealth, renown, or physical pleasure. If individuals preferred a particular course of action to another, it must have been because they thought the same thing—that it would more effectively promote their selfish interests.

These ideas of Locke's "struck at all fundamentals, threw all order and virtue out of the world, and made the very ideas of these *unnatural*."[29] Because he did not recognize anything good in itself about beauty, Locke came to believe that humans lack any natural preference for beauty for its own sake. But that led him to think that beauty of all kinds is merely an instrumental means for advancing one's own interests, which in turn led him to think that virtue (moral beauty) is in and of itself worthless.

Shaftesbury chose not to publish his criticism of Locke. But in *Soliloquy* he reproduces almost verbatim a passage from one of his critical letters, changing it only by omitting Locke's name and putting in its place a hypothetical "Writer" who asserts "That the Measure or Rule of HARMONY was *Caprice* or *Will*, *Humour* or *Fashion*" (C 1.217). At about the same time he was writing the letters, he wrote a passage for the *Essay on Wit* that makes a similar point. It's a passage we've looked at before, the one in which Shaftesbury compares a person who seriously questions why he should avoid being nasty to a knave who acknowledges no reason for action other than self-interest. The first character, the nasty one, doesn't recognize anything bad in itself about being unclean. Being unclean, in and of itself, simply doesn't bother him. He doesn't find it repulsive. To be convinced that it's worthwhile to put in the effort to be clean, consequently, he requires reasons based on the self-interested effects of uncleanliness, such as that other people will shun him or that he'll experience unpleasant olfactory sensations. As a result, if no one else is around and he has a cold that blocks his sense of smell, he won't see any reason to avoid uncleanliness. And even when he does take efforts to be clean, he'll lack the concern for cleanliness characteristic of a decent person. The second character, the knave, doesn't recognize anything bad in itself about being dishonest. Being dishonest, in and of itself, simply doesn't bother him. He doesn't find it repulsive. To be convinced that he ought to put forth the effort to be honest, consequently, he requires reasons based on dishonesty's effects on his own interests, such as that other people will shun him or that he'll be severely punished. As a result, in situations in which he can avoid the ill effects, he'll not recognize any reason to avoid dishonesty. And even when he does act in accord with virtue, he'll lack the beauty of mind of which virtue truly consists.

Shaftesbury didn't think Locke was nasty or knavish. But he thought Locke's philosophy had the troubling implications the nasty and knavish exemplify. Just as the nasty gentleman will invariably be inwardly nasty, the soul of the knave will invariably be bereft of virtue. The knave's ultimate motivation, on which his moral status depends, is always selfish, always unworthy. And Locke's philosophy implies that everyone's ultimate motivation is the same as the knave's. Those who accept Locke's philosophy deny the possibility of real virtue. The danger is that their behavior will end up conforming to that philosophy. Adherents of Locke may, through a self-fulfilling prophecy, blind themselves to the non-instrumental value of beauty and as a result fall into totalizing selfishness.

What's important for our purposes in this chapter is that in the midst of one of his letters, Shaftesbury says this: "Had Mr Locke been a virtuoso, he would not have philosophised thus." As we have seen, Shaftesbury is under no illusion that all virtuosos are paragons of virtue. Many of them are "irregular in their Morals." But all virtuosos are in a vitally important respect superior to the nasty and knavish. Virtuosos appreciate motivating reasons of an entirely different sort. Virtuosos are true lovers of real beauty. They recognize that beauty for its own sake is something to cherish. While the knave reduces all practical considerations to the common coin of profit or pleasure, virtuosos appreciate a good that is not just one more fungible consideration to be tossed on the scales of self-interested calculation. Creating and promoting beauty is for the virtuoso worthy as a final end. The normative universe of the virtuoso has more dimensions than the knave's. The normative universe of the virtuoso includes completely selfless valuing.

What virtuosos need to realize is that the same standards they are committed to in the aesthetic arena apply even more powerfully in the moral realm—that beauty of mind is of the same sort but even more compelling than the beauty of physical things. When the gentlemen of fashion ignore moral beauty, they violate their own principles. They live "at variance with themselves, and in contradiction to the Principle, on which they ground their highest Pleasure and Entertainment" (C 1.85). And if that's not exactly a good thing, it's better than being one of those people whose disregard of moral beauty is perfectly in line with their disregard for the beauty of physical things. If someone loves music or architecture or gardens, and if she cares enough to work hard to improve her skill and refine her taste in those areas, she is primed to love virtue and to work hard to be virtuous. Just as she's averse to deformity in her areas of interest—averse, for instance, to bad music and ugly buildings—she can be moved toward becoming averse to immorality.

A morally frivolous airy spark is to be preferred to those who treat all things, moral and aesthetic, as mere means to advance narrow self-interest. For there may be nothing satisfactory and convincing to say to such people when they ask why they shouldn't commit injustice when they can get away with it. About such beauty-blind lost causes Shaftesbury writes, "With such as these, wherever they shou'd be found, I must confess I cou'd scarce be tempted to bestow the least Pains or Labour, towards convincing 'em of a *Beauty* in *inward Sentiments* and *Principles*" (C 3.109). This is why Shaftesbury is more troubled by Locke's philosophy than by the morally irregular gentlemen of fashion. Within the souls of the gentlemen of fashion are beachheads from which he can try to instill love of moral beauty. To be a virtuoso is to recognize features of the world that can serve as footholds to virtue. The Lockean is a blank slate (see C 1.205).

## 3. The Instrumentalist Interpretation

So Shaftesbury thinks appreciation of artistic beauty can be instrumentally valuable in promoting virtue. But should it be valued in itself, as a fundamental or final good? The instrumentalist interpretation says no. According to the instrumentalist interpretation, artistic appreciation is valuable only as a means to virtue. In and of itself it is dispensable, not truly a part of the good life. We turn now to the reasons for attributing this view to Shaftesbury.

The heart of the instrumentalist interpretation is an idea Shaftesbury attributes to Epictetus: one can achieve true happiness by caring only about what is entirely within one's own control, and the state of one's mind is the only thing that is entirely within one's own control.[30] Shaftesbury takes this idea to underlie Epictetus's dismissive attitude toward fine lamps and everything else besides virtue (see C 3.121–122). All material things are subject to physical insult, to corrosion and breakage and destruction. Only a fully virtuous character is immune to every vicissitude. Beauty of mind—a foundation more solid not only than "Pagaentrys," "Estates," or "Honours" but even than "Stone or Marble"—constitutes the only "lasting and sure Foundation of *Order, Peace*, and *Concord*" (C 2.238).

In his private notebooks Shaftesbury dilates on the importance of focusing only on the state of his mind. He tells himself that any concern he gives to external things will come at the expense of concern for what is internal—that it is impossible to place ultimate value on his internal state without completely withdrawing concern from everything else.[31] All other "Arts are incomplete." They all "stand in need of something exteriour," they all fail to ensure the good life. The art of bringing one's mind into harmony is uniquely "compleat in it self."[32] It is this complete art to which Shaftesbury commits himself: "To thy Work then, thy Art: thy Life. The sole Business. The main Concern. Life itself and all that there is in the Matter of Living."[33] For anything other than the beauty of mind, he tells himself, he should have "no admiration: no search of Order here: no Passions towards this [non-moral] Beauty, or any Beauty of this sort."[34] He resolves not to let "any outward thing to be my Good,"[35] to separate his happiness entirely from "Exterior things."[36] His only concern should be *"The Garden and Groves within."*[37]

[E]ither these internall matters, the cult of Vertue, & the sacred recesses of the Mind, are worthy of admiration, or they are not. If they are not; then cease to admire in this way. If they are; then cease to admire in that other. *a celebrated Beauty*! *a Palace*! *Seat*! *Gardens*! *Pictures*! *Italy*! *a Feast*! *a Carnivall*! What dos this concern thee? If thou admires any of these, as being taken with them, & wishing for them; what is become of Temperance, Continence, & those other Vertues? And where is that Honesty, Faith, Justice, Magnanimity grounded on them?[38]

Pursuing virtue wholeheartedly means rejecting the "Charm & Allurement" of all "exteriour things." Shaftesbury quotes approvingly from the section of Epictetus's *Discourses* where Epictetus contends that one can opt entirely for a life of virtue or turn completely in the direction of pleasure.[39] There can be no concessions made to anything other than virtue. It's all or nothing.[40]

Two passages in *Characteristicks* may appear to express the same dismissive attitude toward art. The first passage is a section of *The Moralists* in which Theocles develops a hierarchy of beauty. The hierarchy consists of "*Three* Degrees or Orders of Beauty" (C 2.227).[41] The first order is the beauty of physical objects—of "*Architecture, Sculpture*, and the rest of that sort" (C 2.228). The second order is the beauty of human minds, which are "*Forms which form*" (C 2.228). The third order is the beauty of God's mind, "which forms not only such as we call mere Forms, but even *the Forms which form*" (C 2.227–228).

In his explication of the hierarchy, according to the instrumentalist interpretation, Theocles claims that beauty belongs only to the creative minds of God and humans, while physical objects are not actually beautiful at all. This claim appears to be the conclusion of a bit of dialogue between Philocles and Theocles that's Socratic to the point of pastiche.

"I know, good Philocles, you are no such Admirer of *Wealth* in any kind, as to allow much Beauty to it; especially in a rude Heap or Mass. But in Medals, Coins, Imbost-work, Statues, and well-fabricated Pieces, of whatever sort, you can discover *Beauty*, and admire the Kind." "True," said I; "but not for the *Metal's* sake." "'Tis not then *the Metal* or *Matter* which is beautiful with you." "No." "But *the Art*." "Certainly." "*The Art* then is the *Beauty*." "Right." "And *the Art* is that which beautifies." "The same." "So that the Beautifying, not the Beautify'd, is the really *Beautiful*." "It seems so." "For that which is beautify'd, is beautiful only by the accession of something beautifying: and by the recess or withdrawing of the same, it ceases to be beautiful." "Be it." "In respect of Bodys therefore, *Beauty* comes and goes." "So we see." "Nor is the Body it-self any Cause either of its coming or staying." "None." "So that there is no Principle of Beauty in *Body*." "None at all." "For Body can no-way be the Cause of Beauty to it-self." "No-way." "Nor govern nor regulate it-self." "Nor yet this." "Nor mean nor intend it-self." "Nor this neither." "Must not *that* therefore, which means and intends for it, regulates and orders it, be the Principle of Beauty to it?" "Of necessity." "And what must that be?" "Mind, I suppose; for what can it be else?" (C 2.226)

Philocles loves beautiful sculpture and metalwork. But Theocles gets him to see that his admiration is not for the physical stuff. He loves the artistry that has brought the physical stuff into a certain form. It's the mind of the artist that has done that. What's "really Beautiful" is the mind that has imposed form on the matter, not the matter that has been formed (C 2.225–226). "[T]he Beautifying, not the Beautify'd, is the really Beautiful" (C 2.226). "[T]here is no Principle of Beauty in *Body*" (C 2.226). "BEAUTY, belonging not to *Body*, nor having any principle of existence except in MIND and REASON, is alone discover'd and acquir'd by this diviner Part" (C 2.238). "Mind alone" is where the "Principle of Beauty" resides. True love of beauty is always love of a designing mind.

Theocles goes on to say that pursuit of things at the lowest level of the hierarchy is "despicable" (C 2.227). The wise person has but "slight regard" for physical things; he "pass[es] over" them (C 2.238). "[W]hen you place a Joy elsewhere than in the Mind," Theocles says, "*the Enjoyment* it-self will be no beautiful Subject" (C 2.237). Pursuit of any physical thing is "*absurd*" (C 2.236). All of this sounds like strong evidence for the instrumentalist interpretation, according to which one ultimately ought to realize that artistic appreciation has no fundamental or final value.

The second passage from *Characteristicks* that appears to support the instrumentalist interpretation is a lengthy footnote to a section of the Miscellaneous Reflections called "Pursuit of *Beauty*.—Preparation for *Philosophy*" (C 3.100). Many people, the footnote says, pursue physical objects they deem beautiful. They pursue beauty "in *outward* Things, and in the *meaner* and *subordinate* Subjects" (C 3.113). But pursuing this "inferior *Species*" of beauty will ruin one's soul (C 3.113). When "we run in search" of elegant physical things, "we grow, in our real *Character* and truer SELF, *deform'd* and *monstrous, servile* and *abject* . . . sacrificing all internal Proportion, all *intrinsick* and *real* BEAUTY and WORTH, for the sake of Things which carry scarce a Shadow of the Kind" (C 3.113–114). A wise person "disdains to be allur'd" by the pursuit of outward things. A wise person "refus[es] to be captivated by any thing less than the *superior, original,* and *genuine* Kind" of beauty (C 3.113). Physical things carry "scarce a Shadow" of real beauty (C 3.114). Pursuing them deforms one's character.

There may be moments when Shaftesbury *seems* to have a more positive attitude toward artistic beauty, when he sounds like he endorses appreciation of beautiful art for its own sake. But such moments, according to the instrumentalist interpretation, are decoys, Shaftesbury's way of sugarcoating a moral message to bring a wider audience along to a position that would have left them cold if it had been delivered unadorned. Dehrmann puts this point well when he says that Shaftesbury's discussions of art are a "means of luring his contemporaries into the philosophical life they shun . . . a ploy."[42] Those discussions are designed to entice readers toward morality by initially giving them to believe that virtue is easier and more pleasant than it really is. "Art is merely the means to a further end."[43] Eventually, Shaftesbury's "readers [should] be brought to step away from their interest in painting in order to grasp the intention of leading a philosophical life according to nature."[44] In support of this decoy reading, the instrumentalist interpretation can point to two of Shaftesbury's notes on *Plasticks*, the unfinished essay on art he was working on in the months before he died.

> Remember still: This the Idea of the Work viz. *Quasi* The Vehicle of other Problemes, i:e. the Praecepts, Demonstrations &c of real Ethicks. But this hid: not to be said except darkly or pleasantly with Raillery upon Self, or some such indirect way.[45]

> To *twist*, as it were, & *interweave* Morality with Plasticks, that supream Beauty, with this subaltern, those high & severe Maxims with these curiouse & *severe* also in their kind.[46]

In a letter Shaftesbury wrote while working on *Plasticks*, he makes the same point:

> I shou'd be sorry to throw away time in such little Works or Compositions [if they could not] serve instead of an agreable *Vehicle* for the *moral Potion*; which by it-self is become mere *Physick*, and loathsome to Mankind; so as to require a little sweetening to help it down.[47]

These passages reveal, according to the instrumentalist interpretation, that Shaftesbury doesn't think art can have value in itself. He writes about art because he thinks it might be useful in enticing his readers to concern themselves with morality. Art has value only as a means to virtue.

What appears to be more evidence for the decoy reading comes in two passages from the third volume of *Characteristicks*, where Shaftesbury recounts the "pretense" of his earlier works.

> He pretends, on this head, to claim the Assent not only of *Orators*, *Poets*, and the higher *Virtuosi*, but even of the *Beaux* themselves, and such as go no farther than the Dancing-Master to seek for *Grace* and *Beauty*. He pretends, we see, to fetch this *natural Idea* from as familiar Amusements as Dress, Equipage, the Tiring-Room, or Toy-shop. (C 3.111)

> His Pretence has been to *advise Authors*, and polish *Styles*; but his Aim has been to correct *Manners*, and regulate *Lives*. (C 3.114)

In the first passage Shaftesbury seems to be revealing that he doesn't really believe his concept of beauty is continuous with the ideas of beauty held by orators, poets, dancers, and other art lovers, or by those who make dresses, saddles, and ornaments. He *pretends* to fetch his idea of beauty from the practices of such people, but actually his idea of beauty is distinct from theirs. It's a bait and switch: he feigns agreement in order to lure the reader to a different position. In the second passage Shaftesbury seems to reveal that he doesn't really intend to advise authors and polish styles. He *pretends* to do that, but he's actually aiming elsewhere. Discussion of polished writing and style is another bait and switch.

Tiffany claims that even *The Moralists*' apotheosis of the beauty of nature is a decoy, part of the ploy to facilitate popular consumption rather than an expression of Shaftesbury's real philosophy.

> If Shaftesbury really loved nature as Theocles does, we should expect to find it prominent in his more personal comments—letters and private notes. But the letters, when they touch on the deeper matters of life, show nothing of this sort. And in the *Regimen*, when in the sanctum of his self-communion we should most surely look to find the man himself, there appears no haunter of shades such as Theocles in *The Moralists*. Here is not Shaftesbury with the woods and field, but Shaftesbury with Shaftesbury, and predominantly, Shaftesbury with Marcus Aurelius and Epictetus.[48]

When Shaftesbury has Theocles and Philocles enthuse ecstatically in the beauty of mountains and forests and seas, he's just adding sugar to the medicine. Aesthetic experiences are a ladder that, once climbed up into the bracing Stoic stratosphere, should be kicked away.

## 4. The Non-Instrumentalist Interpretation

I've explained reasons for thinking that Shaftesbury believes artistic appreciation is truly worthwhile only to the extent that it promotes virtue—reasons for thinking that Shaftesbury believes the wisest and most virtuous person gains nothing of fundamental value from the beauty of physical things. These reasons do exist. Shaftesbury is sometimes drawn to the idea that happiness requires withdrawing ultimate concern from everything other than one's own virtue. And that can lead to a thoroughly instrumentalist and ultimately dismissive attitude toward art. But it's not the whole story. Shaftesbury is also drawn to the idea that appreciation of beautiful things in and of itself enhances life, that art does add something of fundamental value to a human life.

One place Shaftesbury evinces this positive attitude is in his discussion of enthusiasm. Shaftesbury condemns certain kinds of enthusiasm, but he praises others, affirming their value for true religion and happiness. Love of beautiful things is one of the enthusiasms he endorses. Enthusiastic love of beauty is enriching. It lifts the mind from the mundane goings-on of appetite satisfaction to exquisite delight.

> [T]here is a Power in Numbers, Harmony, Proportion, and Beauty of every kind, which naturally captivates the Heart, and raises the Imagination to an Opinion or Conceit of something *majestic* and *divine*. Whatever this Subject may be *in it-self*, we cannot help being transported with the thought of it. It inspires us with something more than ordinary, and raises us above our-selves. Without this Imagination or Conceit, *the World* wou'd be but a dull Circumstance, and *Life* a sorry Pass-time. Scarce cou'd we be said *to live*. The animal Functions might in their course be carry'd on; but nothing further sought for, or regarded. (C 3.20; see also 1.196)

Appreciation of beauty distinguishes human life from the animalistic. Without love of beauty, our existence devolves to the base animal activity of trying to satisfy "our coarsest Appetites at the cheapest rate" (C 3.20). Our ultimate goal sinks to the "supine State of Indolence and Inactivity" in which physical wants have been met (C 3.20). Love of beauty elevates us above the cycle of physical want, satisfaction, physical want. It creates the capacity to admire and love, rather than only "to indulge lust with whoever is at hand" (C 3.21). It enables us to experience meaning and transcendent joy. And Shaftesbury includes in this category appreciation of the beauty of plenty of things other than virtue: "the Enjoyments of *the Lover*, the *ambitious Man*, the *Warrior*, or the *Virtuoso* (as our Author has elsewhere intimated)," as well as "*Admiration* and *rapturous Views* of Nature" (C 3.20–21). We have seen that when Shaftesbury says that beauty and good are one and the same, he means that we will be happiest if we value beauty above all else. Here Shaftesbury maintains that that includes beauty of all sorts, not just the beauty of virtue.

People who love the beauty of things but do not care about morality would be better off if they cared about morality. But it is, nonetheless, entirely possible for them truly to love the beauty of things for their own sakes. About artists who are "idle, dissolute, or debauch'd" but who nonetheless adhere scrupulously to standards of fine workmanship, Shaftesbury says, "This is Virtue! *Real Virtue*" (C 1.163). "[T]he very Passion which inspires 'em, is it-self *the Love of Numbers, Decency and Proportion*; and this too, not in a narrow sense, or after a *selfish* way" (C 1.85). That's not to say that artists' other failings are redeemed or excused by their commitment to the beauty of things. They are fully accountable for any wrongs they commit, and will suffer accordingly. But their love of beauty is a real good for them, even if they'd be better off still if they prioritized morality. Other examples of people who appreciate beauty for its own sake are a mathematician who takes "contemplative Delight" in the beauty of a theorem (C 2.60), and a shepherd whose "Contemplation of the Ocean's *Beauty*" is a joy to him that is entirely independent of any purpose the ocean can serve (C 2.221–222). Their love of beautiful things enables such people to experience something of fundamental value of which the beauty-blind remain forever insensible.

Shaftesbury compares the benefits of artistic appreciation to the benefits of philosophy. The "Virtuosi" who appreciate "*Architecture, Sculpture, Painting, Musick*, and . . . *Poetry*" are importantly similar to "PHILOSOPHERS" (C 3.96). There are "*inferior* VIRTUOSI" who are worthy of ridicule, just as there can be a ridiculously pedantic "*Pretender to* PHILOSOPHY" (C 3.97, 3.100). But true philosophy and true virtuosoship are both above ridicule, for both promote activities essential to a good life. "[T]he Defects of PHILOSOPHY, and those of *Virtuosoship* are of the same nature . . . But as ridiculous as these Studys are render'd by their sensless Managers; it appears, however, that each of 'em are, in their nature, essential to the *Character* of a *Fine Gentleman* and *Man of Sense*" (C 3.99). The true philosopher and the true virtuoso both care about beauty, and this "perfects the *Character* of" both of them (C 3.100).

That's not to say that virtuosoship is on a par with philosophy. Philosophy goes "a step higher" (C 3.99). Philosophy teaches that "a RIGHT MIND, and GENEROUS AFFECTION, ha[ve] more Beauty and Charm, than all other *Symmetrys* in the World besides" (C 3.103; see 3.106–108). But that's consistent with virtuosoship having real value nonetheless. On this non-instrumentalist picture, disinterested appreciation of beautiful things can enhance life in a way that is similar to how unselfish love of others can enhance life. Feeling non-selfish love for others is a final good for a person. It's a fundamental joy that lifts a person above a consternated attention to self that inevitably leads to vexation and choler. A person who cares about others for their own sakes will be happier than those whose concerns always involve thoughts about how others can serve their own selfish ends. Similarly, disinterested appreciation of beautiful things can be a final good for a person. A person who appreciates beautiful things in and of themselves will have joys that a person blind to artistic beauty will lack. Such a person will be happier than those whose consideration of objects inevitably involves thoughts about how they can serve selfish ends.

What of the idea that true happiness requires withdrawing concern from anything that isn't entirely within one's control? There is no doubt Shaftesbury was drawn to that idea, which he associates with Epictetus. But he doesn't consistently take it to the extreme position that virtue alone is sufficient for the best life. He doesn't hold, for instance, that if one is virtuous, an entirely solitary life is as good as a life of communion with others.[49] Humans of all creatures "are least able to bear Solitude." We inevitably crave "Familiarity and Friendship." Isolation creates "Sadness, Dejection, and Melancholy" (C 2.79). A person condemned to an entirely solitary life could make the most of it. Stoic virtue might enable her to be as well off as she can be given her dire circumstances. But she would be happier—she would have a better life—if she were in a human community. Similarly, a person who lives in an environment utterly bereft of natural and artistic beauty will be better off if she possesses Stoic virtue rather than not. But she would be happier still—she would have a better life—if she were able to experience natural and artistic beauty.

This non-instrumentalist picture fits better with *The Moralists* discussion of the hierarchy of beauty than it may at first appear. The instrumentalist interpretation takes the hierarchy to show that physical objects, or "dead forms," do not actually possess beauty at all.[50] But that might not imply a dismissive attitude toward artistic beauty after all. For it might not matter, from a practical perspective, whether a material thing possesses the property of beauty itself, or whether our experience of the material thing is merely the occasion for us to admire the beauty of the mind that has created it. Even if material things are not themselves beautiful but are only occasions for appreciating the beauty of creative minds, there might still be value in the experience of beautiful material things. Say the correct account of the value of seeing a sculpture is that it sparks in us admiration for the mind of the sculptor. That does not imply that seeing the sculpture is valueless. It just locates the value in something other than the merely physical. There will still be a contrast between someone who sees fundamental value in the experience of sculpture, and an aesthetic-less person who disdains fine lamps and any other fine physical thing.

To see how we can deny that beauty is a property of physical objects while still valuing the experience of them, consider Darwall's reading of Shaftesbury. When you are moved by the beauty of a creation, according to Darwall, you experience a mind-meld with the person who created it. "The contemplation of beauty," Darwall writes, "involves a sharing in, or sympathetic union with, the creative intelligent that formed the beauty contemplated."[51] Truly to be moved by the beauty of something is to apprehend its design. And when you apprehend a thing's design, you are in a state of mind that matches the artist's when she was designing it. The idea of the design in your mind is the same as the idea that was in the mind of the designer in the moment of creation. By designing the thing you now contemplate, the artist has projected her state of mind onto yours. Darwall emphasizes Shaftesbury's statement that "all sound *Love* and *Admiration* is ENTHUSIASM" (C 2.223), which he takes to lead to the idea that love of natural beauty is enthusiasm in a literal sense, truly a communion with God, in that when you apprehend part of nature's design you are in glorious "sympathetic union" with nature's creator. Your mind is filled with an idea that was in the mind of God. Appreciation of artistic beauty also involves sympathetic union with another mind, with the human mind of the artist. Less glorious than union with God though this may be, it may be downright uplifting nonetheless. And when we take to heart that the designing human mind was itself created by God—when we are profoundly inspired by the creation of a human artist, and then realize that the mind of the artist is itself God's creation—we see that love and admiration of artistic beauty is literal enthusiastic communion as well. Appreciation of all kinds of beautiful things, including of "Architecture, Musick, and all which is of human invention, resolves it-self into" appreciation of the beauty of the mind of God (C 2.228).

Theocles says that "*Enjoyment* which reaches the *Sense alone*" is "absurd." The instrumentalist interpretation takes this to be an expression of the idea that appreciation of physical beauty is of no real (no fundamental, no non-instrumental) value. But that may not be the best way to understand Theocles's point. For directly after the "absurd enjoyment" comment, Philocles says that he doesn't understand the "absurdity" Theocles is warning him against. The enjoyment Theocles is telling him to avoid is "still mysterious." "I shou'd not be ill satisfy'd," Philocles says, "if you explain'd your-self a little better as to this Mistake of mine you seem to fear" (C 2.221). So Theocles elaborates. The elaboration is one of the most famous passages of *The Moralists*. It's where Theocles contrasts love of beauty for its own sake with self-interested desire. The person who exemplifies love of beauty is the shepherd who delights in the ocean with absolutely no thought whatsoever of its promoting any of his interests. There are several examples of self-interested desire. One is someone who responds to the ocean's beauty by trying to acquire ownership of it (and even to marry it!). A second is someone whose enjoyment of a beautiful "Tract of Country" requires that he gain "*Property* or *Possession* of the Land" (C 2.222). A third is someone who can enjoy "the *Beauty* of *these* Trees" only to the extent that he can satisfy his desire to eat their fruit (C 2.222). These three people are guilty of the "absurd" mistake Theocles is warning Philocles against. The shepherd is not. The shepherd exemplifies the attitude Theocles is urging on Philocles. He loves beauty the right way. He's making beauty his good.

What's the contrast between the shepherd and the other three? It's not the contrast the instrumentalist interpretation requires. The instrumentalist interpretation requires a contrast between a person who delights in the beauty of physical things and a person who disdains the beauty of all physical things and focuses only on moral beauty. But the passage from *The Moralists* describes a contrast between people whose appreciation depends on command and consumption and ownership and profit, and a person who delights in the world's beauty without any thought of what it can do for her. The mistake Theocles calls "the absurd *Enjoyment* which reaches the *Sense alone*" is not the mistake of enjoying physical beauty. It's the mistake of appreciating things only to the extent that they can serve interests. What's absurd is forfeiting transcendent joy in the world's beauty by focusing entirely on how things can redound to your advantage. When Theocles condemns enjoyment from "*Sense alone*," he's referring to possession and the desire for stuff, which is not part of the shepherd's contemplative experience.

Theocles and Philocles return to the topic of "absurd" enjoyment later in the dialogue (C 2.236). They distinguish, again, between absurd enjoyment and enjoyment of mind. But, again, the distinction is not between enjoyment of physical things and enjoyment of purely mental properties. The distinction is between enjoyment of something because it serves the instrumental purpose of satisfying one's desires, and enjoyment of something for its beauty on its own. It's the distinction between appreciating the "beautiful Feather" and delightful song of a bird, and desiring a bird because it tastes good in a "Fricassee"; between enjoying a plant because it is beautiful, and enjoying a plant because it is good to eat. Enjoyment of the beauty of a bird or a plant is inferior to the enjoyment of virtue, but that does not mean it is absurd (C 2.236–237). Nor is it absurd, of course, to desire to eat a bird or a plant because it will satisfy physical desire. What's absurd is to think that there is nothing of value other than the capacity to satisfy physical desire—to fail to realize that there is noninstrumental value in the enjoyment of the beauty of birds and plants.

*The Moralists* is not the only place Shaftesbury excoriates the obsession with possession. In the long footnote to "Pursuit of *Beauty*.—Preparation for *Philosophy*," he uses particularly scathing language to lambaste the upper classes' acquisition of fine objects. He does, in that footnote, briefly criticize "the *Virtuoso*-Passion" that can lead someone to focus entirely on aesthetics and ignore virtue. But the overriding weight of his censure falls not on the mere appreciation of art but on the drive to make things one's own. He pours scorn on young men who must obtain "a *Horse*, a *Hound*, a *Hawk*!"; on princely sorts who seek out the "finer sorts of Apartments, Gardens, *Villas*!"; on "Gentlemen" who have been ensnared by the chase of "a *Palace and Apartments*," "*Equipage* and *Dress*"; on the "Grandee who assembles all these *Beautys*, and within the Bounds of his sumptuous Palace incloses all these Graces of a thousand kinds" (C 3.112–113). For a man of this sort, the pursuit of beauty has collapsed into the drive to acquire. And while such a man imagines he is adding "Lustre, and Value to [his] *Person*," he is in fact growing in his "real *Character* and truer SELF, *deform'd* and *monstrous*, *servile* and *abject*; stooping to the lowest Terms of Courtship" (C 3.113). All of that could be compatible with an endorsement of the love of physical beauty for its own sake, which Shaftesbury seems to imply in his discussions of enthusiasm, the shepherd, and dedicated sculptors, architects, and painters (3.20, 2.222, 1.163).[52]

The instrumentalist interpretation says we should dismiss as decoys the passages in which Shaftesbury seems to endorse appreciation of physical beauty. Shaftesbury's deepest view, on the instrumentalist interpretation, eschews any true concern for artistic beauty, just as Epictetus cared not a whit about any material object. When he speaks of artistic beauty, Shaftesbury is merely sugarcoating his message for an audience not ready to accept his austere conclusion unadorned. But the evidence for this decoy reading is more slender than it might initially appear.

We saw that one way someone might argue for the decoy reading is by pointing out that Shaftesbury says in *Miscellaneous Reflections* that it had been his *pretense* in earlier works "to claim the assent [of] the higher virtuosi" and "to advise authors, and polish styles" (C 3.111 and 3.114). These passages may seem to be evidence for the decoy reading because they imply that Shaftesbury isn't *really* concerned with virtuosoship or polishing styles—that he's merely *pretending* that he is. But the matter becomes more complicated when we examine how Shaftesbury uses the word "pretense" and its cognates in *Miscellaneous Reflections*.

*Miscellaneous Reflections*, it must be said, is a curious performance. It's a commentary—along the lines of very extended footnotes—on the previous five parts of *Characteristicks*. Four of those previous five parts had robustly first-personal narrators, each of whom was different from the other three. The part without a robustly first-personal narrator, the *Inquiry*, had an authorial voice that was distinct again from the other four. *Miscellaneous Reflections* is narrated by still another character, the Miscellanarian.[53] The Miscellanarian acknowledges that although the previous narrators presented themselves as being different people, they were actually all the work of a single author. But the Miscellanarian does not present himself as being that author. To that author the Miscellanarian resolutely refers in the third person. Shaftesbury, in other words, creates five façades, and then, in order to dismantle the previous five, creates yet another.[54] On top of that, the Miscellanarian boasts about writing in a manner that confounds "Simplicity and Conformity of Design." In his writing, "*Patch-work* is substituted. *Cuttings* and *Shreds* of Learning, with various *Fragments*, and *Points* of Wit, are drawn together, and tack'd in any fantastick form" (C 3.5; see also 3.3–7, 3.17, 3.80–82). But that description of the miscellaneous style flagrantly conflicts with the value of unity advanced throughout the earlier parts of *Characteristicks*.

Anyway.[55] The problem with decoy reading of the pretense passages is that it's not obvious the Miscellanarian is using the key word as we would. As we use it today, "pretense" involves deception or falseness. To pretend to do something is not really to do it. To engage in pretense is to try to deceive. The *Oxford English Dictionary* definitions that capture our common uses of the word are: "A false, feigned, or hypocritical profession or show" and "A feigned or pretended aim or purpose; an avowed purpose serving as a pretext." If that were the meaning Shaftesbury had in mind in the two quotations, then it would seem that he is telling us that his concept of beauty *isn't really connected* to that of the virtuosi, that he *isn't really concerned* with advising authors and polishing styles, that he's only pretending those things are the case. Such a confession does seem to support the decoy reading, according to which Shaftesbury uses art merely as a bait and switch to virtue.[56]

At the time Shaftesbury was writing, however, "pretend" and its cognates commonly had another meaning. The other meaning was "the putting forth of a claim," or "an expressed aim or object; an intention, purpose, or design."[57] On this meaning, there is no implication of deception or falseness. To say that one's pretense is to do something is just to say that one intends to do it. To pretend that something is the case is just to claim that it is case. This meaning of the word is flat-footed. "Pretend" and "pretence" in this sense are similar to the verb- and noun-forms of "claim." If this second meaning is operative in the first quotation, Shaftesbury would be straightforwardly reporting that in previous volumes he had argued for the naturalness of the idea of beauty by pointing to its grip on all sorts of people with no philosophical training—its role in the lives of artists and dancers and actors, of people who love clothes and cars and gadgets. In the second quotation, he would be telling us that while he hopes to advise authors and polish styles, he also has a deeper aim of correcting manners and regulating lives. That he pretended to do such things does not mean he didn't really try to do them. There's no decoy on this interpretation, no bait and switch.

Which of the two meanings does Shaftesbury intend? To answer this, we can look to the rest of *Miscellaneous Reflections*, in which, as it turns out, "pretends" and its cognates appear a great many times. There are instances in which the word signifies some kind of deception or falseness (C 3.8, 3.60, 3.69, 3.100, 3.189). There are instances in which it is difficult to say which of the two meanings he had in mind, or if perhaps the usage straddles both meanings (C 3.25, 3.46, 3.64, 3.72, 3.131, 3.139–143). But most of the time, the word is used in the neutral sense of making a claim, without any suggestion of deception or falseness (see C 3.9, 3.31, 3.37, 3.49, 3.64, 3.67, 3.80, 3.83, 3.94, 3.109, 3.143, 3.173, 3.176, 3.181, 3.183, 3.202–203, 3.207). Here are two examples:

> I have very *solemnly* pleaded for *Gaity* and GOOD HUMOUR: I have declaim'd against *Pedantry* in learned Language, and oppos'd

*Formality* in Form. I now find my-self somewhat impatient to get loose from the Constraint of *Method*: And I pretend lawfully to exercise the Privilege which I have asserted, of rambling from Subject to Subject, from Style to Style, in my MISCELLANEOUS manner, according to my present Profession and Character. (C 3.80)

How far the divine Providence might have indulg'd the stubborn Habit and stupid Humour of this People, *by giving them Laws* (as the Prophet says) *which he himself approv'd not*, I have no Intention to examine. This only I pretend to infer from what has been advanc'd; "That the Manners, Opinions, Rites and Customs of the EGYPTIANS, had, in the earliest times, and from Generation to Generation, strongly influenc'd the HEBREW People (their Guests, and Subjects) and had undoubtedly gain'd a powerful Ascendency over their Natures. (C 3.36–38)

These two quotations are interesting in their own right. The first is a good example of Shaftesbury's self-referential jocularity. The second is a good example of his casual anti-Semitism.[58] But the point here is that in these passages he's using "pretend" the way we would use "claim," without any implication of deception or decoy. So what compelling reason is there for taking him to be using "pretend" and "pretence" in the deceptive sense when he is talking about the connection between virtue and the beauty of art? When he says that he *pretends* to show that his idea of beauty is connected to that of the virtuosi and that he *pretends* to polish styles, why not take him to be relating what he was actually doing? Maybe there's no decisive reason to take his use of the word either way in any particular instance. But it would be, at least, a mistake of haste to take the Miscellanarian's uses of "pretend" and its cognate to invariably signify deception or falseness in a manner that supports the instrumentalist interpretation.

Tiffany argues for the decoy reading by claiming that there is "nothing" in Shaftesbury's "letters and private notes" to indicate that he "really loved nature as Theocles does." According to Tiffany, the real Shaftesbury, as opposed to the public persona he deployed as a decoy, didn't care about the physical beauty of the natural world. But she's just wrong about that. When he was on his grand tour of Europe in 1688–1689, Shaftesbury was inspired by the landscapes of Italy. He climbed steeples and took in the panoramas, which he then described in detail in his diary. As we saw in chapter 1, his private notebooks include expressions of admiration for all of nature's beauty—for the beauty not only of woods and seas but also of dunghills and heaps of decomposing matter. He speaks of the "Beautyes... which are so admir'd in Nature & which all but the grosser sort of Mankind are so sensibly mov'd by."⁵⁹ He sees beauty in the "Winter Land-skip" that others do not, and in the "Chang & Vicessitude" of nature that others find unpleasant.⁶⁰ We also saw in chapter 1 that Shaftesbury wrote a letter in which he expressed "inexpressible Satisfaction" in the contemplation of nature's "Design and Execution." The letter was to an agronomist who was not a notable public figure. Shaftesbury sought him out for advice about the management of his farms. It's very hard to see what strategic purpose planting a decoy in that letter would have served. Shaftesbury exerted great effort, moreover, to beautify his estates. A commitment to beautiful gardens was one of the defining features of his entire life. The times he spent writing sentences that disdain external beauty are vastly outnumbered by the times he spent writing about—and actively working to create—external beauty.

Nor was it just gardens and the natural world. In his private notebooks, Shaftesbury expresses admiration for the beauty of art. He describes "a rationall & admir'd Enthoiasme that belongs to Architecture, Painting, Musick."⁶¹ Such love for art is "highly reas'nable," "justifiable & of a right kind." It would be "Folly, Poorness, & Misery . . . to be without It." As examples of rational and admirable enthusiasm for art, he mentions being "seized with admiration at the View of any of those ancient Edifices," being "struck by those plain & obvious Graces, the natural Beauty & Simplicity of a Work of Raphael," being moved "by the Voice of a Siphacio, or the hand of a Corelli." He continues: "Remember the Pantheon, the wonderfull Fabrick of St Peter's, and (at once) the Architecture of Michel Angelo, the Sculpture & Paintings of the Masters, & the Voice of the Eunuchs, with the Symponyes."⁶² Directly after making those statements about human art, Shaftesbury pivots to the "nobler" beauty of the works of God. His point is that as much as we might love those works of human art, the handiwork of the divine mind is even greater. But he doesn't dismiss human art. He expresses a sincere passion for it.

Shaftesbury also acted like a lover of fine art. As a young man, he was deeply moved by the art and architecture he saw on his grand tour. In his late twenties and early thirties, while he was making some of his most ardent Stoic comments about disdaining worldly things in his private notebooks, he also was expending considerable effort in beautifying homes, designing gardens, and cultivating interests in painting and sculpture. Voitle maintains that "it is one of those paradoxes" of Shaftesbury's personality that "during his most intensely Stoic phase he should be turning into a virtuoso," and thus warns of "the dangers of taking much of what is said in [the private notebooks] at face value."⁶³ And while part of the reason he moved to Italy at the end of his life was because of the Mediterranean climate, Shaftesbury also relished the opportunity to see Italian artwork on a regular basis.[64] Italy was also a great place to talk about art. In a 1712 letter about living in Naples, Shaftesbury says, "the sole subject of all [my] conversation is painting and those other arts."[65] He says in another letter to a friend who was thinking of coming to visit him in Naples, "You will find me, if alive, entertaining my-self very busily with Drawings, sketches, Prints, Medals and Antiques; which as well as Pictures and other Virtuoso-implements, are brought often to my Chamber and Bed-side."[66] These are not the letters of a person who, in his heart of hearts, disdains art.[67]

Then there was Shaftesbury's last commission.[68] In January 1713, when he was aware he was dying, Shaftesbury contacted Paolo de Matteis, a Neapolitan painter whom he had earlier commissioned to complete a painting of Hercules (which we'll discuss in the next chapter). Shaftesbury asked de Matteis to execute a portrait at the end of life. Here's Shaftesbury's description of the painting he had in mind:

> A man of distinction, nobleman of a certain kingdom, virtuoso, philosopher, and author well-known through his writings, having retired to a particular health resort to seek relief from his infirmities, still continues with his studies, ill, exhausted, and near to death as he is. This gentleman-philosopher, by his pose, his clothing, and personal insignia, as well as by his mien and looks, renders visible this true character or *personae*; through the view given of the interior of a study or library (decorated with some busts, antique pieces, and pencil drawings), one is able to recognize the subject upon which he employs his present contemplation.[69]

Shaftesbury didn't ask de Matteis to represent the dying philosopher in a room that was art-less. Stoic wisdom had pride of place in the picture of the dying philosopher. But works of art had a place as well.

I find it just about impossible to believe that all of these engagements with artistic and natural beauty were part of a decoy, mere sugarcoating, that Shaftesbury presented himself as a lover of art and nature only to lure others toward a philosophical position that in its pure form disdained art and nature. It also seems to me highly unlikely that he consistently aspired to become someone who didn't care about artistic or natural beauty, that he invariably took his engagement with such things to be a regrettable weakness or a temporary crutch. Much more consonant with the evidence is that he had a genuine heartfelt love for these things, and that he endorsed that love. He took engagement with the arts to be of real value. He was enriched by artistic beauty. He thought such enrichment was part of a good life.

How can we square such an attitude with the passages from the private notebooks in which Shaftesbury seems to endorse an Epictetus-like turning away from everything but the order of his own mind? At least part of the answer must be that Shaftesbury thought different things at different times. Sometimes he urged himself to turn away from everything but the state of his own soul. Sometimes he embraced the experience of artistic beauty. I don't see any warrant for taking the moments when he urged himself to turn away from artistic beauty to represent the more genuine, truer Shaftesbury-self than the moments when he cherished artistic and natural beauty.[70]

## 5. A Reconciling View

We have looked at the instrumentalist interpretation of Shaftesbury's view of artistic beauty, and at the non-instrumentalist interpretation. We have seen that there are some aspects of Shaftesbury's writings that support one, and some that support the other.

I'll now explain a position that I think can consistently combine at least parts of the instrumentalist and non-instrumentalist elements we find in Shaftesbury's writings. I think this position fits better with the texts as a whole than either of the other two. I should acknowledge, though, that I *want* this position to fit better. I find it more appealing. I should also acknowledge that Shaftesbury himself might not have seen this position clearly. I guess my claim is that, based on what he wrote, he would have recognized compelling reasons to embrace this position had it been offered to him.

Here's the position. Appreciation of the beauty of things is a non-instrumental good in a human life. In and of itself, it can make life better. But moral beauty is a non-instrumental good as well. And of the two, moral beauty is categorically superior. To sacrifice virtue for the beauty of things is always a mistake. Appreciation of the beauty of things can also be instrumentally good, in that it can promote the higher good of virtue. But the beauty of things doesn't necessarily promote virtue. It can also detract. And whenever appreciation of the beauty of things would detract from virtue, it's a mistake to indulge the former.

This position has two parts: [1] appreciation of physical beauty is a non-instrumental or final good but of a categorically inferior kind than the final good of moral beauty, and [2] appreciation of physical beauty can be an instrumental good in that it can promote the final good of moral beauty.[71]

Point [1] tells us that there are two things—artistic beauty and moral beauty—that are both final goods and that one of those things always overrides the other. This kind of relation between two things of fundamental value is not unusual. It's characteristic of moral views that hold that there are multiple basic ends that are strictly normatively ranked. Rawls calls this kind of ranking a "lexical ordering." On Rawls's own view, there are two principles of justice—the first concerning political rights and liberties, the second concerning wealth and economic opportunity. Both principles are part of the constitution of a just society. Both matter on their own. But the first principle is categorically superior to—has lexical priority over—the second. Whenever a choice has to be made between satisfying the first principle or the second, it's always a mistake to satisfy the second. Thomas Reid's view of morality has a similar structure. Reid holds that there are multiple fundamental moral rules, but also that there is a strict normative ranking that tells us what to do whenever we have to choose between two of them. As an example, he cites justice and gratitude. Justice and gratitude are both of fundamental moral importance. But if a choice between them has to be made, gratitude should always yield to justice. The same structure can apply to non-moral goods. Say someone is a serious tennis player. She loves tennis and wants to be as good as she can be at it. She also enjoys running and wants to become a better runner. But tennis is categorically more important to her. Tennis and running both matter to her, but whenever she has to make a choice between the two of them, she always chooses tennis.

Point [2] tells us that appreciation of physical beauty can serve a morally instrumental purpose as well as being a final good. There's nothing unusual about holding that something can be valuable both as a means to another end and as an end in itself. As Hume points out, kindness is valued both because of its tendency to produce beneficial results and because of its fundamental goodness.[72] An attending physician might act toward her interns with kindness both because she believes such conduct is the most effective means of instructing her interns so that they are more likely to provide the best treatment to patients, and because she believes such treatment is fundamentally important. Or consider the non-moral example of a person who is a serious tennis player and who also enjoys running. Running might be not only something she enjoys on its own, but also something that makes her a better tennis player. She runs for both the instrumental reason that it improves her tennis game and for the non-instrumental reason that she enjoys it.

The seventeenth-century enemies of the arts went wrong by failing to recognize any value to art. The gentlemen of fashion recognized that art had value in itself, but they failed to recognize the superior value of virtue. Epictetus recognized the superior value of virtue. And Epictetus may have been wise not to care about the loss of a fine lamp. One shouldn't stake one's happiness on possessing objects of any kind. But if Epictetus exited his possession-free hut one morning and, looking toward the hills, observed nature in all its glory, he would have been a fool to ignore its wonders. In nature, God created something beautiful. It's shameful to refuse the exquisite joy it offers. God also created human minds. Those human minds create art. We shouldn't stake our happiness on possessing any of that art. But when we encounter art that is beautiful, we have the same reason to appreciate it that we have to appreciate nature. Through it, the universe offers exquisite joy it would be foolish and shameful to refuse.

Shaftesbury seeks to explain what will make for the best life. Toward that end, he tries to convince us that if we can gain happiness from beauty on its own, we will have a better life than those who value things only to the extent that they serve selfish ends. To make beauty your good is to be enchanted by beauty in the world wherever it is found, simply because it's beautiful, rather than to chase constantly after gains. The instrumentalists are right that Shaftesbury wants to show that artistic pursuits can promote virtue. But that's a rear-guard action, a response to art's seventeenth-century enemies who claimed that the arts have nothing but immoral effects. The forward thrust of his philosophy is that all experiences of beauty are in and of themselves enriching.

An implication of this view is that a life of virtue and appreciation of art is better than a life of virtue alone. That implication conflicts with the idea that virtue is the complete and self-sufficient good, that a person who is truly virtuous will be happy in a way that nothing can subtract from or add to. There is no doubt that Shaftesbury was at times drawn to that idea. At those times, the only way he could see to make room for artistic beauty was to grant it the instrumental value of promoting virtue, and to cast his non-instrumental love of art as a decoy. But at other times, he relished beautiful art and saw it as continuous with the beauty of virtue and nature: love of beauty in every case the experience of soul thrumming in harmony with the mind of God.

CHAPTER FOUR

# Painting

SHAFTESBURY DISTINGUISHES BETWEEN two types of art: art that represents morally significant conduct, and art that doesn't. To be beautiful, art of every type must have unity of design. But art that represents morally significant conduct must meet another criterion as well: it must have unity of design *and* it must convey accurately the true nature of virtue and vice (see C 1.89, 1.172–73, 1.206–207).

In the category of art that is not morally representational are music, architecture, garden design, and craft. Still life and landscape painting also fall into this category; they're representational, but they don't represent morally significant conduct.[1]

In the category of art that is morally representational are various kinds of writing, and a genre of painting called "history painting." Our topic in this chapter is history painting. We'll discuss writing in the next chapter.

## 1. History Painting

History painting was a well-established genre at the time Shaftesbury was writing. History paintings were larger-than-life representations of stories from mythology, the Bible, and the ancient world. They were not intended to be historical records. Their purpose was to convey the message or moral of the stories. Given our current factual understanding of the word "history," it would probably be more helpful to label them "narrative paintings" or "paintings of stories." That's also more in line with the Latin *istoria* from which "history painting" derives.

"History painting" was a term of art used to designate a form clearly defined by the academies and well understood by the artistically educated. This is important to keep in mind when we see Shaftesbury claim that painters should sometimes breach *"historical Truth"* to convey higher poetical truth (C 3.229), and that "Historys" sometimes do a poor job at "teaching the *Truth* of Characters, and Nature of Mankind" (C 1.91). Shaftesbury is not criticizing "history painting" in these passages. He's saying that to be successful at conveying the moral of a story, a history painting (a narrative painting, the painting of a story) may need to alter some of the details of the source text.[2]

The established nature of this genre should also serve as a caution about overgeneralizing from what Shaftesbury says on the subject. When discussing history painting, Shaftesbury was discussing an art form designed to deliver a moral message. It would have been taken for granted that a history painting had overt moral content. It's no surprise, consequently, that Shaftesbury pays considerable attention to how history painting can most effectively convey virtue's benefits and vice's harms.[3] That doesn't mean he thought all art should always be explicitly morally didactic. Many of the points he makes about how a history painting ought to represent a person making a morally significant decision simply don't apply to his views of the enthusiastic joy we experience from the beauty of music, architecture, or nature. The instrumentalist interpretation we discussed in the last chapter may draw in part on a mistaken extrapolation from Shaftesbury's ideas about history painting to his view of beauty in general.

The great masters of history painting were Italian: Da Vinci, Michelangelo, and Raphael were at the top of the list, but there were many others besides, such as Carracci, de Cortano, Giordano. There were prominent French history painters, such as Poussin, Le Brun, and Le Moyne. The Dutch produced Rubens, Rembrandt, van Dyck. But from the list of significant history painters of the sixteenth and seventeenth centuries, English painters are conspicuously absent. As Agliony put it in 1685, "I have often wondred ... that we have never produced an *Historical Painter*, Native of our own *Soyl*."[4] England had some promising sculptors and architects. "But for a *Painter*, we never had, as yet, any of Note, that was an *English Man*, that pretended to *History-Painting*." Agliony might have been overstating matters; there were some seventeenth-century English practitioners of the genre. Their numbers were few, however, and none of them gained distinction.

Agliony blamed the Puritans for this lack. Those *"Bloody-Principled Zealots"* were "Enemies to all the Innocent *Pleasures* of Life." "[U]nder the pretext of a *Reformed Sanctity*," they destroyed the culture that otherwise would have seen the *"Arts* flourish amongst us; and particularly this of *Painting*."[5] The Puritan position Agliony was responding to is well-represented by George Salteren's *A Treatise against Images and Pictures in Churches*. God forbids the creation of graven images, and, according to Salteren, that prohibition "must be extended to all Images, whether molten, carved, or painted."[6] Salteren took admiration of painting to be the idolatry of image worship.

Hostility toward painting eased after the Restoration. But the Puritan tradition continued to influence English attitudes during Shaftesbury's time, with many continuing to think of painting as morally dubious, even if not outright idolatrous. The genre of history painting, because of its associations with Catholicism, suffered more than most.

There were also dismissive English attitudes toward painting that were distinct from the religious objections of the Puritans. Painting was deemed by some to be a physical endeavor more akin to the work of mechanics than to poetry or architecture. Painters in England wouldn't gain the elevated status of fine artists until well into the eighteenth century. Paintings themselves were often considered mere amusements, trifling entertainment, not the sorts of thing worthy of a gentleman's serious concern or concentrated intellectual attention. Italy's first art academy was founded in 1553, France's in 1648. England's Royal Academy of Art didn't open until 1768 (see C 3.248). That's a fair indication of how English attitudes compared to those on the continent.

Shaftesbury wanted to change all that. He wanted to remedy a situation he described as "the Arts and Virtuoso-Sciences" having "never yet rais'd their Heads in Britain."[7] He realized people might wonder why he was pursuing "so vulgar a Science as *Painting*" (C 3.243).[8] He acknowledged that paintings were thought of as "Amusements of such an inferior kind" (C 3.244). But he believed that advancement of English painting would elevate the nation's status and inspire its people. To make his case, he focused on painting of the most exalted kind—on the genre that partook of the "higher, more serious, and noble Part of *Imitation*, which relates to *History, Human Nature*, and *the chief Degree or Order of* BEAUTY" (C 3.245). He would spur his country toward artistic greatness by translating history painting into English.

## 2. *History Painting in Shaftesbury's* Judgment of Hercules

Shaftesbury's fullest treatment of history painting is *A Notion of the Tablature, or Judgment of Hercules*. This "notion," or essay, was a painstakingly detailed description of a painting Shaftesbury himself conceived and commissioned the Italian painter Paolo de Matteis to execute. Shaftesbury considered history painting to be a two-step process: first the intellectual planning, then the physical production. "The good painter (*quatenus* painter) begins by working first *within* . . . [First he] forms his *ideas*: then his hand: his strokes."[9] Shaftesbury's exemplar of mastery of this two-step process was Raphael, of whom he says "His idea before his hand. All other masters their hand before their idea."[10] Lessing had the same idea when he wrote that Raphael would have been the greatest artistic genius even "had he unfortunately been born without hands."[11] In *Judgment of Hercules* we see Shaftesbury completing painting's first step. *Judgment of Hercules* is Shaftesbury painting without hands (C 3.243).

The story of the painting is Hercules at the crossroads. As Xenophon tells it, when Hercules was a young man on the brink of independence, he went to a quiet place in the woods to debate with himself what type of life he was going to lead. While he was there, two women of great stature approached. One woman was Virtue, the other Pleasure or Vice. Each made a speech, trying to persuade Hercules to follow her path. Hercules listened to both. In the end he was convinced by Virtue.

In his account of how to complete this painting, Shaftesbury expresses clearly his two criteria of artistic beauty: the criterion of formal unity that is essential to all beautiful things, and the criterion of truthful representation of virtue and vice that must be met by morally representational works of art.

Formally, the painting should present a single unified picture to the viewer. It should be designed so that it is as easy as possible "for the Eye, by one simple Act and in one View, to comprehend the *Sum* or *Whole*" (C 3.234).[12] The composition should create "*one* Point of Sight" from which all the parts form "an agreeable and perfect Correspondency."[13]

The focus of Shaftesbury's own composition (Figure 1) is the space that encompasses Hercules's eyes and Virtue's finger. The viewer should stand at a distance that allows the gaze to naturally take in that space.

Compare Shaftesbury's picture with Carracci's (more famous) painting of the same scene (Figure 2). Carracci's composition violates Shaftesbury's unity stricture. It fails to give the eye one central resting place. The viewer's gaze wanders from Virtue's finger, to Hercules's eyes, to the scholar with the book, to the emblematic masks on the table, to Vice's arm.

To promote a single, unified effect, the painting should be as simple as possible. The fewer the objects, the better: nothing extraneous, nothing that distracts from the central action. It should aim for "magnificent austerity."[14] This means that in the Hercules painting there shouldn't be any buildings—no temple of virtue for one goddess, nor palace of pleasure

FIGURE 1. Paolo de Matteis, *The Choice of Hercules*

FIGURE 2. Annibale Carracci, *The Choice of Hercules*

for the other. Buildings are "not essential to the Action," and thus are liable to confound and perplex the viewer as to the real point (C 3.231). As well, buildings "wou'd prove a mere Incumbrance to the Eye, and wou'd of necessity disturb the Sign, by diverting it from that which is principal" (C 3.231). Numerous versions of Hercules at the crossroads violate this rule by including temples, fountains, tables, and other objects that draw focus away from Hercules's choice.

The painting should also be without any extraneous symbols of "the *emblematical* or *enigmatick* kind" (C 3.234). The painter should try to engage the viewers' emotions by drawing them in, by absorbing their attention as though the scene were real life. In real life we don't see emblems floating in the sky. An emblem's presence in a painting will break the spell. An example of such an emblem is the sign of the zodiac that floats in the sky of Raphael's *The Judgment of Paris* (Figure 3). Shaftesbury is willing to excuse Raphael for his zodiac, because the design is for an engraving and not a proper history painting. But a similarly fanciful item would be inappropriate in the Hercules composition. It would distract the viewer from the point of the story (C 3.231).

Look again at Carracci's Hercules. There are a number of elements that violate Shaftesbury's rule that the painting be as simple as possible: Pegasus on Mount Helicon, the scholar, the masks, the violin. Many other versions of Hercules at the crossroads also violate simplicity, including as they do not only buildings and temples but also figures other than the three main actors, all of which distract from focused engagement with Hercules's decision.[15] In the worst violations (Figure 4), more than half the painting is occupied by sensual delights illustrating temptations to vice.[16] Shaftesbury explicitly warns against representing Vice's side of the argument this way. The danger is that the painter will "overdo this part, and express the Affection too much to the life" (C 3.237). Vice ought not have a greater draw on the viewer's attention.

A history painting should focus attention on "a single Action" (C 3.237). It's ridiculous to try to represent "two or three distinct Actions" (C 3.237). You can't do it and maintain the unity necessary for "*one* Picture" (C 3.237). Shaftesbury criticizes Rubens for this kind of composition (Figure 5). If the subject of the painting is Mercury escorting Psyche to Olympus, then that's the only action that should be represented. All the other things going on here are distractions. Some of the figures aren't even paying attention to Mercury and Psyche.

It's also ridiculous to represent lots of different people "*all* speaking at once" (C 3.222) (Figure 6). That "must naturally have the same effect on

FIGURE 3. Raphael (engraving by Marcantonio Raimondi), *Judgment of Paris*

FIGURE 4. Pietro Benvenuti, *Hercules at the Crossroads*

FIGURE 5. Peter Paul Rubens, *Mercury Escorting Psyche to Olympus*

FIGURE 6. Sebastiano Ricci, *Hercules at the Crossroads*

the Eye, as such a Conversation wou'd have upon the Ear, were we in reality to hear it" (C 3.222). Shaftesbury stresses that in his painting it should be perfectly clear that Hercules and Pleasure are silent while Virtue alone is talking. In some other versions, in contrast, Virtue and Vice seem to be speaking at the same time, while secondary figures kibbitz and have side conversations.[17] Such scenes are a cacophony in comparison to the simple clarity of Virtue's voice in Shaftesbury's painting.

That's not to say that every history painting has to be as quiet and still as *The Choice of Hercules*. A painting should be as simple as possible, with nothing extraneous. But to convey the essence of certain subjects, painters may need numerous figures and complex scenes. Domenichino's St. Jerome is a prime example (Figure 7). There are at least 16 figures in this painting: St. Jerome himself, six witnesses adoring St. Jerome, the priest, two attendants to the priest, a couple watching through the doorway, four angels hovering by the roof. Domenichino lavishly portrays clothing and church decorations. He shows us fields and trees and two distant buildings. There's certainly a lot more going on here than in Shaftesbury's Hercules, but Domenichino's painting is one of the most esteemed pictures in the world.[18]

Shaftesbury also sings the praises of Raphael's Massacre of the Innocents (Figure 8). The farthest thing from quiet or still, this picture portrays a frantic, chaotic event involving many people and multiple actions. But every element contributes to a single impression on the viewer, to the moral purpose of the piece.[19]

Shaftesbury admired Raphael so much he found a way to praise his Transfiguration even though that painting—with the top half portraying Christ's transfiguration on Mount Tabor and the bottom half portraying the different event of the miracle of an exorcism—violates the unity requirement (Figure 9). This painting is not a unified whole, there isn't a single central focus for the eye. But that's okay because it's a "double Piece"—basically two different paintings, each of which is successful.[20]

An historical painting should represent a single moment in time. It must be possible for everything that occurs on the canvas actually to "happen together in *one and the same* instant" (C 3.217). *Unity of Time* is as essential as unity of action (C 3.217). This principle is violated by many paintings of Actaeon and Diana. According to the myth, Actaeon was hunting one day when he happened on the goddess Diana while she was bathing. As punishment for the indiscretion, Diana turned Actaeon into a stag. His own hounds then tore him apart. Cesari's painting represents the instant Diana first sees Actaeon (Figure 10). Because Diana is

FIGURE 7. Il Domenichino, *The Last Communion of St. Jerome*

FIGURE 8. Raphael (engraving by Marcantonio Raimondi), *The Massacre of the Innocents*

just realizing Actaeon is present, she could not yet have cast her spell. So Actaeon could not yet have begun to turn into a stag. But in Cesari's painting, it is otherwise. A stag's "Horns are already *sprouted*, if not full grown" from Actaeon's head, even though accurate timing dictates that "his Forehead is still sound" (C 3.219).[21] This temporal disunity is a "sin directly against the Law of *Truth* and *Credibility*" (C 3.218). (In another version, Actaeon's entire head has already been transformed into that of a deer![22])

Choosing the single moment to portray is perhaps the most important decision for a history painter. The painter must aim for the exact moment that most effectively conveys the moral message. Shaftesbury gives an expansive account of his own choice. There are, he tells us, four moments he could have opted for.

1. The moment the two goddesses first accost Hercules.
2. A moment in the middle of the goddesses' dispute.
3. The moment when the dispute is far advanced and virtue is just about to win Hercules over.
4. A moment when Hercules is entirely won over by virtue.

FIGURE 9. Raphael, *The Transfiguration of Christ*

FIGURE 10. Giuseppe Cesari, *Diana and Actaeon*

In moment 1, Hercules would be impressed and surprised by the appearance of the goddesses. Representing those emotions has little value. Serious moral engagement would be lacking. In 2, Hercules would be divided and in doubt. Such a state does not convey the superiority of Virtue's case. In option 4, Virtue will have stopped speaking and Hercules will no longer be conflicted. That would drain the picture of its dramatic power, and give the impression that committing to virtue is easy. The right choice is 3: Hercules in the throes, "wrought, agitated, and torn by contrary Passions," at the very moment just before he decides for Virtue (C 3.215). With the drama to engage viewers' emotions, moment 3 maximizes the impact of Hercules's subsequent resolution to live "a Life full of Toil and Hardship, under the conduct of VIRTUE, for the deliverance of Mankind from Tyranny and Oppression" (C 3.215–216). The painting vivifies the moment of moral agency.

Crucial to conveying the dramatic internal action of decision-making is the fact that the body "moves much slower than the Mind" (C 3.218). One can come to a realization a moment or two before one's body fully absorbs the change. Some parts will react more quickly than others. When a person is frightened, for instance, "the Eyes, and Muscles about the Mouth and Forehead" show alarm before "the heavier and more distant Parts [of the body] adjust them-selves, and change their Attitude some moments after" (C 3.218). This gives the painter the ability to represent the "Tracts or Footsteps" of an emotion that is passing and the *"Anticipation"* of an emotion that is just arising (C 3.217, 3.218).

Hercules's body language should reveal his transition between two emotional states. He should be listening to Virtue earnestly and with extreme attention. His face should express for her strong admiration that borders on love—almost to the point of being "excited by an amorous love" (C 3.220). At the same time, he has not yet fully rejected Pleasure. This is indicated by the position of his body, which inclines toward Pleasure. In turning his head away from the low road, there should be bodily regret, a reluctance not wholly overcome. But that's just about to change. We are witnessing him at the very last stage of the process that ends with his committing decisively to Virtue.

With this kind of planning and skill, a painter can reveal in a single instant a morally significant progress of sentiments. And the sentiments should be naturally expressed. The painter must "take care that his Action be not *theatrical*, or at second hand; but *original*, and drawn from NATURE herself" (C 3.225–226). Paintings shouldn't mimic the "study'd Action, and artificial Gesture" of actors on stage.[23] They should mirror real emotion and action. In *Judgment of Hercules*, the goddess Virtue is supposed to look like a person actually speaking to someone, not like an affectedly self-conscious *"fine Talker"* (C 3.225). An example of the offending theatricality Shaftesbury warns against is Carracci's *The Samaritan Woman at the Well* (Figure 11). An even more egregious offender is Van Dyck's *Samson and Delilah* (Figure 12). These paintings don't mirror life. They don't accurately represent the passion and conduct of real people. Their models are scenery-chewers.

But while human figures should be as true to life as possible, other elements of the painting can depart from source details. If, for instance, the event involved "a Confusion, Oppugnancy, and Riot of Colours," the painter might nonetheless rightly use only colors that harmonize with each other (C 3.229). The painter ought to strive for the higher truth of visual unity, rather than for mere historical representation (C 3.229).[24] With regard to his own painting, Shaftesbury notes that, as the story is often told, Hercules is clad in a lion's skin "of a yellow and dusky colour," while Virtue wears "a resplendent Robe of the purest and most glossy White" (C 3.230). But those colors cannot be felicitously combined. The

FIGURE 11. Annibale Carracci, *Christ and the Samaritan Woman*

FIGURE 12. Antony van Dyck, *Samson and Delilah*

painter ought therefore to depart from a "literal" representation of the event. Rather than represent any figure in "extraordinary brightness or lustre," the painter must "make use of such still quiet Colours, as may give to the whole Piece a Character of Solemnity and Simplicity, agreeable with it-self" (C 3.230). The painting is to be of a unified, subdued palate.[25]

Another departure from historical truth that can be salutary is what Shaftesbury calls "Hyperbole," or judicious exaggeration of certain physical features.[26] As an example of effective hyperbole Shaftesbury points to Poussin's *Christ and the Samaritan Woman* (Figure 13).[27] The woman's finger in this painting is longer than it would be in real life. But the elongated finger is apt because it sharpens the viewer's focus on the central action. Shaftesbury also approves of the hyperbolically brutal attack Raphael represents in *The Massacre of the Innocents*. But he didn't approve of all hyperbole. Michelangelo's musculature endowments are right at the edge of acceptable exaggeration. Pietro da Cortona's elongation of arms goes over the line.[28]

Most important is that the painter make decisions in light of what will promote the moral message of the painting. The ultimate goal is accurate representation not of the kind of things that can be photographed, but of "the *moral* and *poetick Truth*" of virtue and vice, of "the higher and nobler Species of Humanity" (C 3.238). Every other consideration "must be sacrific'd to the *real* BEAUTY *of this first and highest* Order" (C 3.232). The natural "must pay homage" to the moral (C 3.232).

Crucial to the moral purpose of Shaftesbury's painting is the representation of the two goddesses. Virtue must be represented as "a Lady of goodly Form, tall and majestic" (C 3.223), "dress'd neither negligently, nor with much study or ornament" (C 3.222). She should be standing firm, "with one Foot advanc'd, in a sort of climbing Action, over the rough and thorny Ground" that leads to righteousness (C 3.224). She speaks with passion and force, but without becoming theatrical or "a mere *Scold*" (C 3.226). With her left hand she urges to the path upward. With her right hand she dismisses the path down. Though neither lean nor tanned, "the Substance and Colour of her Flesh" will reveal that "she was sufficiently accustom'd to exercise" (C 3.223).

The soft flesh of the goddess Pleasure reveals exactly the opposite about her. Though possessing "fond Airs of Dalliance and Courtship," she is tired and lazy (C 3.227). Her left hand points to the road of pleasure, but it's a "slight and negligent" gesture, that of someone who's exhausted herself from talking and now "appears weary and spent" (C 3.238). With her right hand, Pleasure supports "with much ado, the lolling lazy Body"

FIGURE 13. Nicolas Poussin, *Christ and the Samaritan Woman at the Well*

(C 3.227). The biggest challenge in representing Pleasure is to strike the right balance between her effort to persuade Hercules and her supine indolence. If she is seen to be making too much of a persuasive effort, it will fail to convey Pleasure's lazy character, as well as detract from the central focus on Virtue's speech. If she makes no persuasive effort at all, then the conflict that powers the central action—Hercules in the throes—will be diminished. The answer, Shaftesbury thinks, is to make Pleasure one-fifth active and four-fifths lazy. Her left arm is the active part, that which is still trying to persuade. The rest, lazy.

## 3. Reception of Shaftesbury's Judgment of Hercules

*A Notion of the Tablature, or Judgment of Hercules* was first translated into German in 1748, and, as Dehrmann shows, it exerted an outsized influence on German thought in the decades that followed.[29] Mendelssohn, Abbt, and Herder all read it avidly. Gottsched valued it for its lessons on how art can improve society by imparting moral truths in accessible form. Nicolai was influenced by Shaftesbury's idea of an elevated role for painting, as well as by particular guidelines about what makes for a successful painting. Wieland praised the essay, endorsed Shaftesbury's idea of painting's capacity to improve character, and went on to write a play, *Die Wahl des Herkules*, based on the same episode.

Jaffro explains how Shaftesbury's *Hercules* influenced Lessing.[30] In *Laocoon*, Lessing explores how beauty applies to actions and thoughts, as well as to forms. In his discussion of painting, he explores Shaftesbury's idea that the key to planning a painting is identifying the most "fruitful" or "pregnant" moment and the one viewpoint that most effectively captures the essence of the moral message.[31] "[I]t is certain," Lessing writes, "that the single moment, and the single viewpoint of that moment, can never be chosen too significantly."[32] Lessing expands as well on Shaftesbury's idea that a painter should impart to the representations of subjects traces of what has come before and foreshadows of what is yet to come.[33] These ideas of Shaftesbury's also influenced James Harris's *Three Treatises* and Adam Smith's "Of the Nature of that Imitation which takes place in what are called The Imitative Arts." Harris and Smith emphasize a painting's need to capture a *"Punctum Temporis"* or "single instant of action" that conveys to a viewer the essential moral meaning of a story.[34]

Nablow maintains that *Judgment of Hercules* influenced French thinkers such as Voltaire, who was led by the essay to bring the story of Hercules to bear on his own work.[35] And Shaftesbury was at the leading edge of the aesthetic thinking in England in the eighteenth and nineteenth centuries. Hinnant shows that *Judgment of Hercules* was an instrumental influence on Burke's development of the distinction between the beautiful and the sublime.[36] Wittkower argues that Shaftesbury's comments about architecture in the "Letter on Design" that accompanied *Judgment of Hercules* were critical to the development of the New Palladian architectural movement of eighteenth-century England.[37] Two famous paintings—Reynolds's

FIGURE 14. Paolo de Matteis, *Diana and Acteaon* (first version)

*David Garrick between Tragedy and Comedy* (1761) and Westfall's *Shakespeare between Tragedy and Comedy* (1825)—are variations on (or parodies of) Shaftesbury's subject of the choice of Hercules.[38] John Adams was so moved by Shaftesbury's essay that he proposed that Shaftesbury's image of Hercules be used as the Great Seal for the United States of America.[39]

As Pestilli shows, Shaftesbury's ideas on history painting are also reflected in two paintings attributed to de Matteis, Shaftesbury's collaborator on Hercules. The two paintings are of Actaeon and Diana, the story of the goddess who turns the hunter into a stag.[40]

In the first painting, completed before de Matteis's collaboration with Shaftesbury, Actaeon has antlers as he enters Diana's realm (Figure 14). This violates Shaftesbury's *"Rule of Consistency,"* according to which it must be possible for everything represented to "happen together in *one and the same* instant" (C 3.217), for this is the moment when Diana is first surprised by Actaeon, so she could not yet have cast her spell. In this painting, moreover, the figures of Actaeon, Diana, and the nymphs are small, almost incidental. The emphasis of the composition is on a pastoral landscape and irrelevant distant buildings. This violates Shaftesbury's mandate that a history painting focus the viewer on an essential moral conflict.

FIGURE 15. Paolo de Matteis, *Diana and Acteaon* (second version)

In the other painting of Actaeon and Diana attributed to de Matteis, the composition is completely different (Figure 15). As Pestilli puts it, "Two more radically different versions of a subject by the same painter would be hard to find."[41] Everything in this painting is devoted to heightening the moral drama. Natural features are pared down and backgrounded. There are no extraneous buildings, no premature antlers. Figures fill the frame. The expression and posture of the nymphs convey shock at Actaeon's transgression and frightful anticipation of Diana's response. The nymphs also funnel the viewer's eye toward the intense locked gaze from Diana to Actaeon. Diana is vital and active. She's in the final stage of the emotional passage from surprise to anger. It's the moment a split second before the fateful event. The tension is palpable.

Shaftesbury believed that if his instructions were expertly executed, the resulting painting of Hercules would inspire virtue and deter vice. He wished for the painting to be placed in a room in the royal palace where a young prince would see it on a regular basis. Repeatedly viewing "Virtue in this Garb and Action" could encourage the royal youth to his moral duty when one day he had to make a real-world decision similar to Hercules's mythological one—a decision on which not only his own happiness but the fate of Europe and the entire world might depend (C 3.251).

That's an ambitious goal. I can't say I share Shaftesbury's high hopes. My own sense is that Paola de Matteis didn't do a great job executing Shaftesbury's vision. Virtue is supposed to be at the zenith of her speech, when "the highest Tone of Voice and strongest Action are employ'd" (C 3.216). Hercules is supposed to be in the final stage of a monumental internal struggle. But it looks to me more like he's puzzling over her convoluted driving directions to a C-grade tourist site he's not sure he wants to visit.[42] Maybe I would have a stronger response if Shaftesbury had commissioned Titian to paint the upward path, Rubens to paint Pleasure's body, Velasquez to paint Hercules's expression, and van der Meer to paint the face of Virtue.

Then again, I have doubts about whether even the most expertly executed Hercules painting would have on twenty-first-century viewers the effect Shaftesbury hoped for. History paintings just don't seem to have the same impact today. Their technical aspects may impress. Their place in the history of art might be of interest. But the intended emotional and moral uplift tends to fall flat. There are loads of moral messages in contemporary painting. But the methods and subject matter Shaftesbury focused on no longer seem as effective at conveying them.

Shaftesbury's discussion of history painting also conflicts with our moral sensibilities in its portrayal of women. It is not just that the women are often nude and on display for the male gaze. They are also typically represented as bewitching, inhuman creatures whose entire purpose is to pose a challenge to the ineluctably male protagonist. Nor is this attitude anomalous in Shaftesbury's writing. He routinely extols what is admirable about the masculine by contrasting it with what is shameful about the feminine. His recommendations concerning history painting amply illustrate a morally archaic view of women that makes appearances throughout Shaftesbury's thought.

## 4. History Painting and the Movies

The contemporary art form that I think comes closest to conveying Shaftesbury's conception of history painting is moviemaking, especially moviemaking of the mid-twentieth century. The auteur-director is akin to

Shaftesbury's designer of a history painting—someone who has a vision, storyboards it in a manner similar to Shaftesbury's *Hercules*, and then brings in a cinematographer, actors, and editors to realize it. And, like Shaftesbury's ideal of history painting, many of the great movies use narrative images to pack punches of stupendous moral power.

De Sica's *Bicycle Thieves* is a prime example. It's the story of a poor man named Antonio Ricci who needs a bicycle for the only job he can find that will enable him to feed his family. His bicycle is stolen. The main action of the movie consists of Ricci and his son Bruno trying to get the bicycle back. At the movie's climax, Ricci, having lost any hope of recovering his own bicycle, spots an unattended bicycle by the side of a building. He tells Bruno to take the bus home. We then see within Ricci a struggle between the reluctance to steal and a desperate desire to keep his job so he can feed his family. He walks toward the bicycle, then away from it, toward the bicycle, then away, agony manifest in face and body. Eventually he gives in. He grabs the bicycle. As he's pedaling away, a man runs out of the building and yells that his bicycle is being stolen. Shouting "Thief! Thief!" a crowd chases Ricci down. His son Bruno, who has failed to board the bus, hears the commotion. He turns. We see the boy's face contort in confusion and shock and pain as he realizes that the bicycle thief is his father (Figure 16). Bruno's close-up at that moment could be the subject of a Shaftesburean history painting.

I suspect, though, that Shaftesbury would think an even better choice would be Ricci in the final throes of intense moral struggle (Figure 17). This is the moment that immediately precedes Ricci's crossing the line (as represented by the lamppost in the middle of the frame), stealing the bicycle—and paying for his transgression.

Another example is David Lean's 1957 film, *Bridge on the River Kwai*. It's the story of a World War II British battalion that has been captured by the Japanese and put to work building a railway bridge for the Japanese military. The British commanding officer, Colonel Nicholson, makes building the bridge a point of pride for the British soldiers, because it will give his men a sense of purpose that will carry them through their trying circumstances, and because it will prove to their Japanese captors the superiority of British discipline and efficiency. Nicholson eventually becomes deeply invested in the success of the bridge, coming to think of it as his personal legacy, even though it is designed to help the Japanese defeat the British. The day after the bridge is completed, the rest of the British soldiers are sent away while Nicholson and the Japanese await the first military train. Meanwhile, a British commando force arrives with

FIGURE 16. *Bicycle Thieves*

FIGURE 17. *Bicycle Thieves*

FIGURE 18. *The Bridge on the River Kwai*

plans to destroy the bridge. Minutes before the train is to arrive, Nicholson discovers the commandos' explosives. He tries to cut the fuse, which alerts the Japanese, who kill the commando positioned to detonate the bomb. A second commando swims across the river to try to take over, but he too is shot. Just before he dies, the second commando confronts Nicholson. The commando's dying accusation opens Nicholson's eyes to the true nature of the situation. The camera zooms in as Nicholson comes to the realization he has made a terrible mistake. "What have I done?" he whispers. We see Nicholson's face change from moral anguish to the moral resolution to do his duty by destroying the bridge (Figure 18). The next second a mortar explosion knocks Nicholson down. He stands, injured, and makes his way toward the detonator. He is shot, but he continues to stagger forward. With his last breath, just as the train reaches the bridge, he falls on the plunger. The bomb detonates. The bridge explodes. The train careens into the river.

Or consider Akira Kurosawa's film from 1963, *High and Low*. The main character is Kingo Gondo, an executive at a large shoe company. Gondo has mortgaged all he owns to arrange a secret buyout of the company, so that he can wrest control from a faction that he believes is subverting its long-term success for short-term gain. Just before Gondo is about to put his plan into action, he receives a phone call from someone who says he has kidnapped Gondo's son. But Gondo's son is safe. The kidnapper has abducted the chauffeur's son by mistake. The kidnapper says that Gondo has to pay nonetheless, or the boy will be killed. If Gondo hands over the money he secured for the corporate coup, he'll be completely ruined. He'll lose his job. He'll go into ruinous debt. His family will suffer great hardship. Initially, he decides he won't pay. Then comes the scene that Shaftesbury would highlight. As Gondo's associate is getting ready to leave with the money for the buyout, his chauffeur begs Gondo to pay the kidnapper. Also in the room are Gondo's own wife and child. For a moment, Gondo engages in a monumental internal struggle. Then he decides to pay the kidnapper.

Shaftesbury would have loved the way these pivotal scenes convey internal moral conflict. Like his painting, these scenes vivify the moment that the struggle between virtue and vice reaches maximal intensity. To effect that portrayal, Shaftesbury gave de Matteis detailed instructions on the figures' facial expressions and body language. De Sica, Lean, and Kurosawa would have given comparable instructions to their actors. Of course De Sica, Lean, and Kurosawa also had at their disposal many other techniques. The medium of film bestows vast powers of control on viewers' experience. In the pivotal scenes of *Bicycle Thieves* and *Bridge on the River Kwai*, De Sica and Lean use close-ups to devastating effect. But it's Kurosawa who is most like a history painter in the way he uses blocking to convey moral tension. Like a larger-than-life history painting, *High and Low* is shot in very wide format (Tohoscope, a Japanese version of Cinemascope). This enables Kurosawa, in the pivotal scene, to encompass everyone in the large room together in one stationary mid-range shot (Figure 19). Within the frame he places the figures—Gondo, the chauffeur, the business associate, Gondo's family—in a configuration that highlights Gondo's choice. Kurosawa's blocking of this scene is a twentieth-century version of Shaftesbury's instructions in *Judgment of Hercules*.

With those examples in mind, I'd like to revisit the topic of the last chapter. Our question there was whether Shaftesbury believed that artistic beauty had non-instrumental value; or whether he saw art as having only the instrumental value of promoting virtue, and as such should be dispensed with when it no longer served an edifying purpose. I argued that Shaftesbury thought art could serve the instrumental purpose of promoting virtue, but that he also valued it non-instrumentally. I want to say now that we can appreciate the nature of this attitude by imagining the same attitude in a morally concerned filmmaker. This filmmaker may make movies with a strong message, perhaps about political or social issues. She may be deeply committed to using film toward that end. Her political and social convictions might be of the utmost importance to her. At the same time, she may truly love the medium of film. Its purely aesthetic qualities may be for her a great thrill, a delight. She may think of film as not merely of instrumental value, not merely something for people at a lower level

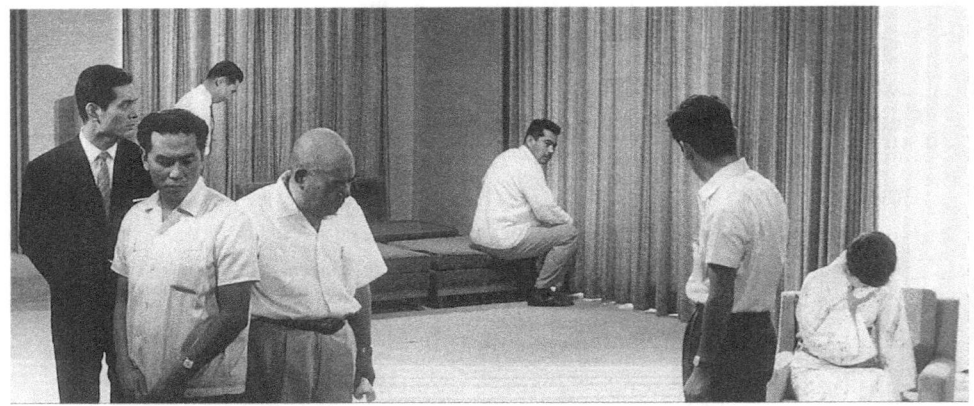

FIGURE 19. *High and Low*

of characterological development that can be dispensed with by moral adepts. A world without movies, no matter how morally upright, would be one she doesn't want to live in. I believe that's the attitude Shaftesbury had toward painting. He exerted great effort to view paintings and to build a collection when doing those things was for an Englishman logistically difficult and culturally unusual. And he wrote about painting—about elements of it both small and large—with a passion that bespeaks a soul enchanted by art.

Few people today can be expected to gain inspiration from the allegorical didacticism of history paintings. But Shaftesbury's conception of that genre turns on the same elements that power some of the most affecting visual storytelling of our time. A narrative in paint, as Shaftesbury understands it, should convey the same drama and internal conflict that continues to arrest our emotional and moral attention today.

This idea of successful narrative is also evident in something Shaftesbury says about theater. He praises Shakespeare's *Hamlet* as being the work that has "most affected English hearts" (C 1.171). Why did he think that play in particular was so compelling? It's far from an allegory or morality play. It's not even clear what moral message it's meant to deliver. Shaftesbury thought the play was compelling because it focused so thoroughly on the psychological/spiritual/moral anguish of the main character. Every aspect of *Hamlet* draws us into "a Series of deep Reflections, drawn from *one* Mouth, upon the Subject of *one* single Accident and Calamity, naturally fitted to move Horror and Compassion" (C 1.171). He loved *Hamlet* for its portrayal of sustained internal conflict.

*Hamlet* may have resonated with Shaftesbury for another reason as well. The high-born Hamlet is both self-flagellating and prodigiously gifted. His soul is the scene of struggle between reflection and action, between the inclination to withdraw and the duty of a noble station. He adopts various personae and is acutely aware of the difference between his public face and his innermost thoughts. He tells tricky stories, and stories within stories. It's a character easy to imagine Shaftesbury identifying with.

CHAPTER FIVE

# Writing

BEAUTIFUL PAINTING should inspire virtue. Good writing should too. Just as a painter should represent accurately "not only *Men,* but *Manners,* and human Passion," a writer should accurately "describe both *Men* and *Manners,* and give to an *Action* its just Body and Proportions" (C 3.214, 1.129). *A Notion of the Historical Draught or Tablature of the Judgment of Hercules* is Shaftesbury's instruction to history painters about how to design compositions that will inspire virtue. *Soliloquy: or, Advice to an Author* is Shaftesbury's instruction to authors.

Shaftesbury discusses poems and plays in *Soliloquy,* but he does not address himself chiefly to poets and playwrights. He addresses himself chiefly to writers who advise us how to live. His aim "is not so much *to give Advice,* as to consider of the *Way and Manner of advising*" (C 1.98). This meta-advice, Shaftesbury thought, was sorely needed. For a great many advice-giving authors produced books that were utterly awful. The offenders included essayists, memoirists, and "super-speculative" philosophers. In this chapter we'll look first at how these writers fail, and then at what Shaftesbury thinks they need to do to succeed.

## 1. Bad Writing: Philosophy

Shaftesbury thought ancient philosophy was the source of the most inspiring writing in the history of humankind. But scholastic and modern philosophers turned philosophy into something worse than worthless, attacking the tree of wisdom with turgid pedantry.

The sins of philosophical writing start with tedious organizing introductions that are more likely to tire us than win our attention. A thesis is proposed, "the Subject divided and subdivided"—and "instantly we begin a Strife with *Nature*, who otherwise might surprize us in the soft Fetters of Sleep" (C 1.161).

More important, super-speculative philosophers discuss matters that are in and of themselves useless to a person trying to live the best human life. The "Natures, Essences, and Propertys" the super-speculative philosophers expound on have no bearing on what will make a person more virtuous or happy (C 1.178; see also 1.189). It may take great cleverness to produce systems of thought on these matters. But true philosophy is distinguished by its unique capacity to teach us to how to live, not as a mere show for "Subtlety and Nicety" (C 1.184).

Shaftesbury compares the super-speculative philosophers to a "notable *Enthusiast*" who thought he could become the world's greatest "Master of Voice and Language" by determining the shape a mouth must make to form various sounds (C 1.177). Toward that end, the enthusiast strenuously exalted his voice while forming every configuration of throat and mouth.[1]

> And thus bellowing, roaring, snarling, and otherwise variously exerting his Organs of Sound, he endeavour'd to discover what Letters of the Alphabet cou'd best design each Species, or what new Letters were to be invented, to mark the undiscover'd Modifications. He found, for instance, the Letter *A* to be a most genuine Character, an original and pure Vowel, and justly plac'd as principal in the front of the alphabetick Order. For having duly extended his under Jaw to its utmost distance from the upper; and by a proper Insertion of his Fingers provided against the Contraction of either Corner of his Mouth; he experimentally discover'd it impossible for human Tongue under these Circumstances to emit any other Modification of Sound than that which was describ'd by this primitive Character. The Vowel *O* was form'd by an orbicular Disposition of the Mouth; as was aptly delineated in the Character it-self. The Vowel *U* by a parallel Protrusion of the Lips. The other Vowels and Consonants by other various Collisions of the Mouth, and Operations of the active Tongue upon the passive Gum or Palat. (C 1.178)

Shaftesbury doesn't deny that such phonetic investigation may be useful to grammar, nor that grammar can be useful to rhetoric and other arts of speech and writing. But the enthusiast became so enamored of his "speculative Science of *Articulation*" that he stopped looking for anything more elevated (C 1.179). He became convinced that his discoveries were the pinnacle of what could be learned about human language.

Not every intellectual endeavor has to have direct implications for making us better people. Mathematics is entirely worthwhile even though it doesn't have immediate practical moral benefits. But that's because mathematicians are under no illusion that their proofs on their own improve human life. They have the "Modesty and good Sense" to seek such improvement from "other Studys and Practice" (C 1.180). In contrast, super-speculative philosophers, like the enthusiastic phonetician, mistakenly believe that their systems are the alpha and omega of wisdom, preventing them from attending to other, improving studies. The only purpose their super-subtle speculations serve is thus "to shut the door against better Knowledge, and introduce Impertinence and Conceit with the best Countenance of Authority" (C 1.180). Such philosophizing is "more delusive and infatuating, on account of its magnificent Pretension" (C 1.179). It is a "choking Weed" that strangles the search for real wisdom, its practitioners, like Narcissus at the pool, forever captured by adoration of their own cleverness (C 1.177).

One way some super-speculative philosophers go wrong is by trying to understand human passions entirely in terms of bodily causes and effects. Such mechanistic accounts may qualify someone "to give Advice to an Anatomist or a Limner," but on their own they don't provide any useful advice about how to live (C 1.181).[2] They tell us nothing about the "regulation and Government of those Passions, on which the Conduct of a Life depends"—nothing about how to command our passions, about how to free ourselves from superstition and vain fears, about how to withstand imposture and delusion (C 1.182). A super-speculative philosopher may tell us, for instance, that the passion of fear "determines the Spirits to the Muscles of the Knees, which are instantly ready to perform their Motion; by taking up the Legs with incomparable Celerity, in order to remove the Body out of harm's way" (C 1.182). But learning those mechanisms of blood and muscle won't help me "diminish my Fears, or raise my Courage" (C 1.182). Similarly, purely mechanistic accounts of how I form ideas do not on their own help me regulate my mind. Such accounts have no more bearing on my conduct and inner state than the super-speculative debate between atomists and plenitudinarians has on a craftsman. Just as the craftsman can "proceed as well on one Hypothesis as the other," my mind "will proceed either way alike" (C 1.186). Learning about such things is no more compelling than learning "how, and by what Motions of my Tongue or Palat, I form those *articulate Sounds*, which I can full as well pronounce, without any such Science or Speculation" (C 1.187). Shaftesbury compares the super-speculative philosophers who produce mechanistic accounts of passions and ideas to someone who examines the inner workings of a watch only to determine the kind of metal each part is composed of (C 1.181). Without a view of the watch's telos—without a normative framework that explains what the watch is for, and thus when the watch is working properly—these examinations won't enable anyone to make a better watch. Similarly, mechanistic accounts of thought and feeling on their own, without wisdom about virtue and happiness, won't help us lead better lives.

When discussing the counter-productivity of super-speculative philosophy, Shaftesbury makes one of his most oft-quoted statements: "The most ingenious way of becoming foolish, is by a *System*" (C 1.180). Commentators often point to this as indicative of Shaftesbury's whimsy, frivolity, and blithe inconsistency. But while Shaftesbury is not the most rigorous, sober, opposite-of-whimsical writer you're ever going to read, his "foolish by a system" comment is part of a sharper point than the quotation of that single sentence might suggest. Here's the full passage.

> As for other Ability or Improvement in the Knowledge of human Nature or the World; [the mathematician] refers himself to other Studys and Practice. Such is *the Mathematician's* Modesty and good Sense. But for *the Philosopher*, who pretends to be wholly taken up in considering his higher Facultys, and examining the Power and Principles of his Understanding; if in reality his Philosophy be foreign to the Matter profess'd; if it goes beside the mark, and reaches nothing we can truly call our Interest or Concern; it must be somewhat worse than mere Ignorance or Idiotism. The most ingenious way of becoming foolish, is *by a System*. And the surest Method to prevent good Sense, is to set up something in the room of it. The liker any thing is to Wisdom, if it be not plainly *the thing it-self*, the more directly it becomes *its opposite*. (C 1.179–180)

This is not Walt Whitman boasting "Do I contradict myself? Very well then I contradict myself." Shaftesbury is not dismissing systematic thinking in general. He believes in "good Sense." He is criticizing those who are so enraptured by their untethered speculations that they ignore matters of real importance.

## 2. Bad Writing: Memoirs and Essays

A second category of authors Shaftesbury thinks sorely in need of meta-advice are "Writers of Memoirs and Essays." One group in the forefront of his mind are English authors who publish what they call their "*Meditations, Occasional Reflections*, [and] *Solitary Thoughts*" on religious and moral subjects (C 1.103).³ The offenses of these writers begin with their irksome prefaces. Here are some examples.

- In *Occasional Reflections on Several Subjects*, Boyle calls what will follow immature "Trifles" that are "unfinished and unpolished."⁴ By "way of Apology" for the book's incoherence, unevenness, and lack of precision, Boyle notes that the contents were pulled together from among "loose and forgotten papers" that were "written for my own private Amusement" in "a loose and Desultory way."⁵ The book's many flaws may thus be excusable, as is "a Careless Dress, when a man intended not, nor expects, to go out of his study, or let himself be seen."⁶ Boyle also apologizes for his apologies, acknowledging that "some may think that in this Preface I employ Excuses that seem (some of them) not to agree with another."⁷
- In *Mid-Night Thoughts*, William Killegrew tells the reader that he is publishing things he scribbled down when he awoke in the middle of the night. Killegrew "was perswaded by some Friends, to transcribe these loose Papers as they were first writ, and tacked together, without any method of coherence observed, as appears by the frequent repetitions of the same expressions in many of them."⁸
- In Mathew Hale's *Contemplations, Moral and Divine*, the editor explains that the contents were written "ex tempore . . . [A]s things came into [Hale's] thoughts, so he put them into writing."⁹ Hale had not "revised them for that purpose; nor so much as read over some of them since he wrote them; nor indeed so much as finished some of them . . . [T]he Reader must know that they are published . . . in their native and primogeneal simplicity."¹⁰
- In the first of his *Essayes or Moral Discourses on several Subjects*, Thomas Culpeper forewarns the reader that the book lacks polish because it is "but the result of private thoughts."¹¹

On the surface, these comments are all humility and self-deprecation, "preface" for the authors seeming to have "become only another word to signify *Excuse*" (C 1.203). But the modesty is false. Each author's underlying message, in actuality, is that even his aimless, careless jottings are so wonderful that he cannot in good conscience deny humankind their stupendous benefits. There is as well an annoying affectedness to it all, a "coquetry" that draws attention away from the subject to the writer himself.

At least as offensive is the easy resignation to incoherence and gracelessness. Authors who care about producing true work will hew to a plan and concern themselves with tone. They'll tend to the organizing structure of a piece, and to variations in style that hone its desired effect. There is a morality of authorship. It's a subset of the virtue of true workmanship. A mechanic wouldn't boast about delivering to a customer a shoddy product. A painter wouldn't boast about not having finished a painting. An author shouldn't boast about publishing unpolished writing. An author ought to "fix his Eye upon that consummate *Grace*, that Beauty of *Nature*, and that *Perfection* of Numbers" (C 1.204). As difficult as it may be to "bring *Perfection*" to his work, that nonetheless ought to be his constant aim (C 1.204). Criteria of balance and integrated composition apply "in every Writing, from the *Epopee* or *Heroick-poem*, down to the familiar Epistle, or slightest Essay" (C 3.160). But these memoirists and essayists just sit down and start writing, without any thought to effective variation or unifying theme (C 3.18). The results are "*Cruditys*," misshapen "Miscarriages and Abortions" that are "beget in publick" (C 1.103). Then the author attaches to the work a preface "to reconcile his Reader to those Faults which he chuses rather to excuse than to amend" (C 1.203).

These authors are also guilty of the offense of oversharing. They invite us to watch them work through problems they should have "kept to themselves" rather than expose "on the Stage of the World" (C 1.103). They come forth covered in "scum" that ought to be cleansed in private. Shaftesbury compares them to quack doctors who illustrate to their audiences in disgusting detail the benefits special supplements have had on their digestive systems. "The Proverb, no doubt, is very just, *Physician cure thy-self*," but no one wishes to be present when a physician is actually engaged in his purgative "bodily Operations" (C 1.103). Nor is a reader "any better entertain'd" by the "experimental Discussions" of a writer who is "in reality doing no better, than taking his Physick in publick" (C 1.103).

As unpalatable as he finds secular memoirists and essayists, Shaftesbury is even more appalled by "Candidates for Authorship" who "*happen to be of the sanctify'd kind*"—of the published religious reflections of ministers and priests (C 1.104). Like the secular writers, these "*holy Advisors*" exhibit appalling self-aggrandizement, presuming that any random thought that pops into their heads is of such value that they can't in good conscience *not* publish it (C 1.105). In a characteristically sarcastic passage, Shaftesbury says that most of us cannot imagine how far the "Charity [of these religious writers] is apt to extend. So exceeding great is their Indulgence and Tenderness for Mankind, that they are unwilling the least Sample of their devout Exercise shou'd be lost" (C 1.104). They "can allow nothing to lie conceal'd" that happens to pass through their minds during their private religious ruminations (C 1.104). The sanctified authors also write very badly, delivering for publication crudities that have never been given the order and polish of the writing art. But rather than even make a show of apologizing for the ugliness of their writing, the sanctified authors aggressively defend it. "A *Saint*-Author of all Men least values Politeness. He scorns to confine that Spirit, in which he writes, to Rules of Criticism and profane Learning. Nor is he inclin'd in any respect to play the Critick on himself, or regulate his Style or Language by the Standard of good Company, and People of the better sort. He is above the Consideration of that which in a narrow sense we call *Manners*" (C 1.104). As an illustration of the rejection of politeness in writing, Shaftesbury points to the letters of Pope Gregory, whose disdain for polite expression led him to carry on "a kind of Massacre upon every Product of human Wit" (C 3.146). Gregory condemned the teaching of grammar, eschewed elegant expression, and boasted of his own cacophonousness. "I have scorned observing the art of eloquence," Gregory writes. "I do not avoid the clash of m-sounds; I do not steer clear of a mingling of barbarisms; I spurn careful attention to positionings and changings of prepositions and inflections" (C 1.146). Gregory brandishes his lack of revision like a badge of honor, when in fact it is nothing but ugly writing.

## *3. Solution for Bad Writing: Soliloquy*

Shaftesbury advises authors to avoid these writing offenses by practicing intensive self-reflection. We saw in chapter 2 that Shaftesbury believes that gaining critical distance on one's own passions and ideas is essential to moral agency. His claim in *Soliloquy* is that critical distance is also necessary for good writing. An author must "multiply himself into *two Persons*, and be *his own Subject*" (C 1.99). Only after that process has been completed should he reveal his writing to the world.

Shaftesbury develops several comparisons for the reflective work authors ought to engage in. One comparison is to self-surgery. To become effective at surgery, doctors need to practice. They gain this practice by performing surgery on patients in hospitals. There is no hospital where a would-be author can test his advice, no patients he can expect to operate on. But he can operate on himself. He can try out his own advice. He will then be in a position to assess which aspects work and which do not.

Shaftesbury also compares the author's process to dramatic soliloquy on the stage, from which the title *Soliloquy* originates. In a play, a character can appear alone, then submit himself to severe *"Self-dissection."* He can become in effect "two distinct *Persons*. He is Pupil and Preceptor. He teaches, and he learns" (C 1.100). That self-dissection is exactly the kind of activity an author ought to cultivate. Indeed, Shaftesbury suggests that "soliloquy" isn't just a metaphor. He thinks it can be useful for authors to take themselves away from other people and, like Hamlet, literally talk to themselves out loud.

And Shaftesbury compares the author's process to the way a person uses a mirror. Before a person makes a public appearance, he looks at himself in the mirror, notes the things that could look better, and makes a judgment about what to do to achieve improvement. He takes conscious measures to refine various of his aspects. Then he looks at himself again, making further refinements if necessary. The writing process should involve a kind of mirroring analogous to this conscious, self-reflective method of putting oneself together in preparation for a public appearance. An author ought to hold his thoughts up to "a kind of *vocal* Looking-Glass" (C 1.108). This comparison is evident in the image Shaftesbury designed as the emblematic illustration for *Soliloquy*. It's a triptych of mirrors. On the left panel is represented a beautiful and well-proportioned figure. The figure is looking directly into a hand-mirror, and the landscape around him is bright and open. The landscape on the right, in contrast, is dark and ugly, and the figure is misshapen, scared, and hounded by harpies. The figure on the right has a mirror in his hand, but unlike the figure on the left, he is "turn'd strongly away from it," refusing "to look at himself."[12] The large central panel of the triptych represents a desk in a study. Looming over the desk is a massive mirror. No one is present, but a scroll and pen are there, awaiting use. The message is clear. If writers wish to align with the right and good, and avoid the evil and dismal, they must use a mirror. They must try out their ideas on themselves.

Let's look now at how this process is supposed to work for philosophers, and for memoirists and essayist.

## 4. Soliloquy for Philosophers

The soliloquy Shaftesbury prescribes for philosophers consists of Stoic exercises that look a lot like contemporary cognitive behavioral therapy. He tells philosophers to interrogate their own passions to determine what beliefs underlie them. They then ought to work to eradicate the false beliefs that are influencing them, and strengthen the true. Over time, if they stick with it, their passions will fall in line with an accurate perception of reality. Since reality is a unified, coherent system, a set of passions in line with reality will be unified and coherent as well. Soliloquy of self-interrogation can thus dissolve internal strife, as well as eliminate the disappointment and despair that comes from expecting what will not happen and desiring what cannot be. The philosophical writing that results should explicate this process of psychological improvement.

Shaftesbury sketches how this process would play out with regard to various emotions. When I feel fear, I should ask myself what belief underlies it. If upon thorough search and examination I find that the belief is false, "the Passion it-self must necessarily diminish, as I discover more and more the Imposture which belongs to it" (C 1.183). When I am afflicted by vanity, I should reflect on "the imaginary Advantages, and inconsiderable Grounds" that give rise to it; if I persist in focusing on these facts, "'tis impossible I shou'd not in some measure be reliev'd of this Distemper" (C 1.183). The same process can be followed "in respect of *Anger, Ambition, Love,* [and] *Desire*" (C 1.183). I should conduct an internal examination of each, a "Search and Scrutiny of my *Opinions*." By so doing, I will bring my emotions in line with the "just Value of everything in Life" (C 1.183–184).

Philosophy that follows this "*self-conversant Practice*" will be "more practical" than the super-speculative investigation of plenitudes and vacuums, of animals spirits and muscles, of substances, essences, and properties (C 1.181). Philosophy of this kind will promote "Acquaintance, Friendship, and good Correspondence with *our-selves*" (C 1.181). It will enable us to live in accord with "a right Idea of *Life*" (C 1.184).

Rivers says that Shaftesbury's philosophy is grounded in psychology more than the natural sciences.[13] I think Shaftesbury does rely on the natural sciences when he is elucidating the beauty of God's creation. But I think Rivers's point is spot-on when applied to Shaftesbury's meta-advice to advice-giving authors. He urges them to view themselves through the lens of psychology rather than of metaphysics, epistemology, or physics.

## 5. *Soliloquy for Memoirists and Essayists*

The memoirists and essayists pose a different problem from the philosophers. The memoirists and essayists don't need any encouragement to focus on themselves. They're happy to do that. The problem is what they think it means to write about their true selves.

Writers like Gregory think the most accurate reflections of their true selves are first thoughts. They think publishing one's ideas in the form in which they initially occur is more authentic—truer to one's real nature, truer to who one really is—than elegant revision. They scorn the self-editing process necessary for eloquence. If all beauty is truth, then the most beautiful writing consists of immediate reactions because those are the truest representation of an author's mind. Revision and self-editing falsify. Conventions of polite writing are incompatible with honesty.

Gregory is far from the only one to see an opposition between politeness and honesty. Boyle expresses a similar idea when he humblebrags that his aim is not "to express Eloquence, but only to cherish Piety."[14] The puritan hostility to art and ritual is a version of the same opposition, based as it is on the belief that solicitude toward any external show is incompatible with true concern for the internal state of one's immortal soul. Rousseau may be the patron saint of this idea, interpreted as he often is as condemning mannered society and apotheosizing natural man. An extreme example of this principled impoliteness is the ancient Greek Cynic Diogenes, as pungently portrayed in Bayle's *Dictionnaire*, whose thorough rejection of the polite niceties that normal people use to hide their true selves led him to conceal absolutely nothing, not even his sexual relations, which he had with his wife "in the middle of the street."[15] In his unpublished *The Adept Ladys*, Shaftesbury strikes a similar note, imagining an enthusiastic sect who carry around with them their own feces and excreted bodily fluids.[16] Or consider MTV's *Real World*, the first American reality TV show, which promised "to find out what happens when people stop being polite and start getting real."[17]

Shaftesbury opposes this opposition of honesty and politeness. He holds that the results of the mirror method of revision are more true to who one is—more true to one's real nature—than unreflective responses. If writers wish that "their Composition and Vein of Writing be natural and free," they must engage in the "Preliminary of *Self-study* and *inward Converse*" (C 1.172). Practicing soliloquy on oneself before airing one's thoughts is the honest approach. Polite revisions are more accurate reflections of self than unreflective responses.

How can this be? Shaftesbury's brutally frank opponents claim that sophisticated refinements conceal what they really are, that eschewing such refinements is the best way to truthfully reveal their true nature. If thoughts naturally arrive in one's head in inelegant language, how can it be unnatural to reproduce them on the page? In what sense can Shaftesbury hold that the artful is more natural than the artless?

It's a question we can ask of Shaftesbury more generally. He equates virtue and nature. He exhorts us to live in accord with our nature. But he also stresses the importance of politeness and manners. And he insists on the need to work hard on ourselves in order to become virtuous. He says that virtue is natural, yes, but also that the "Perfection of Virtue is from long *Art* and *Management*" (C 3.160). What can he have in mind when making the seemingly paradoxical assertion that we need to exert *"Force on* Nature" in order to "become *natural*" (C 1.208)? That *"Labour and Pains* are requir'd, and *Time* to cultivate a natural Genius" (C 2.224)? What concept of human nature explains his lament that it is very "hard to find a Man who lives NATURALLY, and as a Man" (C 2.56)? The answer is to be found in Shaftesbury's concepts of nature and self.

## 6. The Revised as More Natural Than the Unrevised

Shaftesbury's concept of nature is teleological and aspirational. What's natural for an organism to do, on this understanding, is what it's built to do, the end for which the organism is designed. Reaching that end is not a foregone conclusion. It can require a great deal of effort and skill, and perhaps luck. Many individuals may fail at it. Most may fail. That doesn't mean that those who succeed at achieving what they are built to do are thereby *unnatural*. Just the contrary. It's the few who do what they are built to do who are the most natural.[18]

Consider the Olive Ridley turtle, which buries its eggs on the beach. When the eggs hatch, the baby turtles make a mad dash for the sea. But gulls and other predators are at the ready, and a majority of the baby turtles are eaten before their feet ever touch the water. Maybe only one out of a thousand manages to escape predation, head out to the open sea, and live a long, productive turtle life. But the turtle that achieves this end is not thereby unnatural. It's that turtle that is living the way turtles are designed to live. That turtle is doing—is accomplishing—what is natural.

Or recall the story we looked at in the introduction, about the Ethiopian at carnival (C 1.52–53). The masked visage of almost every person the Ethiopian observed was grotesque, ridiculous. But that didn't mean the face of the single person he saw without a mask was unnatural. The person without a mask was the most natural of all. Similarly, according to Shaftesbury, it's possible for the internal character of the majority of a population to be distorted, unnatural. Truly natural character may be rare.

It takes a great deal of effort for a person to achieve the pinnacle of virtue and taste. Many people may fail to achieve it. Some may not even try. But the few who do succeed are not thereby conducting themselves unnaturally. The few who succeed are living the most natural lives of all. As Shaftesbury writes,

> The Perfection of Virtue is from long *Art* and Management, *Self-Controul*, and, as it were, *Force on Nature*. But the common Auditor or

> Spectator ... comprehends little of the Restraints, Allays and Corrections, which form this *new* and *artificial Creature*. For such indeed is the *truly virtuous Man*; whose ART, tho ever so *natural* in it-self, or justly founded in *Reason* and *Nature*, is an Improvement far beyond the common Stamp, or known Character of Human Kind. (C 3.160)

Those who achieve the pinnacle of virtue and taste are like athletes whose physical prowess is unusual and yet also paradigmatic of the nature of the human body. They are like turtles that make it to the ocean and go on to lead long, productive turtle lives. This natural end should not be modeled on the untutored taste of "an innocent Child's Eye."[19] It should be modeled on that sensibility that is "well & truly form'd," when "the original first rude Taste [is] corrected by rule, & reduc'd to a yet more simple & natural Measure."[20]

Shaftesbury's most developed example of such an individual is Theocles from *The Moralists*—the moral equivalent of an Olympic athlete. On Shaftesbury's teleological view, Theocles conducts himself more naturally than Diogenes (he of the street sex), and that would be the case even if Diogenes-like behavior were more common. The conscious effort Theocles puts into the perfection of his character enables him to achieve the end for which he was designed, while Diogenes, by wallowing in primitive crudity, is a sea turtle who never makes it out of the sand. Possession of "natural *good* TASTE" is neither inevitable nor easy (C 1.208). We have to "endeavour to form it" (C 1.208). We have to work hard to "become *natural*" (C 1.208).

This teleological conception of human nature is not without its problems. But to follow Shaftesbury in affirming the honesty of polite writing, we may need to accept only one aspect of his teleological view: namely, that humans are naturally *self-reflective* creatures. The idea here is that humans are built not merely to have immediate affections and motives but also to think consciously about their affections and motives, and to modify their conduct and character in light of those thoughts.[21] If such practically efficacious self-reflection is natural to human beings, then polite revision might be more natural—more true to who we really are—than unedited expression. Henry Frankfurt's concept of bullshit helps explain this point.

Bullshit, as Frankfurt explains, is speech that has no connection to the truth.[22] Bullshit is distinct from both sincerity and deception. If you ask me how much money I have in my wallet and my goal is to be sincere, I will look in my wallet and give you an accurate account; what I say will non-accidentally represent how the world is. If my goal is to deceive you, I will purposely give you an inaccurate account; what I say will non-accidentally misrepresent how the world is. But the third possibility—the case of bullshit—is that I don't care at all whether what I say is accurate or inaccurate. In this third case, I will tell you that I have a certain amount of money without looking in my wallet or giving any thought at all to what is there. A prime example of bullshit is a campaigning politician's declaration of love for his country. It's not that the politician *doesn't* love his country, it's not that he's lying. Rather, he's saying something that is completely untethered from actual feelings or beliefs. He would say the same thing regardless of what he felt or believed. He declares his patriotism because it is easy and convenient, not because it is accurate or inaccurate.

What's important to realize is that bullshit is often easier than honesty. When speaking about certain matters, clichés can come to one's lips almost unbidden. Uttering well-worn phrases is as simple as can be. What takes considerably more effort is finding the words to capture what one truly thinks. For what one truly thinks about things that are truly worth thinking about is almost always more complex than well-worn phrases and clichés can express. "One wou'd think, there was nothing easier for us, than to know our own Minds . . . But our Thoughts have generally such an obscure implicit Language, that 'tis the hardest thing in the world to make 'em speak out distinctly" (C 1.107). The words that accurately represent, the honest words, are often not the first ones that come to mind. Rather than reflecting accurately one's real feelings, uttering the first thing that comes to mind may bypass what's actually in one's heart. It may just pass on the surrounding bullshit. Accurate and honest words are more likely to be the ones someone comes to finally, after careful, conscious introspection—through reflections and revision. It's harder to say what one thinks than most people think.

The word Shaftesbury uses for bullshit is *froth*. People who never engage in reflection or revision, he tells us, exhibit a "Frothiness or Ventosity in Speech" (C 1.100). They manifest a "frothy Distemper" (C 1.103). "[T]heir Froth abounds" (C 1.105). Free of the trouble of having to submit their thought to reflection and revision, these *"great Talkers"* produce an "Exuberance of Conceit and Fancy," inflating every conversation they're a part of with *"Tumour* or *Flatulency"* (C 1.105). Shaftesbury's aim in expounding polite revision is to teach writers to produce writings that are more sincere and authentic—that are truer reflections of an author's mind—than the froth that "engross[es] the greatest part of the Conversations of the World" (C 1.105).

Writers like Gregory and vulgarians like Diogenes privilege their initial impulses. They believe that any alteration to their unrefined responses would falsify who they really are. Like a music fan who insists that the unreleased demo is superior to the final production, like a reader who prioritizes an author's private jottings to the polished manuscript, they assume that first expressions more truly reveal the artist's mind than considered revisions. That's a mistake. Reflection and refinement are essential to artistry. The truer work of art is the reflective and refined.

This truth of reflection and refinement holds not only for the arts of music and writing but also for the self-improving art of life. It is the nature of human beings to be reflective, to look at themselves and judge what they see. The capacity for self-refinement such scrutiny opens up is truer to what makes us distinctively human than impulsive, unreflective responses. Self-refinement is essential to the development of a truly human self. This is what explains Shaftesbury's seemingly paradoxical assertion that a great deal of effort is needed in order to "become *natural.*"

Those who equate honest self-expression to unrevised first responses have a primitive understanding of self. They think of the self as a preexistent enduring simple that needs only to be uncovered to be seen—that truthful portrayal of self is a matter of mere revealment. Shaftesbury's self is far from anything so simple.[23] As Shaftesbury understands it, there are many aspects to a human being, different beliefs, inclinations, and goals. If these aspects fail to cohere, the human being will lack a true self. Unity is necessary for identity, necessary for selfhood. And the unity that's necessary must obtain through time as well as at any given moment. If people's minds change willy-nilly from one day to the next, they will be "in reality transform'd and lost" (C 1.176). Having a self—a true self, a unified character—is not a foregone conclusion. It's a hard-won accomplishment.

To bring one's thoughts into synchronic and diachronic coherence— to make up one's mind—one must engage in the reflection and revision that is distinctive of human nature. Conscious self-recollection is necessary for a person to gain "*a Will*, and insure him *a certain Resolution*; by which he shall know where to find himself; be sure of his own Meaning and Design; and as to all his Desires, Opinions, and Inclinations, be warranted *one and the same* Person to day as yesterday, and to morrow as to day" (C 1.116). Reflection and revision don't uncover the self. They form it. If honesty is the accurate representation of who one really is, it is the result of conscious reflection that is most honest, not unrefined first responses. Recall the passage we looked at in the introduction in which Shaftesbury explains why we take it to be the highest compliment to be told that we have acted in accord with who we really are: it's because we identify who we really are with the best we can be (C 1.173–176).

Shaftesburean politeness is polish, not a mask.[24] A mask conceals features rather than altering them (C 1.52–53). Polishing alters. When a sculptor polishes the stone, the stone changes. The polishing makes the sculpture. Diogenes and Gregory consider the effort to make behavior and writing more polite to be akin to wearing a mask at carnival. Shaftesbury considers it part of making of one's self a beautiful work of art.

Shaftesbury himself clearly engaged in plenty of polite polishing prior to publication. His private notebooks are replete with circuitous and tormented self-dialogue, rough in tone and substance. They contain excoriating self-criticism—at times, self-disgust—and the writing is often raw, crude, even ugly. The contrast with Shaftesbury's finished *Characteristicks* could not be greater. Each individual treatise follows its own intricate design, with argumentative progressions whose pacing and reversals, twists and turns, are plotted with care. There are robustly realized narrative voices. And the prose throughout is polished to a high gleam. Even the miscellaneous digressions and conversational asides are the result of effortful art. Shaftesbury sought to "give an *extemporary* Air to what was writ, and make the *Effect* of Art be felt, without discovering the *Artifice*" (C 3.15; see also 3.88). He aimed for a kind of writing that "conceals the Artifice as much as possible: endeavouring only to express the effect of Art, under the appearance of the greatest Ease and Negligence" (C 1.160). Shaftesbury also planned fastidiously the illustrations. He attended closely to all aspects of the book's physical appearance.

Most significant of all might be the very act of gathering all his writings together into one work. Another writer might have been content to let the different pieces he'd published over the course of his career remain forever in separate covers. The effort Shaftesbury exerted to create a single emphatic book—with cross-referencing notes and a unifying index—bespeaks his intense desire to bring his thoughts together into a whole. The alternative would have been unfinished, disparate, disunified.

Shaftesbury's avidity to form a single work is of a piece with his lifelong aspiration to fashion from the conflicting aspects of his personality a unified whole. Collecting his essays was continuous with the task of a "Recollection of himself" (C 2.35). The art of writing was particularly well-suited to this. For writing, he thought, had a special feature not shared by other arts. Sculptors and painters who portray great physical beauty will never as a result "grow a jot more" physically beautiful. But by writing about "the Graces and Perfections of *Minds*," an author may hope to achieve a more beautiful mind (C 1.28). Writing about what kind of person to be is itself a way of becoming a better self.

# Conclusion

AS WE SAW in the introduction, Shaftesbury's thought was met with intense criticism in the eighteenth century. That's par for the course for any successful philosophical work. But there was an unusual element to the criticism of Shaftesbury. Some of it involved ad hominems of a particularly literal kind—attacks on Shaftesbury himself, claims that his philosophy was vitiated by his personal idiosyncrasies.

Shaftesbury's philosophical failings, according to critics, were due to his "crazy constitution" and "his rank."[1] Constitutionally, he was deemed to be lacking the appetites of a normal human being. He was born with a "Quiet Indolent Nature," an "unactive Spirit." He disliked "sensual Enjoyment."[2] With regard to rank, he was born to great privilege. His life was one of complete "Ease and Affluence."[3]

As a result of his constitution and rank, critics claimed, Shaftesbury had no problem being virtuous. He wanted very little, and what he did want was handed him on a silver platter. The fundamental philosophical mistake this led Shaftesbury to was the pernicious separation of morality from motives of reward and punishment. Because of his privilege and inborn disposition, Shaftesbury himself did not need the promise of reward and the threat of punishment in order to avoid wrongdoing. But normal people—people with typical appetites and without great wealth— do require those incentives. Shaftesbury thought that virtue was entirely easy and pleasant, a matter of simply giving in to one's natural tendencies. But such a philosophy was a narcissistic reflection of his peculiar state, not helpful advice for how humans ought to live. If his philosophy were widely propagated, it would lead normal people to all manner of vicious conduct. And this mistake was of the highest significance. The consequence of such immorality would be the eternal damnation of the masses.

There can be no denying Shaftesbury's psychological peculiarity, nor his economic privilege. But it can be denied that Shaftesbury advanced the simplistically silly philosophy such criticism attributes to him.

Shaftesbury may have had a personal reputation for moderation and calm. His authorial voices may be serenely self-assured. But both of those were effects he put in a great deal of self-conscious effort to produce. He was well aware of obstacles to virtue and of the difficulty of overcoming them. Shaftesbury might have been unusual in that carnal and materialistic temptations were not the most significant obstacles he himself faced; his detractors might have had a point there.[4] He was, however, tormented by pessimism, social hostility, and self-loathing—all of which were diametrically opposed to the character to which he thought human beings ought to aspire. The resounding positivity of his philosophy was something he worked extremely hard to achieve. The need for significant moral effort is, as well, conspicuous in the substance of his published philosophy, with its extended explorations of the challenges to self-improvement and to living in accord with one's nature. Becoming virtuous—in Shaftesbury's personal experience and in his *Characteristicks*—takes a tremendous amount of work. Making one's self into a beautiful work of art is as much a hard-earned accomplishment as sculpting a stone or writing a book.

What of the charge that Shaftesbury's philosophy is suitable only for the rich? That he was blithely ignorant of the moral challenges people without great wealth must face? There is almost certainly considerable truth to the charge that Shaftesbury was out of touch with the lives of common folk. When we look at the competing views, however, Shaftesbury's critics do not emerge as the greater champions of working people.

Shaftesbury dealt with working people and attended to worldly matters more closely than is implied by, for instance, the airy caricature at the center of Berkeley's *Alciphron*. He was personally involved in the details of his tenancies, his farmland, his gardens, his houses. And in his writing, Shaftesbury rates the working people he interacted with as morally superior to the economically privileged. Here's an example from the 1699 version of the *Inquiry*:

> It happens with *Mankind*, that some by necessity are ty'd to Labour, whilst others are provided for in an abundance of all things at the expence of the Labors of the rest. Now, if amongst those of the easy sort, there be not something of fit and proper Imployment rais'd in the room of what is wanting by such a vacancy from common Labor and Toil . . . but that there be a settled Idleness, Supineness, and a relax'd

and dissolute State; it must needs produce a total disorder of the Passions, and must break out in the strangest irregularities imaginable. It is not thus with those who are taken up in honest and due Imployment, and have bin well inur'd to it, as amongst the industrious sort of common People; where it is rare to meet with any instances of those irregularities of Affection that are known in Courts, and where Idleness reigns.[5]

Shaftesbury's point is that the idle rich are often much more corrupt and contemptible than working people. He makes the same point when contrasting the "Honesty" and *real Virtue* of a poor mechanic with the compromised pandering of learned writers (C 1.163), and when praising a "poor Shepherd's" appreciation of beauty in comparison with a gentleman's abject desire for possession and status (C 2.221). One might contend that such comments are just gauzy romanticizations that only go to show how out of touch with real life Shaftesbury was. But it's also possible that Shaftesbury was actually acquainted with working people who really did exhibit the commitment to true work and the appreciation of beauty on which he modeled virtue.

This possibility is relevant when considering the criticism of Shaftesbury based on his privilege. Berkeley says that Shaftesbury's error is thinking that common folk can have ultimate concern for anything other than their own skin. The truth, according to Berkeley, is that we can keep common folk from vice only by instilling in them selfish fear of the consequences. Astell advances the same criticism: because most people are incapable of appreciating the intrinsic excellency of moral laws, the "terror of punishment" is necessary to motivate them to do the right thing.[6] Balguy agrees: Shaftesbury's disengagement of morality from self-interest will do more harm than good, for it is only the "few" who are "capable of being drawn by the fine intellectual Cords of Moral Beauty, Order, Proportion. A vast Majority must be driven by Authority, and managed by the Springs of Hope and Fear."[7] Continues Balguy, "The Bulk of our Species are too corrupt to be influenced or wrought upon by the intrinsick Worth and Excellence of Virtue."[8] "A great Part of the World, in respect of their duty, want Discipline as much as Children; and without Promises or Menaces, will not be prevailed upon, or even moved."[9] The "Generality of Men can only be considered as in an Infant State of Virtue."[10]

Berkeley, Astell, and Balguy have a lower view than Shaftesbury of the moral psychology of common folk, a lower view of the life to which most people can aspire. Berkeley, Astell, and Balguy think most people are moral infants—that the highest they can ever achieve is obedience based on physical punishment and hedonistic reward. Shaftesbury thinks ordinary minds can elevate considerably higher than that. The beauty of the ocean, of workmanship, of selfless love of others: such truly disinterested considerations can and do motivate shepherds, mechanics, and friends. And this amounts to a different view not only of morality but of the point of life itself.

According to Astell, the motivation to continue living requires belief in God's reward and punishment. If she lost her belief in God, Astell says, she "wou'd not stay a Day longer."[11] "Human Nature is exposed to" so much "Pain and dissatisfaction" there would be no point in carrying on.[12] Earthly life is disgusting and painful. The only thing that makes it tolerable—the only reason not to commit suicide—is the prospect of a hereafter.

Shaftesbury, in contrast, asserts that great beauty is accessible to us here and now. Cherishing and creating such beauty is what makes earthly life worth living.

ACKNOWLEDGMENTS

THERE ARE MANY FRIENDS and colleagues who helped me tremendously in the writing of this book. At the risk of leaving someone out, I express here my profound gratitude to Alix Cohen, Guy Fletcher, Aaron Garrett, James Harris, Jenann Ismael, Laurent Jaffro, Rachana Kamtekar, Sandeep Kaushik, Matt Kilman, Chris Lydgate, Brad Miller, Shaun Nichols, Hal Ratner, and Mark Timmons. I am also grateful to my family: David, Sam, Jesse, Hannah, and Sarah.

Earlier versions of parts of this book have been previously published. I thank the publishers for permission to use the material, and the editors and referees for their comments, which helped me improve it.

- Parts of chapter 1 are from "Shaftesbury on the Beauty of Nature," *Journal of Modern Philosophy* 3 (2021), 1–28.
- Parts of chapter 2 are from "Shaftesbury's Claim the Beauty and Good Are One and the Same," *Journal of the History of Philosophy* 59 (2021), 69–92. Copyright © 2021 Journal of the History of Philosophy, Inc. Published with permission by Johns Hopkins University Press.
- Parts of chapter 2 are from "Shaftesbury on Life as a Work of Art," *British Journal for the History of Philosophy* 26 (2018), 1110–1131. Reprinted by permission of the publisher (Taylor & Francis Ltd., http://tandfonline.com).
- Parts of chapter 2 are from "Love of Humanity in Shaftesbury's *Moralists*," *British Journal for the History of Philosophy* (2016), 1117–1135. Reprinted by permission of the publisher (Taylor & Francis Ltd., http://tandfonline.com).
- Parts of chapter 2 are from "Shaftesbury on Selfishness and Partiality," *Social Philosophy and Policy* 37 (2020), 55–79.
- Parts of chapter 5 are from "Shaftesbury on Politeness, Honesty, and the Reason to be Moral," in *New Ages, New Opinions: Shaftesbury in his World and Today*, edited by Patrick Muller (Frankfurt: Peter Lang, 2014), 167–184.

The images of artwork in chapter 4 are used with the following permissions:

Fig. 1. Paolo de Matteis, *The Choice of Hercules*. Alamy.com.
Fig. 2. Annibale Carracci, *The Choice of Hercules*. Alamy.com.
Fig. 3. Raphael (engraving by Marcantonio Raimondi), *Judgment of Paris*. National Galleries of Scotland. Provenance unknown, 2010.
Fig. 4. Pietro Benvenuti, *Hercules at the Crossroads*. Alamy.com.
Fig. 5. Peter Paul Rubens, *Mercury Escorting Psyche to Mount Olympus*. Alamy.com.
Fig. 6. Sebastiano Ricci, *Hercules at the Crossroads*. Alamy.com.
Fig. 7. Il Domenichino, *The Last Communion of St. Jerome*. Alamy.com.
Fig. 8. Raphael (engraving by Marcantonio Raimondi), *Massacre of the Innocents*. Metropolitan Museum of Art.
Fig. 9. Raphael, *The Transfiguration of Christ*. Alamy.com.
Fig. 10. Giuseppe Cesari, *Diana and Actaeon*. Museum of Fine Arts–Hungarian National Gallery.
Fig. 11. Annibale Carracci, *Christ and the Samaritan Woman* or *The Woman at the Well*. Wikipedia.
Fig. 12. Antony van Dyck, *Samson and Delilah*. Alamy.com.
Fig. 13. Nicolas Poussin, *Christ and the Samaritan Woman at the Well*. Museum of Fine Arts–Hungarian National Gallery.
Fig. 14. Paolo de Matteis, *Diana and Actaeon* (first version). Bayerishce Staatsgemaldesmmlunger—Alte Pinakothetk, Munchen.
Fig 15. Paolo de Matteis, *Diana and Actaeon* (second version). Christie's.

# NOTES

The following is a list of abbreviations used to refer to works by Shaftesbury:

A   *Askemata*. Edited by Wolfram Benda, Christine Jackson-Holzberg, Patrick Müller, and Friedrich A. Uehlein, as part of the *Standard Edition* (II.6). Stuttgart-Bad Cannstatt: Frommann-Holzboog, 2011.

C   *Characteristicks of Men, Manners, Opinions, Times, with a Notion of the Historical Draught, or Tablature of the Judgment of Hercules and a Letter Concerning Design*. In three volumes. Indianapolis: Liberty Fund, 2001. The first number after the "C" represents the volume, the second number, the page.

M/SE   *The Moralists, a Philosophical Rhapsody; The Sociable Enthusiast, a Philosophical Adventure*. Edited by Wolfram Benda and Gerd Hemmerich, as part of the *Standard Edition* (II.1). Stuttgart-Bad Cannstatt: Frommann-Holzboog, 1987.

PRO   Letters and other writings from the Shaftesbury Papers in the Public Record Office, the National Archive.

R   Shaftesbury, Anthony Ashley Cooper, the third Earl of. *The Life, Unpublished Letters, and Philosophical Regimen*. Edited by Benjamin Rand. London: Swan Sonnenschein, 1900.

SC   *Second Characters*. Edited by Wolfram Benda, Wolfgang Lottes, Friedrich A. Uehlein, and Erwin Wolff, as part of the *Standard Edition* (I.5). Stuttgart-Bad Cannstatt: Frommann-Holzboog, 2001.

V   *An Inquiry Concerning Virtue, in Two Discourses*. London: A. Bell and S. Buckley, 1699.

W   Preface to *Select Sermons of Dr Whichcot. In Two Parts*. London: Awnsham and John Churchill, 1698.

## *Introduction*

1. The biographical sketch that follows is deeply indebted throughout to Voitle, *Third Earl of Shaftesbury*, which is the standard biography.

2. See Anthony, Lord Ashley to Andrew Percivall, May 27, 1691, PRO 30/24/22/2.

3. January 22, 1705, PRO 30/24/20/110 (quoted in Voitle, *Third Earl of Shaftesbury*, 244).

4. May 28, 1694, in Locke, *The Correspondence of John Locke* V, 66.

5. Locke, *The Correspondence of John Locke* V, 66.

6. For discussion of Locke and the first Earl's role in slavery in Carolina, see Farr, "Locke, Natural Law, and New World Slavery"; Brewer, "Slavery, Sovereignty, and 'Inheritable Blood'"; Hinshelwood, "The Carolina Context"; Glausser, "Three Approaches to Locke and the Slave Trade"; Bernasconi, "Locke's Almost Random

Talk of Man"; Welchman, "Locke on Slavery and Inalienable Rights"; Bernasconi and Mann, "The Contradictions of Racism: Locke, Slavery and the Two Treatises"; Uzgalis, "'The Same Tyrannical Principle'"; Lewis, "Locke and the Problem of Slavery"; Armitage, "John Locke, Carolina, and the Two Treatises of Government."

7. Recent scholarship has examined Shaftesbury's Whig political commitments and their role in his philosophical work. See Klein, *Shaftesbury and the Culture of Politeness*, 131–142; Müller, "'An Equal Commonwealth'"; Jaffro, "Psychological and Political Balances." Klein, Jaffro, and Müller valuably identify important political themes in Shaftesbury's thought. By focusing in this book on Shaftesbury's views of beauty, I do not mean to imply that beauty was the only matter of importance to him, and that political concerns were irrelevant to his thought. At the same time, I think Shaftesbury had philosophical views that were independent of Whig commitments, and that there is a danger of overreading politics into his philosophy as a whole. I discuss these issues in Gill, "Shaftesbury on Selfishness and Partisanship."

8. Voitle, *Third Earl of Shaftesbury*, 77.

9. Toland, "Introduction to *Letters from the Right Honourable the late Earl of Shaftesbury to Robert Molesworth*," viii.

10. Earl of Shaftesbury to Jacques Basnage, January 21, 1707; PRO 30/24/22/4/pp. 32–22 (quoted in Voitle, *Third Earl of Shaftesbury*, 221).

11. Earl of Shaftesbury to Jacques Basnage, January 21, 1707.

12. Earl of Shaftesbury to Jacques Basnage, January 21, 1707.

13. Earl of Shaftesbury to Jacques Basnage, January 21, 1707.

14. Thomas Stringer to Anthony, Lord Ashley, May 5, 1699; PRO 30/24/44/77 (quoted in Voitle, *Third Earl of Shaftesbury*, 97–98).

15. Earl of Shaftesbury to Benjamin Furly, December 29, 1701; PRO 30/24/20/49 (quoted in Voitle, *Third Earl of Shaftesbury*, 211).

16. Earl of Shaftesbury, July 9, 1703; PRO 30/24/20/73 (quoted in Voitle, *Third Earl of Shaftesbury*, 212).

17. Earl of Shaftesbury, July 9, 1703; PRO 30/24/20/73 (quoted in Voitle, *Third Earl of Shaftesbury*, 212).

18. Earl of Shaftesbury to Benjamin Furly, November 1702; PRO 30/24/20/66 (quoted in Voitle, *Third Earl of Shaftesbury*, 214).

19. Earl of Shaftesbury to Benjamin Furly, November 3, 1708; PRO 30/24/21/161 (quoted in Voitle, *Third Earl of Shaftesbury*, 284–285).

20. Earl of Shaftesbury to Robert Molesworth, July 19, 1709; PRO 30/24/22/4/pp. 128–129 (quoted in Voitle, *Third Earl of Shaftesbury*, 296).

21. Earl of Shaftesbury to John Wheelock, July 9, 1709; PRO 30/24/22/4/p. 130 (quoted in Voitle, *Third Earl of Shaftesbury*, 297).

22. Earl of Shaftesbury to John Wheelock, July 9, 1709; PRO 30/24/22/4/p. 130 (quoted in Voitle, *Third Earl of Shaftesbury*, 297).

23. Earl of Shaftesbury to John Wheelock, August 8, 1709; PRO 30/24/21/177 (quoted in Voitle, *Third Earl of Shaftesbury*, 298).

24. PRO 30/24/46/83 (quoted in Voitle, *Third Earl of Shaftesbury*, 375). See also A 475–476.

25. Felix Paknadel, "Shaftesbury's Illustrations of *Characteristics*," *Journal of the Warburg and Courtauld Institutes* 37 (1974), 290.

26. Voitle, *Third Earl of Shaftesbury*, 339. For a comprehensive account of Shaftesbury's work on the second edition while he was in Naples, see O'Connell, "Shaftesbury in Naples: 1711–1713."
27. SC 18.
28. Astell, *Bart'lemy Fair*.
29. Mandeville, *The Fable of the Bees*, 323–369.
30. Balguy, *A Letter to a Deist*.
31. Berkeley, *Alciphron*.
32. Butler, *Fifteen Sermons*, xxiii–xxv.
33. Harris, *Hume: An Intellectual Biography*, 44–46.
34. Rivers, *Reason, Grace, and Sentiment*, 241.
35. Den Uyl, "Shaftesbury and the Problem of Modern Virtue," 275.
36. See Axelsson, *Political Aesthetics*.
37. Moore, "Shaftesbury and the Ethical Poets in England, 1700–1760." James Harris was Shaftesbury's nephew.
38. Moore, "Shaftesbury and the Ethical Poets in England, 1700–1760," 313.
39. Robertson, "Introduction," in *Characteristics of Men, Manners, Opinions, Times*, xxv.
40. See Solomon, "Shaftesbury's *Characteristics*"; Ryan, "Keats's 'Hymn to Pan.'"
41. See Hinnant, "Shaftesbury, Burke, and Wollstonecraft."
42. See Allen, *Wordsworth and the Passions of Critical Poetics*, 1–25.
43. Boyer, "Schleiermacher, Shaftesbury, and the German Enlightenment," 182.
44. Leibniz, *Philosophical Papers and Letters*, 635.
45. Leibniz, *Philosophical Papers and Letters*, 633.
46. Dehrmann, *Das "Orakel der Deisten"*; Elson, *Wieland and Shaftesbury*; Varsamaopoulou, "'Et in Arcadia Ego'," 45–68.
47. Jaffro, "Le choix d'Hercule."
48. Von Herder, Letter 33 in *Sammtliche Werke*, VVII, 158. Quoted and translated by Amir, *Humor and the Good Life in Modern Philosophy*, 13.
49. Weiser, *Shaftesbury und das Deutsche Geistesleben*, 254; Corbeau-Parson, *Prometheus in the Nineteenth Century*, 2020.
50. See Carter, "Schiller and Shaftesbury"; Walzel *Das Prometheussymbol von Shaftesbury zu Goethe*, viii–x, lxxxiii; Cassirer, "Schiller und Shaftesbury," 51. For detailed discussion of how Schiller was—and was not—influenced by Shaftesbury, see Beiser, *Schiller as Philosopher*, 20–21 and 91–93. For Shaftesbury's influence on Schleiermacher, see Boyer, "Schleiermacher, Shaftesbury, and the German Enlightenment."
51. See Jourdain, "The Boldest of the English Philosophers," 367.
52. See Crisafulli, "Montesquieu's Story of the Troglogytes"; Crisafulli, "Parallels to Ideas in the *Lettres persanes*"; Gonthier, "Persians, Politics and Politeness."
53. See Robb, "The Making of Denis Diderot." See also Legros, "Diderot et Shaftesbury."
54. Brown, *Essays on the Characteristics*, 1–2.
55. Walpole, *A Catalogue*, vol. IV, 55. For discussion, see Alderman, "Bibliographical Evidence," 58–59.
56. Thomas Gray to Richard Stonehewer, August 18, 1758.

57. For discussion of the philosophical relationship between Shaftesbury and Smith, see Otteson, "Shaftesbury's Evolutionary Morality and its Influence on Adam Smith." See also Den Uyl, "Shaftesbury and the Problem of Modern Virtue," 314–316.

58. Smith, *Lectures on Rhetoric*, 56.

59. Smith, *Lectures on Rhetoric*, 8.

60. Smith, *Lectures on Rhetoric*, 7.

61. Smith, *Lectures on Rhetoric*, 60.

62. Smith, *Lectures on Rhetoric*, 61.

63. De Quincy, *Biographical Essays*, 11.

64. Strohminger and Nichols, "The Essential Moral Self."

65. This passage from *Sensus Communis* is also interesting because it shows how Shaftesbury's literary ambitions evolved. In the 1699 version of the *Inquiry concerning Virtue*, he sought to make the same point as I've just described in the *Sensus Communis* passage. But in that earlier work, instead of spinning a playful tale about an Ethiopian at carnival, he put the same point in straightforward polemical form: "[W]hilst we see in all other Creatures around us so great a proportionableness, constancy and regularity in all their passions and affections . . . Man in the mean time, vicious and unconsonant man, lives out of all rule and proportion, contradicts his Principles, breaks the Order and Oeconomy of all his Passions, and lives at odds with his whole Species, and with Nature: so that it is next to a Prodigy to see a Man in the world who lives NATURALLY, and as a MAN" (V 98–99; see also C 2.56).

66. I think the order Shaftesbury chose for the volumes and works in *Characteristicks* makes it more difficult for a twenty-first-century reader to enter into Shaftesbury's thought. In my opinion, the most accessible approach for someone coming to the book for the first time is to read the works in this order: *Inquiry, Moralists, Soliloquy, Sensus Communis, Enthusiasm, Miscellaneous Reflections*.

## Chapter 1: Nature and God

1. The definitive account of Burnet's work and its influence, both positive and negative, is Marjorie Hope Nicolson, *Mountain Gloom and Mountain Glory*.

2. Burnet, *Sacred Theory*, 11.

3. Burnet, *Sacred Theory*, 15.

4. Burnet, *Sacred Theory*, 19.

5. Burnet, *Sacred Theory*, 22.

6. Burnet, *Sacred Theory*, 21–22. Some might claim that the Flood was a miracle, that God contravened the laws of nature by creating new waters "*to make the Deluge, and then annihilated them again when the Deluge was to ease*" (23). Burnet wanted no part of such miraculous explanations. He sought "to give an Account of these Phaenomena" that coheres with the rest of our understanding of nature (38). The deus ex machina of a miracle is not an explanation but a failure to explain. To resort to a miracle, moreover, is to discredit God, for it is to imply that God's original design of the world was imperfect, in need of ad hoc alteration. "We think him a better Artist that makes a Clock that strikes regularly at every Hour from the Springs and Wheels which he puts in the Work, than he that hath so made his Clock that he must put his Finger to it every Hour to make it strike" (131–132). As we'll see, Burnet's opposition to miracles was a great positive antecedent of Shaftesbury.

7. Burnet, *Sacred Theory*, 174 and 36.
8. Burnet, *Sacred Theory*, 65.
9. Burnet, *Sacred Theory*, 214.
10. Burnet, *Sacred Theory*, 62.
11. Burnet, *Sacred Theory*, 341.
12. Burnet, *Sacred Theory*, 80.
13. Burnet, *Sacred Theory*, 82.
14. Burnet, *Sacred Theory*, 88.
15. Burnet, *Sacred Theory*, 92.
16. Burnet, *Sacred Theory*, 40.
17. Burnet, *Sacred Theory*, 119.
18. Burnet, *Sacred Theory*, 136.
19. Burnet, *Sacred Theory*, 136.
20. Burnet, *Sacred Theory*, 156.
21. Locke, *Two Treatises*, 113 (Second Treatise § 32).
22. Locke, *Two Treatises*, 115 (Second Treatise § 37).
23. Locke, *Two Treatises*, 116 (Second Treatise § 37).
24. Locke, *Two Treatises*, 119 (Second Treatise § 43).
25. Locke, *Two Treatises*, 118 (Second Treatise § 42).
26. Locke, *Two Treatises*, 117 (Second Treatise § 40).
27. Locke, *Two Treatises*, 115 (Second Treatise § 36).
28. Locke, *Two Treatises*, 118 (Second Treatise § 42).
29. Locke, *Two Treatises*, 116 (Second Treatise § 37).
30. While Burnet and Locke might both believe uncultivated wilds can only be improved by cultivation, Locke's view of human nature differs from Burnet's. On Burnet's lapsarian view, humans were originally created entirely good and have since the Fall become entirely corrupt. Locke has a more complex, ambivalent view of human nature, thinking that pre-civilized people were in some ways better and in some ways worse. See, for instance, Locke, *Two Treatises*, 39 (First Treatise § 58). For Locke, movement toward civilization is not entirely a value gain with regard to human nature, even if it is a value gain with regard to the land.

31. As I discussed in the introduction, Shaftesbury had a close personal relationship with Locke but disagreed with much of his philosophy. I discuss Shaftesbury's view of Locke's philosophy in chapters 2 and 3. For full accounts of Shaftesbury's objections to Locke, see Carey, *Locke, Shaftesbury and Hutcheson*, 98–149; Uehlein, "Whichcote, Shaftesbury and Locke"; Stuart-Buttle, *From Moral Theology to Moral Philosophy*, 89–117. As far as I can tell, Shaftesbury did not have any personal connection with Burnet, but he owned a copy of Burnet's *Archaeologiae Philosophicae*, and it is extremely likely that he was aware of *The Sacred Theory of the Earth*. For discussion of Burnet's possible influence on Shaftesbury's moral theory (and on Shaftesbury's rejection of Lockean philosophy), see Tuveson, "The Origins of the 'Moral Sense.'"

32. Shaftesbury also mentions polytheism (C 2.7), which I do not discuss here.

33. Shaftesbury's point here anticipates Adam Smith's impartial spectator: see Smith, *Theory of Moral Sentiments*, 185 (3.2.29).

34. A 96–97.
35. A 98.
36. A 97–98.

37. A 97.
38. A 94.
39. A 100.
40. A 536.
41. A 535.
42. A 536.
43. A 537.
44. A 120. When I speak of emotions, affections, and passions in Shaftesbury, I mean to refer to phenomenologically robust features of mind that move us to action. When I speak of rationality and reason, I mean to refer to the faculty that forms beliefs based on evidence. As John Spurr explains in "'Rational Religion,'" in the religious debates that occurred in the decades leading up to Shaftesbury, writers used "reason" and its cognates in many different and incompatible ways, sometimes to argue for tolerance of free inquiry, sometimes to further an Anglican endorsement of revelation, sometimes to describe moral character, sometimes to describe discursive ratiocination. Shaftesbury's uses are not completely free of their own ambiguities. The main point I wish to make is that Shaftesbury thinks reason and passion come together into a single response to the creator of nature's beauty. But Shaftesbury also clearly thinks that there is a use of reason that can assess truth based on evidence rather than feeling (C 1.121–122, 2.162, 2.166–163, 2.187–188; A 120), and a use of passion that feels and motivates distinct from reason (C 2.8, 1.35, 2.8, 2.203). Modern deism is an example of dispassionate reason. Vulgar enthusiasm is an example of unreasonable passion. Shaftesbury's goal is to merge the best and to lose the worst of both: a reasonable enthusiasm, a passionate deism.

45. Shaftesbury's views on enthusiasm are influenced by Henry More, *An Antidote against Atheisme*, and *Enthusiasmus Triumphatus*. See C 3.42–44.

46. Spurr elucidates the central role in religious thinking in Restoration England played by the belief that Scripture was the word of God. Spurr explains that to maintain that religion was rational was typically to assert that there are rational grounds for believing that the claims of Scripture came from God, rather than to assert that the claims of Scripture could be independently established by reason alone. Shaftesbury's attack on scriptural revelation is thus an attack on the cornerstone of much of the Christianity of his day. Spurr writes, "Restoration Englishmen were repeatedly told that divine mysteries were above, not contrary to, reason, and they were warned not to confuse faith and science" (Spurr, "'Rational Religion,'" 577). The following quotation from Howell is a good example of the view Shaftesbury opposes: "If we will believe no more than we can demonstrate to be true, our Assent is not Faith, but Science; for it is not built up the foundation of Gods Testimony, but on Demonstrations from the Nature of the things testified, and so it honours not God at all; because it receives not the Truth for his sake, but Him for the Truths sake" (Howell, *The Spirit of Prophecy*, 225).

47. In Shaftesbury's index for the *Characteristicks*, under "Scripture," two of the subheadings are: "Scripture interpolated, suppress'd, controverted, manag'd" and "Variety of Readings, controverted Passages, Books, Copys, Catalogues" (C 3.285).

48. Whichcote, *Eight Letters*, 99.

49. See Whichcote, *The Works*, 1.205–207 and 1.220–221.

50. See Whichcote, *The Works*, 1.385, 2.62, 2.293, and 2.306.

51. See Whichcote, *The Works*, 3.302 and 3.307–308.

52. I discuss this issue in Gill, "The Religious Rationalism of Benjamin Whichcote."

53. Uehlein describes well Shaftesbury's relationship to Whichcote when he writes, "Shaftesbury definitely does not philosophize in accordance with Whichcote's unity of natural (rational) and revealed religion. However close he comes to him, however much he draws from the sermons, quotes him verbatim and repeats his notions with apparently the same meaning, there still remains a decisive difference . . . Shaftesbury philosophizes within the bounds of *scientia naturalis*. He does not envision the fall and restitution of man" (Uehlein, "Whichcote, Shaftesbury, and Locke," 1046). But then Uehlein says something that baffles me: "On the other hand, revealed religion is not dismissed by Shaftesbury; he is silent about it" (1046). At least to the extent that revealed religion is identified with religion based on scriptural revelation (the Bible) or direct revelation (enthusiasm), Shaftesbury says a great deal about it. Uehlein must have something else in mind by "revealed religion," but I'm not sure what it is.

54. Berman maintains that Toland himself did not really believe these scriptural claims—that the passages in which he seems to endorse them are a subterfuge, a lie, an artful concealment of his actual beliefs and real anti-Christian intentions. See Berman, "Deism"; and Berman, "Disclaimers." If that is the case, it is noteworthy that Shaftesbury also had such anti-Christian intentions and was less willing than Toland even to pretend otherwise. (Perhaps Shaftesbury, because of his higher social position, had the luxury of being less concerned about the personal ramifications of pretending otherwise.) At the same time, I believe that Pfeffer makes a strong case for reading Toland as less subversive or radical than Berman maintains—which makes Shaftesbury's more thorough rationalism stand out even more clearly. See Pfeffer, "Paganism."

55. Toland, *Christianity not Mysterious*, 131.

56. Toland, *Christianity not Mysterious*, 92–95 and 130.

57. As we'll see in chapter 4, Shaftesbury thought that "history paintings" of significant events from antiquity were powerful tools for moral instruction. But he focused his attention on Greek and Roman mythology, not on the biblical events that so many history paintings of his day took as their subjects. In his notes for *Plasticks*, he expresses particular doubts about the moral value of representations of Christ and the crucifixion. Of painting Christ he writes, "Wretched Model! Barbarean No Form, no grace of Shoulders Breast . . . no *Demarche*, Air, Majesty, Grandeur . . . God the Father a Broken, wrapt up, nurs'd, old Man: consumptive-Look, haggard, broken, with Carcass in Lap, a Dead Christ held forth in Winding-Sheet: a Pigeon in Bosom, and a lubberly *Hoberde hoy* or two, of an Angel" (SC 202–203; see also SC 247).

58. A 442, 453.

59. Chalmers, *General Biographical Dictionary*, Vol. VII, 98.

60. Stuart-Buttle explains well Shaftesbury's opposition to the Christianity of his day. See Stuart-Buttle, *From Moral Theology to Moral Philosophy*, 89–117.

61. Shaftesbury's view of beauty is fundamentally classical, in line with Greek ideals of balance, proportion, and harmony. See Klein, *Shaftesbury and the Culture of Politeness*, 199–206; and Axelsson, *Political Aesthetics*, 204, 213–214.

62. In *Alciphron*, Berkeley misrepresents Shaftesbury as holding that judgments of beauty are simply immediate unreflective emotional responses—responses "without a

reason" based on "free untutored judgment" (Berkeley, *Alciphron*, 59–60). That is not Shaftesbury's position. He does say that there are simple beauties that even infants can judge immediately, but he spends a great deal of time arguing that there are complicated beauties that require great discernment and learning to judge accurately. One indication of Berkeley's misrepresentation is that he attributes to Shaftesbury the idea that judgments of beauty are based on "a certain *je ne sais quoi*" (Berkeley, *Alciphron*, 62, 71). But Shaftesbury explicitly argues that it is only the unknowing who believe that beauty's cause is "the *Je-ne-scay-quoy*, the unintelligible, or the I know not what; and suppose [it] to be a kind of *Charm*, or *Inchantment*" (C 2.204). The knowing realize that there are content-ful principles of beauty that can be learned and understood. As he writes in his notes to *Plasticks*, "Tis not the *je ne scay quoy* to which *Idiots* & the ignorant of Art would reduce every thing. Tis not the [mere belief]: the *I like* & *You like*. But *why do I like*? And if not with reason & Truth I will refuse to like, dislike my Fancy, condemn the *Form*, search it, discover its *De-formity* & reject it" (SC 186). He even says of the French term itself that it is "not in our Language: nor I hope ever will be. But for us something better reserv'd" (SC 198). Berkeley's interpretation can point to a passage in *Sensus Communis* where Shaftesbury says, "Mens first Thoughts, in this matter, are generally better than their second" (C 1.83; see Berkeley, *Alciphron*, 73). But Shaftesbury is there criticizing "*Casuists*" and super-speculative philosophers, not endorsing ignorant unreflective emotional responses. He's arguing that the casuistical arguments for morality can be counterproductive, not that moral judgments ought to be independent of reasoning.

63. But see footnote at C 1.89.

64. Hume was dismissive of the *The Moralists*' claims about identity, writing, "If the reader is desirous to see how a great genius may be influenc'd by these seemingly trivial principles of the imagination . . . let him read my Lord *Shaftesbury*'s reasonings concerning the uniting principle of the universe, and the identity of plants and animals [in] his *Moralists, a Philosophical Rhapsody*" (Hume, *Treatise*, 166 [1.4.6.6]). It seems, however, that Hume did learn from Theocles's views on identity. For Hume's own view, like Theocles's, relies on the idea that there is no single "constant and invariable" mental item that can fund personal identity: compare Hume, *Treatise of Human Nature*, 164 (1.4.6.2) and C 2.350–351. Hume and Theocles seem to draw different conclusions, with Theocles moving from the premise that there is no constant and invariable mental item to the conclusion that personal identity must consist of something other than a mental item, and Hume moving to the conclusion that there is no personal identity. But it's not entirely clear that the "uniting principle" (C 2.200) or "sympathy of parts" (C 2.196) that underlies Shaftesburean identity is all that different from the kind of organizational principles that Hume would use to explain congregations, nations, and selves (C 2.200). Perhaps Hume was responding to Shaftesbury's notion that because nature is a single unified system, nature is a *self*; but in that case, Hume might be reading the relevant passage too literally, not taking into account the self-consciously fanciful way Theocles sometimes puts his points. For discussion of personal identity in Shaftesbury, Winkler, "'All Is Revolution in Us,'"; U. Thiel, *Early Modern Subject*; Jaffro, "Cyrus' Strategy"; Boeker, "Shaftesbury on Persons"; and Boeker, "Shaftesbury on Liberty."

65. Hume's comments in *Dialogues concerning Natural Religion* about the rotting of a turnip seem to me to be a variation on Shaftesbury's *Moralists* discussion of decay

and rotting; compare C 2.205–206 with Hume, *Dialogues*, 185 (part 12, paragraph 7). Hume seems to riff on Shaftesbury's theme of our world's being only one of many created worlds; compare C 2.168 with Hume, *Dialogues*, 24 (part 5, paragraph 12). The narrative tone of Hume's dialogue also seems to be very similar to the first night of *The Moralists* (with Demea adopting a tone similar to Shaftesbury's old Gentleman, and Philo adopting a tone similar to Philocles). Given these similarities, Shaftesbury's prominence at the time, and Hume's close acquaintance with *Characteristicks*, it seems to me very likely that Hume had *The Moralists*' argument from design very much in mind when composing the *Dialogues*.

66. Important predecessors of Shaftesbury in this wave of scientific design arguments were More, *An Antidote against Atheisme*; Ray, *Wisdom of God*; and Bentley, *A Confutation*. Influential works following on Shaftesbury's include Derham, *Physico-Theology*; Collins, *Discourse*; and Tindal, *Christianity*. Newton expresses a view of nature that is similar to *The Moralists* in its rational requirements for religious belief (Newton, *Opticks*, 377–379). Rivers has a different view of Shaftesbury's place in this line of thought, writing that for Shaftesbury, belief in God "is not reached by metaphysical speculation (although Theocles engages Philocles in metaphysical argument before summarising the faith of theism, Shaftesbury's methods are not like Cudworth's). Nor is it demonstrated through minute empirical observation of the hand of the divine artificer in natural phenomena (the enormously influential method of Ray and Derham). The basis of Shaftesbury's epistemology is psychological" (Rivers, *Reason, Grace, and Sentiment*, 141). I am claiming that Shaftesbury *does* reach appreciation of God's design through the observational method of Ray and Derham. But I agree with Rivers that Shaftesbury also uses psychology to make his point. The second part of the *Inquiry* is Shaftesbury at his most psychological. The second day of *The Moralists* is Shaftesbury at his most naturally scientific.

67. In contrast to my interpretation, Stuart-Buttle and Axelsson argue that Shaftesbury was hostile to the science of his day. See Stuart-Buttle, *From Moral Theology to Moral Philosophy*, 89 and 97; and Axelsson, *Political Aesthetics*, 190. I am more in agreement with Glauser, who writes, "[I]t is impossible for this disposition to be exercised with regard to the beauty of a great many things in the absence of considerable scientific, psychological, moral and theological knowledge. Even given the last three, a person wishing to discover the beauties of the material world would need a great deal of knowledge in physics, geology, and cosmology. Although Shaftesbury does not stress this point, it is fair to say that whatever his conception of aesthetic experience is, it is bound to rely heavily in many cases on the accumulation of a great deal of rational knowledge. This is important to stress in the face of romantic interpretations of Shaftesbury. Rather, his whole approach to beauty leans on the hopeful promise of important progress in scientific, psychological and moral knowledge. This is why he is a figure of the Enlightenment" (Glauser, "Aesthetic Experience in Shaftesbury," 34–35).

68. A 125.

69. A 125.

70. But with regard to miracles, Shaftesbury follows entirely in Burnet's footsteps. See note 6 above.

71. Toland, *Christianity not Mysterious*, 146.

72. Toland, *Christianity not Mysterious*, 146.

73. Toland, *Christianity not Mysterious*, 146.
74. Toland, *Christianity not Mysterious*, 147.
75. Locke, *Reasonableness*, 91.
76. Locke, *Reasonableness*, 91.
77. Cudworth, *True Intellectual System*, 150.
78. Cudworth, *True Intellectual System*, 150.
79. Cudworth, *True Intellectual System*, 150.
80. Shaftesbury's hostility toward relying on anything other than natural laws makes especially telling his statement that "Christianity is a super-naturall Religion" (Letter to Lord Somers October 20, 1705, PRO 30/24/22/4).
81. Some of Shaftesbury's narrators, however, do seem to allow for the occurrence of miracles in ancient times, even if they reject that God would produce any miracles in the current age. See C 2.184 and C 3.46. Notable in this regard is Shaftesbury's index entry for "Christianity," which reads (in its entirety): "*no way concern'd in modern Miracles*. ii. 326, 30, &c. *Not founded in Miracle merely*. Ibid. *and* i. 297, 8."
82. Müller, "Dwell with honesty & beauty & order," 224.
83. Müller, "Dwell with honesty & beauty & order," 227.
84. McAteer, "Silencing Theodicy with Enthusiasm," 789. McAteer claims Shaftesbury's view is similar to the Book of Job, in which God gives Job "a kind of mystical vision of the natural world, a vision of things 'too wonderful' for human beings to understand" (789). As I explain in the body of the text, Shaftesbury himself uses the Book of Job to argue for religious rationalism.
85. McAteer, "Silencing Theodicy with Enthusiasm," 791.
86. Liu, *Seeds*, 224–225.
87. Michael Prince argues that Philocles is not converted to Theocles's view, and that the dialogue remains poised between the opposing positions of the two characters (Prince, *Philosophical Dialogue*, 54–60). I think Philocles is converted based on the passage that includes: "O Theocles! said I, well do I remember now the Terms in which you engag'd me, that Morning when you bespoke my *Love* of this *mysterious Beauty*. You have indeed made good your part of the Condition, and may now claim me for *a Proselyte*" (C 2.223–224). I discuss this matter in Gill, "Love of Humanity."
88. For discussion of cognitively rich aesthetic experience, see Carlson, *Aesthetics*, 7; and Parsons and Carlson, *Functional Beauty*, 31–61.
89. Nicolson explains how Shaftesbury's claim that there is great beauty in rugged, jagged, foreboding places (see C 2.214, 2.217–218; SC 278–279) was of great historical significance, marking a turning away from the popular view of the time (exemplified most clearly by Burnet's *Sacred Theory*) that mountains and grottoes and dark forests were ugly reflections of human depravity (Nicolson, *Mountain Gloom and Mountain Glory*, 170–179 and 289–300). Nicolson also explains how Shaftesbury helped spark the rise of Romantic views of beauty and conceptions of the sublime that would come to exert strong philosophical and literary influence in the centuries to come.
90. Shaftesbury's view resembles a position in contemporary environmental philosophy called "positive aesthetics" (Carlson, *Aesthetics*, 73–102). Positive aesthetics holds that wild nature is completely beautiful—that "the natural world untouched by humanity is essentially aesthetically good" (Budd, "The Aesthetics of Nature," 137), that "all untouched parts of nature are beautiful" (Kinnunen, "Luonnonestetiikka,"

49), that "landscapes always supply beauty, never ugliness" (Rolston III, *Environmental Ethics*, 237).

91. SC 67.

92. See Myers, "'Wise Substitute of "Providence"!'."

93. Leatherbarrow and Myers argue—correctly, I believe—that Shaftesbury's characters are not saying that landscape gardens are better than formal gardens. See Leatherbarrow, "Character, Geometry, and Perspective"; and Myers, "Shaftesbury, Pope, and Original Sacred Nature." Shaftesbury's characters are saying that no garden compares favorably to anything wild. For an alternative view, see Liu, *Seeds*, 115–117.

94. Gatti writes, "The artistically beautiful in fact reveals the work of the human mind, whereas the naturally sublime is a manifestation of the divine mind: this is why the "Rude *Rocks*, the mossy *Caverns*, the irregular unwrought *Grotto's*' are preferable to 'the formal Mockery of Princely Gardens'" (Gatti, "The Aesthetic Mind," 74).

95. Voitle, *Third Earl of Shaftesbury*, 265.

96. The Earl of Shaftesbury to Mr Eyre, December 17, 1707 (PRO 30/24/22/4, pp. 55–56).

97. A 198.

98. A 200; see also 163–164.

99. One of the most splendid expressions of the attitude toward natural beauty that Shaftesbury describes can be found in John Muir's "A Near View of the High Sierra," a description of an excursion Muir took to the Sierra Nevada mountains in October 1894. It begins with Muir going into town to gather provisions. There he meets two painters who ask him to guide them into the mountains to "a landscape suitable for a large painting" (Muir, "High Sierra," 51). Muir takes them to a spot that meets their needs and then leaves them to paint their pictures while he strikes out on his own for an ascent of Mount Ritter. In the course of his narration, Muir explains the difference between the painters' view of nature's beauty and his own. The painters are looking for "a typical alpine landscape" that can be enclosed easily "in a frame"— for a vista with features "regular and evenly balanced" (50, 52, 49). But most parts of the Sierra Nevadas are too rugged and massive to make a pretty picture of. Muir writes, "[T]he general expression of the scenery—rocky and savage—seemed sadly disappointing [to the artists]; and as they threaded the forest from ridge to ridge, eagerly scanning the landscapes as they were unfolded, they said: 'All this is huge and sublime, but we see nothing as yet at all available for effective pictures'" (52). But that is exactly the scenery Muir loves. And his profound response to the mountains is cognitively rich—inextricably linked to his scientific understanding of them, to the time he's spent "measuring and studying" their glaciers and their "movements, trends, crevasses, moraines, etc., and the part they had played during the period of their greater extension in the creation and development of the landscapes" (48). The climax of Muir's narration is his summiting of Mount Ritter. Here's what he says:

[G]enerally, when looking for the first time from an all-embracing standpoint like this, the inexperienced observer is oppressed by the incomprehensible grandeur, variety, and abundance of the mountains rising shoulder to shoulder beyond the reach of vision; and it is only after they have been studied one by one, long and lovingly, that their far-reaching harmonies become manifest. Then, penetrate the wilderness where you may, the main telling features, to which all the surrounding topography is subordinate, are quickly perceived,

> and the most complicated clusters of peaks stand revealed harmoniously correlated and fashioned like works of art—eloquent monuments of the ancient ice-rivers that brought them into relief from the general mass of the range. The cañons, too, some of them a mile deep, mazing wildly through the mighty host of mountains, however lawless and ungovernable at first sight they appear, are at length recognized as the necessary effects of causes which followed each other in harmonious sequence. (Muir, "High Sierra," 68–69)

An "inexperienced observer" may not appreciate the beauty of the scene, but Muir's understanding of the natural processes enables him to see the "far-reaching harmonies," how all the different elements are "harmoniously correlated." He appreciates that "however lawless and ungovernable at first sight they appear, [they] are at length recognized as the necessary effects of causes which followed each other in harmonious sequence." His painter-friends are delighted by a visual harmony that is on the surface, something that can be captured in a picture frame. Muir is transfixed by an order of forces that requires scientific understanding to appreciate and that cannot be represented in a picture. While the painters fixate on scenes that are static, Muir's elevated experience involves flux:

> Standing here in the deep, brooding silence all the wilderness seems motionless, as if the work of creation were done. But in the midst of this outer steadfastness we know there is incessant motion and change. Ever and anon, avalanches are falling from yonder peaks. These cliff-bound glaciers, seemingly wedged and immovable, are flowing like water and grinding the rocks beneath them. The lakes are lapping their granite shores and wearing them away, and every one of these rills and young rivers is fretting the air into music, and carrying the mountains to the plains. (Muir, "High Sierra," 69)

Shaftesbury's and Muir's love of nature is a love of the manifestation of the laws of change, a love of the order that underlies the never-ending transformations wild places undergo. Shaftesbury and Muir also both see in nature's beauty the creation of a divine mind. "Deep views of nature" uncover the handiwork of a "sovereign Genius" (Shaftesbury). Watching day turn into night alone in the mountains will reveal to you "the terrestrial manifestations of God" (Muir). For both of them, full appreciation of the beauty of the natural world is a religious experience.

    100. In this passage Philocles is initially talking about what he perceives to be his inability to love all of humanity. It's only later that the discussion shifts to the question of whether Philocles can love all of nature (which is the only part of the question I describe here). I discuss this shift in "Love of Humanity in Shaftesbury's *Moralists*."

    101. For Shaftesbury and the early novel, see Prince, *Philosophical Dialogue*, 43.

    102. Shaftesbury's appreciation of nature makes him a forebear of the views of later environmental thinkers such as Ralph Waldo Emerson, Henry David Thoreau, John Muir, and Aldo Leopold. These environmentalists share with Shaftesbury the belief that nature is fundamentally unified and the idea that such unity makes all of nature beautiful. Emerson speaks of the "intimate" unity of nature and finds "a rule of one art, or a law of one organization, holds true throughout nature" (Emerson, "Nature," 53). Muir says that "none of nature's landscapes are ugly so long as they are wild" (Muir, *Our National Parks*, 4). Leopold holds that the highest value is that which promotes "the integrity, stability, and beauty of the biotic community" (Leopold, *Sand County Almanac*, 189). Also like Shaftesbury, these later environmental

thinkers believe that nature's systematic beauty is complex, and that as a result full appreciation of it comes through scientific understanding. They agree with Shaftesbury that the experience of nature's beauty is cognitively rich. A part of nature may strike us as "a tangle of chains so complex as to seem disorderly," says Leopold (*Sand County Almanac*, 181). But if it is a natural system, it will have a "stability" that "proves it to be a highly organized structure," the beauty of which we can come to realize by learning about the "cooperation and competition of its diverse parts" (181). Muir says that "the mind" is necessary for appreciating natural beauty, and not merely "our physical senses" ("An Unpublished Journal of John Muir," 43). Senses give us awareness of only those phenomena immediately present, while the mind can recognize the invisible, inaudible, and historical forces that create the deep beauty. Thoreau refers to the kind of investigation of nature when he says, "My profession is to be always on the alert to find God in nature, to know his lurking-places, to attend all the oratorios, the operas, in nature" (Henry David Thoreau, Journal Entry, in *I To Myself*, 99). When describing the science whose aim is to develop a theory of nature, Emerson writes: "[N]ature is already, in its forms and tendencies, describing its own design. Let us interrogate the great apparition, that shines so peacefully around us" (Emerson, "Nature," 35).

103. See Leatherbarrow, "Character, Geometry, and Perspective," 339–341.

104. Gould explains that Darwinian evolution doesn't proceed with nearly as much elegance as Shaftesbury contends nature exhibits. Rather than "optimal design," evolution produces "an astonishing variety of 'contrivances,'" "odd arrangements and funny solutions." Evolution proceeds down twisty paths "a sensible God would never tread." Gould cites as examples the way evolution has led orchids and pandas to repurpose parts that originally served very different functions. "If God had designed a beautiful machine to reflect his wisdom and power, surely he would not have used a collection of parts generally fashioned for other purposes. Orchids were not made by an ideal engineer; they are jury-rigged from a limited set of available components" (Gould, *Panda's Thumb*, 20). For a comprehensive discussion, see Gould and Lewontin, "Spandrels of San Marco."

105. M/SE 247. There's another change on the next page. In the later versions, Theocles's praise continues thus: "[B]y Thee (O *Sovereign* Mind!) I have been form'd such as I am" (C 2.194). In the earlier version, the parenthetical part of that sentence is absent. It's just: "[B]y Thee I was made such as I am" (M/SE 247).

## Chapter 2: Virtue

1. A 142–143.
2. A 208, 241–242.
3. A 288.
4. A 73.
5. A 151.
6. A 73.
7. A 207.
8. A 132.
9. A 207.
10. A 206–208.

11. A 180, 328; 207–208, 433; 65, 80, 119, 183, 225, 245, 247, 275, 437, 439, 441. See also A 65, 80, 119, 180, 183, 207–208, 225, 245, 247, 328, 433, 437, 439, 441.

12. Filonowicz provides an insightful account of the difference between the two versions of the *Inquiry* (*Fellow-Feeling and the Moral Life*, 65–103). Filonowicz contends that the early version is superior to the later one, taking Shaftesbury's comparison to beauty to be a philosophical deterioration.

13. Shaftesbury was opposed to Descartes's view that animals were mere mechanism, automata, without any conscious states. He rejects the "modern Hypothesis of *animal Insensibility*," opting instead "to believe firmly and resolutely, 'That other Creatures have their Sense and *Feeling*, their mere *Passions* and *Affections*, as well as our-selves'" (C 3.129–130).

14. Although the term "moral sense" is not one he emphasizes or explains in detail (see Rivers, *Reason, Grace, and Sentiment*, 124). There is little evidence that he thinks the moral sense is a distinct psychological faculty in the way that Hutcheson did.

15. Shaftesbury's insistence on the naturalness of the beauty-deformity distinction is a direct counter to Locke's denial of innate ideas; see C 2.229–230. For explication of Shaftesbury's rejection of Locke's view of innate ideas, see Peter Carey, *Locke, Shaftesbury, and Hutcheson*, 98–149; and Stuart-Buttle, *From Moral Theology to Moral Philosophy*, 88–117.

16. Santayana, *Sense of Beauty*, 16.

17. Xenophon, *The Shorter Socratic Writings*, 147.

18. Xenophon, *The Shorter Socratic Writings*, 148.

19. Plato, *Symposium*, 497 (215d).

20. Plato, *Symposium*, 497–498 (215e).

21. Plato, *Symposium*, 499 (217a).

22. Plato, *Symposium*, 500 (218e).

23. Xenophon, *The Shorter Socratic Writings*, 159–160.

24. Hume, *Treatise of Human Nature*, 265–266 (2.3.3.2–3), 294 (3.1.1.5–7), 307 (3.2.1.2–3).

25. Hume, *Treatise of Human Nature*, 266 (2.3.3.4).

26. Schneewind, *Invention of Autonomy*, 302.

27. Irwin, *Development of Ethics: Volume 2*, 866–867.

28. There are other possibilities, such as whether moral properties could be rigidly designated or be based on ideal dispositions rather than actual responses. But I don't think Shaftesbury's texts will shed much light on those questions, or vice versa.

29. W 7.

30. Grote has argued that Shaftesbury himself advances egoistic hedonism. According to Grote, when Shaftesbury attacks Hobbes, the voluntarists, and other "selfish" theorists, he is not attacking the view that pleasure-based self-interest is our only reason to be virtuous but rather is attacking the view that pleasures accrued from externally bestowed rewards and punishments are our only reason to be virtuous. See Grote, "Shaftesbury's Egoistic Hedonism." For discussion of Grote's view, see section 2c of my "Shaftesbury" entry in *Stanford Encyclopedia of Philosophy*.

31. W 12.

32. Lepper, Greene, and Nisbett, "Undermining," 130.

33. Shaftesbury's concerns about the partiality of the herding principle are in the same spirit as concerns about empathy in Prinz, "Against Empathy"; and Bloom, *Against Empathy*.

34. For a wealth of evidence for the existence this tendency, see Hamlin et al., "Not Like Me = Bad."

35. See Gill, *British Moralists*, 181–197.

36. Greene, *Moral Tribes*, 14.

37. Greene, *Moral Tribes*, 54.

38. Hume, *Treatise of Human Nature*, 4–5 (introduction, paragraph 7).

39. There's also a direct line from Shaftesbury's view of the content of virtue to Utilitarianism. Shaftesbury says that to be virtuous is to "love the Publick, to study universal Good, and to promote the Interest of the whole World, as far as lies within our power" (C 1.23). This statement is an antecedent to Hutcheson's proto-Utilitarian claim that "that Action is best, which procures the greatest Happiness for the greatest Number; and that, worse, which, in like manner occasions Misery" (Hutcheson, *Inquiry*, 125). Levy-Eichel points to Shaftesbury's coinage of *"Moral Arithmetic"* (C 2.99) as a crucial part of the pre-history of Utilitarianism, and its use of mathematics in moral subjects (Levy-Eichel, "Moral Arithmetic"). For further discussion of Shaftesbury's influence on Utilitarianism, see Driver, "The History of Utilitarianism." For a view of Shaftesbury's difference from classic Utilitarians, see Crisp, *Sacrifice Regained*, 86.

40. See Hutcheson, *Essay*, 137–155.

41. Hume's view of justice and other artificial virtues may be different, with morally explicit thoughts having motivational force in those cases. See Gill, "Hume on Moral Motivation."

42. Shaftesbury also illustrates this perspective in his story of two friends trying to resist amorous temptation (C 1.110–115). For discussion, see Jaffro, "Cyrus' Strategy"; Boeker, "Shaftesbury on Persons"; Boeker, "Shaftesbury on Liberty and Self-Mastery."

43. A 476. He also writes: "Begin therefore; and, as a Legislatour to thy Self, establishing that Economy or Commonwealth within, according to those Laws which thou knowst to be just; Swear never to transgress what thou hast solemnly decreed, & hast appointed to thy self" (A 191).

44. Kant does, however, affirm that we have some control over the sentimental aspects of our character (albeit less control than Shaftesbury thinks we have), and that we ought to work to shape our sentimental dispositions so that they are more conducive to morality. See Cohen, *Kant and the Human Sciences*, 84–108. But having certain sentimental dispositions is, for Kant, valuable only as a means to the end of a (rational) good will, whereas for Shaftesbury, having harmonious dispositions is non-instrumentally valuable, valuable in itself.

45. Kant, *Groundwork*, 15.

46. Shaftesbury explicitly contends that we have the power to form our own taste (C 3.114). For more on the self-improvement aspect of Shaftesbury's work, see Garrett, "Seventeenth-Century Moral"; and Amir, *Humor and the Good Life in Modern Philosophy*, 28.

47. One might wonder if the value a person places on moral beauty is agent-relative or agent-neutral. (For account of this distinction, see Ridge, "Reasons for

Action.") Will the Shaftesburean agent place ultimate value on the moral beauty of her own soul, or will she aim to maximize moral beauty in the world (which could conceivably entail becoming worse oneself in order to cause several other people to become better)? I think we should attribute to Shaftesbury a special agent-relative reason to make yourself virtuous, even if he did not have the agent-relative/agent-neutral distinction at hand. Just as an artist recognizes an agent-relative reason to create beautiful art herself (not just maximize beautiful art, regardless of who makes it), so too a person recognizes an agent-relative reason to make her own soul beautiful (not just maximize beautiful souls). I discuss this issue in connection with Hume in Gill, *Humean Moral Pluralism*, 58–61 and 71–73.

48. Nietzsche is associated with self-creation by, for instance, Jaspers, *Nietzsche*, 140, 151, 154; Nehamas, *Nietzsche*, 141–199; and Rorty, *Contingency*, 27–28, 98–99, 108, 174–175. For discussion of the complexity of Nietzsche's idea of self-creation and its apparent tension with his fatalism, see Leiter, "Fatalism," 217–257.

49. Nietzsche, *Beyond Good and Evil*, 62 (section 31).

50. Nietzsche, *The Gay Science*, 170 (section 299).

51. Nietzsche, *The Gay Science*, 189 (section 335).

52. Nietzsche, *Human, All-Too-Human*, 6 (introduction, section 3).

53. Nietzsche, *The Gay Science*, 189 (section 335).

54. Nietzsche, *Human, All-Too-Human*, 6; Nietzsche, *Beyond Good and Evil*, 156, section 226; Nietzsche, *The Gay Science*, 171 (section 301).

55. Nietzsche, *The Gay Science*, 104 (section 107).

56. From *Oxford English Dictionary Online*, https://www-oed-com.ezproxy.is.ed.ac.uk/view/Entry/11237?isAdvanced=false&result=1&rskey=SQ5epE&. Accessed February 18, 2022.

57. Burnet: "We think him a better Artist that makes a Clock that strikes regularly at every hour from the Springs and Wheels which he puts in the work, than he that hath so made his Clock that he must put his finger to it every hour to make it strike" (Burnet, *Sacred Theory of the Earth*, 72). Hume: "A peasant can give no better reason for the stopping of any clock or watch than to say that it does not commonly go right: But an artist easily perceives, that the same force in the spring or pendulum has always the same influence on the wheels; but fails of its usual effect, perhaps by reason of a grain of dust, which puts a stop to the whole movement" (Hume, *Enquiry concerning Human Understanding*, 66 [8.13]).

58. This line from *Sensus Communis* seems to have been a significant influence on Yeats's "Ode to a Grecian Urn," which ends with "Beauty is truth, truth beauty,—that is all Ye know on Earth, and all ye need to know." See Solomon, "Shaftesbury's *Characteristics*." I think Shaftesbury means something more flatfooted than Yeats. Shaftesbury is maintaining that works of art are successful when they are unified and when they represent accurately the nature of virtue and vice.

59. From *Oxford English Dictionary Online*, https://www-oed-com.ezproxy.is.ed.ac.uk/view/Entry/206884?rskey=j5AmSF&result=1#eid. Accessed February 18, 2022.

60. See Sellars, "Shaftesbury, Stoicism, and Philosophy as a Way of Life," 408.

61. But Shaftesbury does write, "Were a Man to form himself by one single Pattern or Original, however perfect; he wou'd himself be a mere *Copy*. But whilst he draws

from various Models, he is *original, natural,* and *unaffected.* We see in outward Carriage and Behaviour, how ridiculous any one becomes who imitates another, be he ever so graceful. They are mean Spirits who love to copy *merely.* Nothing is agreeable or natural, but what is *original.* Our Manners, like our Faces, tho ever so beautiful, must differ in their Beauty" (C 3.161). His point here is not that we should invent new values. His point is that we should instantiate existing values in an original way. But it would be fair to raise a challenge about how much of a coherent difference from Nietzsche this amounts to in the end.

62. For a thorough account of how Shaftesbury's Prometheus comparison was received in German thought, and of the significant differences between Shaftesbury's comparison and the later German Prometheus comparisons, see Dehrmann, *Das "Orakel der Deisten,"* 341–360.

63. Shaftesbury also uses Prometheus in another context, when discussing the problem of how to reconcile an omnipotent benevolent God with human cruelty and depravity (C 2.114–115). He says that some people try to explain human depravity by attributing it to Prometheus's creation of humans, but that's a failure because it just pushes the question back to why God created Prometheus or didn't use his power to prevent Prometheus's errors. It no more explains human evil than one explains "how this huge Frame of World is supported" by contending that the world rests on the back of an elephant, and then by explaining that what supports the elephant is that it rests on the back of a tortoise (C 2.115).

64. For clear discussion of these arguments, see Crisp, *Sacrifice Regained,* 86–91. Crisp explains how Shaftesbury uses the distinction between higher and lower pleasures in a manner that clearly anticipates Mill's arguments in chapter 2 of *Utilitarianism.*

65. V 83.
66. V 87.
67. V 85.
68. V 199.
69. V 87.
70. V 198.
71. V 199.
72. V 199.

73. V 199. Butler agrees with much of Shaftesbury's moral philosophy, but he singles out as a fundamental mistake Shaftesbury's claim that virtue is obligatory because it will make a person happy. This claim, Butler argues, commits Shaftesbury to holding that if it did turn out that a person could be happier by being vicious, that person would be obligated to be vicious (Butler, *Fifteen Sermons,* xxiii). But we could never be obligated to act viciously. We are always obligated to act in accord with our second-order principle of reflection (which Shaftesbury calls the "sense of right and wrong" and Butler calls "conscience"), independent of whether or not doing so will make us happier. It is that second-order principle of reflection that is the entire ground of moral obligation, not the considerations concerning happiness that occupy Shaftesbury in Book II of the *Inquiry* (Butler, *Fifteen Sermons,* xxv).

74. V 197.
75. V 108–109.

76. V 102–103, 105.
77. V 192.
78. V 192; see also 160.
79. V 113.
80. V 114.
81. V 114.
82. V 137.
83. V 115.
84. V 118.
85. V 116. I think Shaftesbury came to have a different view from this, eventually coming to think that human partiality could produce very strong sincere attachment to the subset of people in one's charmed circle while holding large swaths of other humans in contempt. In the early version of the *Inquiry* he was focused on the problems with the egoist, but in later works he developed a more nuanced psychology that included a focus on non-egoistic partiality (see C 1.69–73).
86. V 125.
87. V 126.
88. I think Shaftesbury developed a more nuanced view of bearing one's own survey as well, coming to think that while half-knaves will suffer internal contradiction, there could be a full knave who has no problems with himself (see C 1.82 and 1.107–108; but see also 1.159). Shaftesbury's view that there might be nothing to say to convince a full knave to be moral anticipates Hume's discussion of the sensible knave (Hume, *An Enquiry concerning Morals*, 81–82 [9.22–25]).
89. V 120.
90. V 126.
91. V 128.
92. V 129.
93. V 131–133.
94. V 120.
95. V 182.
96. V 184.
97. V 184.
98. V 194.
99. V 194.
100. V 193; see also C 1.159.
101. V 133.
102. V 129.
103. V 121.
104. V 140.
105. V 122–123.
106. V 123.
107. V 122.
108. V 136.
109. V 136–137; see also C 1.191–192.
110. V 138.
111. V 147.

112. V 115.

113. V 148. Shaftesbury's emphasis on the human craving of company is similar to Hume, *Treatise of Human Nature*, 234–235 (2.2.5.15).

114. See also P 167–168.

115. Rivers, *Reason, Grace, and Sentiment*, 147.

116. Fowler, *Shaftesbury and Hutcheson*, 126.

117. Berkeley, *Alchiphron*, 62.

118. Brown, *Essays on the Characteristics*, 162.

119. Martineau, *Types of Ethical Theory, volume 2*, 498.

120. Albee, "Review," 183.

121. Tiffany, "Shaftesbury as Stoic," 667.

122. Filonowicz, *Fellow-Feeling and the Moral Life*, 101–102.

123. Stolnitz, "On the Significance of Lord Shaftesbury," 101.

124. Stolnitz, "On the Significance of Lord Shaftesbury," 103–104.

125. Rivers, *Reason, Grace, and Sentiment*, 143.

126. John Andrew Bernstein, "Identification," 325.

127. For further discussion of Shaftesbury's view of pleasure, and different interpretations of it in the secondary literature, see section 2c of my "Shaftesbury" entry in *Stanford Encyclopedia of Philosophy*.

128. In earlier editions, this passage read: "So that *Beauty*, said I, and *Good*, with you, I see, are the same." I do not know why Shaftesbury added "still" to the sentence, as this passage, so far as I can tell, is the first time his characters explicitly draw the beauty-good conclusion.

129. A similar locution occurs in *Miscellaneous Reflections*: every human's constitution is such "That VIRTUE is his *natural Good*, and VICE his *Misery* and *Ill*" (C 3.136).

130. See Axelsson, *Political Aesthetics*, 220 and 235.

131. See also A 127–128.

132. Hume's "Of the Standard of Taste" can be read as a direct rejoinder to Theocles's claim here that disagreement about what is beautiful establishes a mind-independent standard of beauty ("Of the Standard of Taste").

133. Shaftesbury is here attacking Locke's denial of innate ideas. See Carey, *Locke, Shaftesbury, and Hutcheson*, 98–99; Uehlein, "Whichcote, Shaftesbury, and Locke," 1031–1048; and Stuart-Buttle, *From Moral Theology to Moral Philosophy*, 90–102.

134. As additional evidence of its being natural for us to value moral beauty, Shaftesbury points to our reactive moral emotions. This argument is intended to show that his view that we naturally care about moral beauty explains observable emotional phenomena better than the competing egoist view that we naturally have only entirely self-interested affections. If we were entirely self-interested, then we would feel unhappy only about what thwarts our own interests. But we feel guilt and shame about immoral things we have done even when they have no deleterious effects for us (C 2.234–235). What thwarts our interests makes us feel grief and fear, but it does not make us blush. Conversely, when we think we have done something morally worthy we feel pride, regardless of whether our own welfare is advanced. And toward people we think have wronged us, we feel resentment, an emotion we do not feel toward "a Stone, or Madman" that has caused us the same harm (C 2.234). We may seek revenge

on someone we think has treated us unjustly us even when doing so runs counter to "all other interests, and even to Life it-self" (C 2.234). We do not seek revenge to further our own welfare but "out of hatred to the imagin'd Wrong." The best explanation of these phenomena is that humans have a natural "Love of Justice," independent of self-interest. There is "*a Sense of Wrong*, natural to all Men" (C 2.234). We have a "*natural* and *just* Sense of Right and Wrong" (C 2.23). And since we will be happiest when we live in accord with our nature, we will be happiest when we live in accord with moral beauty.

135. Hutcheson, *An Essay*, 5.

136. See Martineau, *Types of Ethical Theory*, 508; and Wiley, *The Eighteenth Century Background*, 74.

137. See Sidgwick, *Outlines*, 185; Peach, "Shaftesbury's Moral Arithmeticks"; Trianosky, "Obligation to be Virtuous"; Grote, "Shaftesbury's Egoistic Hedonism." For discussion of Shaftesbury's views on hedonism, see Crisp, *Sacrifice Regained*, 84–85 and 91.

138. Den Uyl, "Shaftesbury and the Problem of Modern Virtue," 292; Schneewind, *The Invention of Autonomy*, 302–304; Irwin, *The Development of Ethics*, 257.

139. See Annas, "Virtue Ethics." See C 1.760.

140. Leibniz singled out this point in Shaftesbury as one of the most significant (Leibniz, *Philosophical Papers and Letters*, 631).

141. Of course rationalist moral philosophers—Clarke, Balguy, Kant, etc.—will claim that if the nasty gentleman does not recognize his moral obligations, then he certainly is guilty of some kind of irrationality. Immorality, for rationalist philosophers, does imply a violation of reason. My point is just that in this passage, Shaftesbury is suggesting a different picture, one in which the problem with an immoral person is his sentimental constitution, not his reasoning. The painting of that picture, needless to say, does not on its own disprove the rationalist position.

142. See Slote, *The Ethics of Care and Empathy*; Prinz, *The Emotional Construction of Morals*; Haidt and Graham, "When Morality Opposes Justice"; May, "Does Disgust Influence Moral Judgment?".

143. For perspicuous explication of the "self-help" character of the work of Shaftesbury and his predecessors, see Garrett, "Seventeenth Century Moral Philosophy."

144. Anthony, Lord Ashley to John Locke, September 29, 1694; in de Beer, *The Correspondence of John Locke*, volume V, 151.

## *Chapter 3: Art*

1. See the Earl of Shaftesbury to a Friend, December 2, 1704; PRO 30/24/22/2 (quoted in Voitle, *Third Earl of Shaftesbury*, 229). Shaftesbury printed a woodcut of the family crest and "Love, Serve" motto on the first page of *Characteristicks* (C 1.xxi).

2. See A 72–73.

3. PRO 30/24/27/14. p. 145 (quoted in Klein, *Shaftesbury and the Culture of Politeness*, 108).

4. Anthony, Lord Ashley to the second Earl of Shaftesbury, St. John's Court, July 1689; PRO 30/24/22/2 (quoted in Voitle, *Third Earl of Shaftesbury*, 43–44).

5. Anthony, Lord Ashley to Andrew Percivall, May 27, 1691, PRO 30/24/22/2. Here's more of this revealing letter: "I having in me so much desire and love to perfect retirement and otherwise too having been so involved, against my wish, in such troubling affairs at home, as would have made me to have shunned all other business, and avoiding any engagement here which yet notwithstanding the danger of this country has thus drawn me to: and were I not deeply sensible that my duty here to mankind obliged me in some manner to them and against my self in such a perilous and urgent condition of a country and government in which not voluntarily, but by birth I find myself engaged: and were it not from an unmoveable principle of duty in my mind I should not be now doing what I am and be formally concerned with the governing laws of the world which (as the spirit of it now is) is the thing in it that my nature most strives to be exempt from and that nothing but the uttermost Principle of duty and necessity can drive me to."

6. Anthony, Lord Ashley to the Countess of Shaftesbury, 1696; PRO 30/24/22/2 (quoted in Voitle, *Third Earl of Shaftesbury*, 79).

7. Trumbach seeks to explain Shaftesbury's reluctance to marry by arguing for a "homosexual reading" of Shaftesbury's *Askemata* (Trumbach, *Sex and the Gender Revolution*, 441). Klein says some of Shaftesbury's letters suggest "homosexual longings and attachments" that social convention and obligation kept him from acting on (Klein, "Cooper, Anthony Ashley, Third Earl of Shaftesbury"). Branch also finds suggestions of homosexuality in his writing (*Rituals of Spontaneity*, 264). Klein and Tierney-Hynes ("Shaftesbury's Soliloquy") both emphasize the "homosocial" character of Shaftesbury's view of elevated human society, such as in the friendship between Theocles and Philocles of *The Moralists*. Voitle disputes the homosexual readings of Shaftesbury's notebooks and letters (Voitle, *Third Earl of Shaftesbury*, 242–244). Müller also argues against those readings, maintaining that they misinterpret key passages by failing to take into account the surrounding features of Shaftesbury's own texts, the early eighteenth-century context in which Shaftesbury was writing, and the ancient Greek subjects Shaftesbury was discussing (Müller, "Shaftesbury on the Psychoanalyst's Couch").

8. The Earl of Shaftesbury to Benjamin Furly, December 29, 1701; PRO 30/24/20/49 (quoted in Voitle, *Third Earl of Shaftesbury*, 211).

9. The Earl of Shaftesbury to Sir Rowland Gwin, January 23, 1704; PRO 30/24/22/4/pp.1–2 (quoted in Voitle, *Third Earl of Shaftesbury*, 223).

10. The Earl of Shaftesbury to Lord Somers, December 25, 1704; PRO 30/24/22/2 (quoted in Voitle, *Third Earl of Shaftesbury*, 231).

11. The Earl of Shaftesbury to Awnsham Churchill, January 29, 1705; PRO 30/24/22/2 (quoted in Voitle, *Third Earl of Shaftesbury*, 231).

12. I discuss Shaftesbury's attitude toward politics and partisanship in Gill, "Shaftesbury on Selfishness and Partisanship."

13. A 431.

14. Thomas Stringer to Anthony, Lord Ashley, May 5, 1699; PRO 30/24/44/77 (quoted in Voitle, *Third Earl of Shaftesbury*, 97–98).

15. For discussion of how Shaftesbury used the gardens of St. Giles for the kind of peripatetic philosophizing with friends that he describes Theocles and Philocles engaged in in *The Moralists*, see Myers, "Wise Substitute of Providence!" and Fleming, "The 'Convenience of Husbandry.'"

16. Collier, *Short View*.

17. Salteren, *A Treatise Against Images*.

18. Boyer, *The English Theophrastus*, 70.

19. It has been suggested that the small book (the title of which we cannot see) Shaftesbury holds in his frontispiece portrait is by Epictetus. As I noted in chapter 1, in his private notebooks Shaftesbury copied hundreds of quotations of Epictetus.

20. The difference I describe between the instrumentalist and non-instrumentalist interpretations more or less tracks a divide in the scholarly literature. Corresponding to the instrumentalist camp are those who attribute to Shaftesbury the view that art has value merely as an instrument for the promotion of virtue. The editors of *Second Characters* express this view when they write in their preface to their volume on Shaftesbury's aesthetics, "for Shaftesbury the enjoyment of art was never to be an end in itself, but had always to serve a moral purpose" (SC 18). Derhmann says that Shaftesbury believed that "art is merely the means to a further end," where that end is moral improvement (Dehrmann, "Transition," 48). Mortensen claims that Shaftesbury's goal was to give a "moral defense of the appreciation of art," according to which art appreciation is justified by its capacity to improve moral character (Mortensen, "Shaftesbury and the Morality of Art Appreciation," 631). Tiffany ("Shaftesbury as Stoic") and Stuart-Buttle (*From Moral Theology to Moral Philosophy*, 89–117) make similar claims. The commentators in this camp take much of Shaftesbury's philosophy to be fundamentally Stoical, as do Gatti, "The Aesthetic Mind," and Sellars, "Shaftesbury, Stoicism, and Philosophy as a Way of Life." For further discussion of Stoicism and Shaftesbury, see Klein, *Shaftesbury and the Culture of Politeness*, 60–101. See also Laurent Jaffro and Christian Maurer, who argue that Shaftesbury's philosophy has Stoic elements but also some elements that depart away from Stoicism ("Pathologia, A Theory of the Passions"). I discuss these issues in section 1d of my "Shaftesbury" entry in *Stanford Encyclopaedia of Philosophy*.

Corresponding in certain (but not all) respects to the non-instrumentalist interpretation is the position of Stolnitz. Stolnitz argues that Shaftesbury's great philosophical contribution is to be the first to develop the idea that artistic appreciation is of fundamental contemplative value that is entirely independent of any other consideration. On this view, Shaftesbury initiates the separation of artistic appreciation from practical concern, which separation would become the cornerstone of the aesthetic thought of Herder, Lessing, Schiller, Kant, Goethe, and much of modern philosophy of art. Shaftesbury, according to this way of thinking, originates the idea of art for art's sake, and thus essentially invents modern aesthetics.

Stolnitz first developed his interpretation in 1961 (in "On the Significance of Lord Shaftesbury" and "On the Origins of 'Aesthetic Disinterestedness'"). For two decades or so, Stolnitz's interpretation was the closest thing to a received view. In recent decades, however, most commentators have rejected Stolnitz's interpretation, with Stoical or instrumentalist interpretations becoming considerably more predominant. For criticisms of Stolnitz, see White, "Metaphysics of Disinterestedness"; Townsend, "Shaftesbury's Aesthetic Theory"; Mortensen, "Shaftesbury and the Morality of Art Appreciation"; Arregui and Arnau "Shaftesbury: Father or Critic of Modern Aesthetics?"; Rind, "Concept of Disinterestedness." For a comprehensive recent discussion of the issues, see Axelsson, *Political Aesthetics*, 180–184, 202.

I agree with recent commentators that there are numerous aspects of Stolnitz's view of modern aesthetics that it is simply a mistake to attribute to Shaftesbury. On Stolnitz's view, for instance, modern aesthetic value is sui generis or autonomous; for Shaftesbury, in contrast, the beauty of physical things is continuous with the beauty of virtue, both of them based on unity and occupying a single value hierarchy. On Stolnitz's view, modern aesthetic experience is purely contemplative, without any practical implication; for Shaftesbury, in contrast, true appreciation of artistic beauty promotes virtue. On Stolnitz's view, modern aesthetics is concerned with the value of art as it exists in and of itself; Shaftesbury, in contrast, focuses on how appreciation of artistic beauty can be good for a person. But I think there is a kernel of important truth in Stolnitz's interpretation nonetheless: Stolnitz rightly credits Shaftesbury as an originator of the idea that appreciation of beautiful things is worthwhile on its own, distinct from any other considerations—that aesthetic experience is of profound value in itself.

21. See Rivers, *Reason, Grace, and Sentiment*, 147.

22. Bernstein, "Shaftesbury's Identification of the Good with the Beautiful," 314. See also Filonowicz, *Fellow-Feeling and the Moral Life*, 102.

23. Some have taken passages such as those in the previous paragraph to be evidence that Shaftesbury thinks that judgments of beauty are "'immediate,' in the sense that [they take] place without discursive reflection" (Stolnitz, "'Beauty': Some Stages in the History of an Idea"). (See also Berkeley, *Alciphron*, 59–60; Tuveson, *Imagination as a Means of Grace*, 53; Filonowicz, "Ethical Sentimentalism Revisited.") On this reading, all that Shaftesburean judgment amounts to is an emotional response, involving no more intellectual content than the typical distinguishing of blue from red. This is a misreading. Shaftesbury clearly contends that intellectual reflection is often necessary to get judgments right. Immediately after the *Moralists* passage I quoted in the previous paragraph, he has Theocles say, "All own the Standard, Rule, and Measure: But in applying it to Things, Disorder arises, Ignorance prevails, Interest and Passion breed Disturbance" (C 2.232). To apply the concept of the beautiful correctly requires an unbiased, accurate rational understanding of that to which it is applied. Our response to moral beauty is emotional, yes, but an emotional response can fail to accurately reflect whether something is truly beautiful because of "a Defect in the application of that unavoidable Impression and first natural Rule of Honesty and Worth" (C 3.185). To judge an object correctly—including judgments of moral character—we need to learn what the object is actually like. In non-simple cases, the "use of Reason, sufficient to secure a right application of the Affections" is necessary for that (C 2.20).

24. See also A 234.

25. Kant, *The Metaphysics of Morals*, 207

26. This point of Shaftesbury's also aligns with recent psychological research that claims to show that the experience of awe in nature can be morally improving because it tends to make people more patient and altruistic. See Rudd, Vohs, and Aaker, "Awe Expands People's Perception of Time."

27. See Den Uyl, "Shaftesbury and the Problem of Modern Virtue."

28. According to Dabney Townsend, Locke's "indifference to aesthetic questions is legendary," and "this indifference was apparently well known even by Locke's

admirers" ("Lockean Aesthetics," 349). See also Stolnitz, "Locke and the Category of Value."

29. June 3, 1709; printed in R 403. For discussion of this letter, see Carey, *Locke, Shaftesbury, and Hutcheson*, 98.

30. See A 7–8; 57. According to Annas, however, the Stoic view does not rest on the claim that happiness must be based only on what is within one's own control (Annas, *The Morality of Happiness*, 405). Annas's reading may constitute an objection to Shaftesbury's understanding of Stoicism, although perhaps Shaftesbury would attribute this view of withdrawing concern only to what is within one's control to Epictetus alone and not to Stoic philosophers in general.

31. A 383–389.
32. A 303.
33. A 305.
34. A 382. See also 99 and 383–389.
35. A 157.
36. A 156. See also 99.
37. A 382–383.
38. A 192. See also A 198, 221.
39. A 386.
40. Epictetus, *Discourses*, 237 (section 4.2).
41. See also C 2.61, 3.22 and 3.111–114, where Shaftesbury has a more complex hierarchy (with more than three degrees of beauty).
42. Dehrmann, "Transition," 47. See also Tiffany, "Shaftesbury as Stoic"; and Stuart-Buttle, *From Moral Theology to Moral Philosophy*.
43. Dehrmann, "Transition," 48.
44. Dehrmann, "Transition," 47.
45. SC 163.
46. SC 166.
47. SC 384.
48. Tiffany, "Shaftesbury as Stoic," 650–651.
49. See Jaffro and Maurer, "Pathologia," 214–215.
50. Glauser argues that in the passages that seem to deny the beauty of physical things, Theocles has been "carried away by his own rhetoric" (Glauser, "Aesthetic Experience in Shaftesbury," 29). According to Glauser's reading of Shaftesbury, because a material thing really can possess a unified form, a material thing really can have the property of beauty. Because works of art "are temporarily beautified by their respective principles, they do have beauty, although in some lesser measure" (30). And Theocles acknowledges the beauty of things in other passages, such as when he says that that "which is beautify'd, is beautiful only by the accession of something beautifying," and that what we admire is "mind or the effect of mind" (C 2.226).
51. Darwall, *The British Moralists and the Internal 'Ought'*, 190.
52. But see A 378–381, where Shaftesbury makes points similar to those in the footnote at C 3.112–114, and where he includes in his criticism "seeing & admiring," which corresponds to what in the footnote he calls the "*Virtuoso*-Passion, the Love of *Painting*, and the *Designing* Arts" that involves "no Possession, no Enjoyment or Reward, but barely seeing and admiring" (C 3.112–113).

53. Volume 3 of *Characteristicks* is the first and only site of the *Oxford English Dictionary*'s example of usage for the word "miscellanarian."

54. Actually it's even more Russian doll–complicated than that, because characters in one of the previous four works (*The Moralists*) talk in third person about "our friend" who wrote another of the previous works (*Inquiry*) (C 2.148–158). And in the last reflection, the Miscellanarian comments on the style of the miscellaneous reflections (C 3.193) and goes on to nest his final claims three narrative voices deep (the Miscellanian recounts something said by someone else who is himself recounting what someone else said [C 3.194–209]). And then there's the fact that the *Miscellaneous Reflections* are like a series of footnotes on the previous four works, but are themselves longer than any one of those other works. And the *Miscellaneous Reflections* themselves have some very long footnotes. It all strikes me as very *Pale King* David Foster Wallace-esque.

55. For discussion of the novelistic aspects of *Characteristicks*, see Prince, *Philosophical Dialogue in the British Enlightenment*, 23–73.

56. Although how does an esoteric reading work when the supposed subterfuge is revealed in the third volume? Also, the Miscellanian is just one more voice in the volumes. Why should that voice be authoritative, especially when it conflicts with earlier discussions of beauty as unity of design? Maybe it's better for the decoy reading if it turns out Shaftesbury never let the pretense slip in his published writings, because the decoy is something that separates all his published works from his private self. See Jaffro, "Shaftesbury on the 'Natural Secretion' and Philosophical Personae."

57. All the quoted definitions are from the *Oxford English Dictionary*.

58. Shaftesbury frequently expresses disdain for Jews: see C 1.19, 1.175 2.186, 3.35, 3.72; P 203.

59. A 146. See also A 228 and 278–229.

60. A 163.

61. A 114.

62. A 115.

63. Voitle, *Third Earl of Shaftesbury*, 108–109. See also Voitle, *Third Earl of Shaftesbury*, 20–37, 365, 398, 406.

64. As well, Shaftesbury expressed a love of art in his notes for "Plasticks." Writing at the end of his life, he explains how valuable it is to view great art when one is "*sick* and under Pains, Watches, *Insomnia* &c: as also disturbing Business or Affaires"; viewing art in these circumstances raises "pleasing specters" and drives away "other species & haunting Forms of Faces, Grimaces &c in weak stomachs, Indigestions, Head-Akes" and helps "the Passions, calming, allaying" (SC 205).

65. SC 373.

66. SC 376.

67. He also writes, "The Collector of a Cabinet & intense Virtuoso, still more secure as nearer Order, Virtue, (Truth), Beauty" (SC 229).

68. See Wind, "Shaftesbury as a Patron of Art"; and Sweetman, "Shaftesbury's Last Commission."

69. SC 421. Thanks to Brad Miller for his help in understanding Shaftesbury's letters to de Matteis.

70. Klein suggests that Shaftesbury's Stoicism in his notebooks resulted from a temporary personal crisis (Klein, *Shaftesbury and the Culture of Politeness*, 18, 71–73, 89).

According to Klein, the moments Shaftesbury cherishes art align better with his settled character and conduct, while the turning-away moments, which were part of a regimen of Stoic exercises he undertook at certain points in his life, are more isolated. For the alternative view that Shaftesbury remained committed to Stoicism throughout his life, see Stuart-Buttle, *From Moral Theology to Moral Theory*, 95–96.

71. Another possible interpretation is that Shaftesbury is a Stoic through and through, and that his Stoicism allows for the pursuit of beautiful art because beautiful art is a "preferred indifferent." A Stoic preferred indifferent is something that is not fundamentally good but that there is nonetheless a reason to go for. Preferred indifferents have a value that makes them rational and natural to select, but it is a value that is different and inferior in kind from the value of virtue. If the resulting view implies that we ought to select for beautiful art just so long as it does not detract from virtue, then it does seem to be co-extensive with much of what Shaftesbury recommends. But it's notable that he says repeatedly that beauty and good are one and the same, which implies that all beauty shares an evaluative property rather than there being the strict distinction the concept of preferred indifferents implies. As well, Shaftesbury places art on the hierarchy of beauty that also contains virtue and the mind of God, which suggests that he thinks there is more commonality between all kinds of beauty than the categorical distinction between virtue and indifferents implies. It's also notable that even in the most Stoical passages of the private notebooks and his explication of Stoic ideas in *Pathologia*, Shaftesbury (so far as I can tell) makes no use of the concept of preferred indifferents.

72. Hume, *Enquiry concerning Morals*, 163 (7.19). See also Hume, *Enquiry concerning Morals*, 161 (7.11).

## Chapter 4: Painting

1. In his notes for *Plasticks*, he says that even in paintings of animals, fruit, and flowers, there is "in truth & strictness *historical, Moral Characteristick* (SC 182). I don't know what he has in mind here, nor how it fits with his other statements of the difference between history painting, on the one hand, and portraits or landscapes, on the other. (See also C 1.90, 1.181; SC 292.)

2. SC 225.

3. When Hume talks about the moral improvement effected by painters, it seems very likely he is thinking of producers of the kind of history painting Shaftesbury discusses. See Hume, *Treatise of Human Nature*, 395 (3.3.6.6); and Hume, *Enquiry concerning Understanding*, 8 (1.8).

4. Agliony, *Painting*, unnumbered preface 14.

5. Agliony, *Painting*, unnumbered preface 12–13.

6. Salteren, *A Treatise Against Images and Pictures*, 2.

7. The Earl of Shaftesbury to Thomas Micklethwayte, February 23, 1712; PRO 30/24/23/8/149–50 (quoted in Voitle, *Third Earl of Shaftesbury*, 391).

8. See also SC 161.

9. SC 184. See also SC 254.

10. SC 184.

11. Lessing, *Emilia Galotti*, 6.
12. See also C 1.89 and SC 177–178, 180, 224, 231.
13. SC 235 and C 3.235. See also SC 409.
14. SC 380.
15. See, for instance, Giovanni Francesco Romanelli's version: https://www.christies.com/lot/lot-giovanni-francesco-romanelli-viterbo-c-1610-1662-the-6068913/.
16. See, for instance, Benvenuti's version: https://www.kunst-fuer-alle.de/english/fine-art/artist/image/pietro-benvenuti/9915/1/145845/hercules-at-the-crossroads/index.htm.
17. See, for instance, Ricci's version: https://upload.wikimedia.org/wikipedia/commons/0/0c/Sebastiano_Ricci_-_Hercules_at_the_crossroads.jpg.
18. SC 226.
19. Shaftesbury also praised Raphael's Incendio nell Borgo, which represents an even more complex scene than *Massacre of the Innocents*.
20. SC 185.
21. See, for instance, the versions by Cesari and by Rembrandt: https://upload.wikimedia.org/wikipedia/commons/6/6e/Giuseppe_Cesari_-_Diana_and_Actaeon_-_Google_Art_Project.jpg https://en.wikipedia.org/wiki/Diana_Bathing_with_her_Nymphs_with_Actaeon_and_Callisto#/media/File:Rembrandt,_Harmenszoon_van_Rijn_-_Diana_mit_Aktäon_und_Kallisto_-_c.1634-1635.jpg.
22. The version by Balducci: https://augusta-stylianou.pixels.com/featured/diana-and-actaeon-giovanni-balducci.html
23. See SC 286, 412.
24. See SC 206.
25. See SC 270–277.
26. See SC 181, 202, 236–238, 285.
27. See SC 285.
28. See SC 238–239.
29. Dehrmann, *Das "Orakel der Deisten,"* passim.
30. Jaffro, "Le choix d'Hercule," 25.
31. Lessing, *Laocoon*, 36, 37, 81.
32. Lessing, *Laocoon*, 37. See 38, 49–51.
33. Lessing, *Laocoon*, 80–81.
34. Harris, *Three Treatises*, 63–65. Smith, *Essays on Philosophical Subjects*, 208. Jaffro also explains how Lessing, Harris, and Smith elaborated on Shaftesbury's concept of beauty as unity. They pointed out that while the beauty of painting consists of the unity of parts that all exist simultaneously (synchronic, spatial unity), the beauty of poetry and music consists of unity of parts that exist in succession (diachronic, temporal unity). See Lessing, *Laocoon*, 80; Smith, "The Imitative Arts," 204–208; Harris, *Three Treatises*, 31–33.
35. Nablow, "Voltaire, 'Sesostris', and Prodicus' 'Choice of Hercules.'"
36. Hinnant, "Shaftesbury, Burke, and Wollstonecraft," 17–35.
37. Wittkower, *Palladio and English Palladianism*, 103, 179. See also Summerson, *Architecture in Britain*, 197–208; and Ayres, "Pope's *Epistle to Burlington*: The Vitruvian Analogies." Alexander Echlin and William Kelley dispute Shaftesbury's influence

on the New Palladian architecture movement, claiming that he could not have played that role ("A 'Shaftesburian Agenda?'").

38. See Cannon-Brooks, *The Painted Word*, 130; Mannings, "Reynolds, Garrick, and the Choice of Hercules."

39. Letter from John Adams to Abigail Adams, August 14, 1776.

40. Pestilli, "Ut Pictura Non Poesis."

41. Pestilli, "Ut Pictura Non Poesis," 135. It may be the case, however, that the two paintings were *not* by the same painter. Schleier argues that the second painting is a "Pseudo de Matteis," and that it was actually the work of Nicola Vaccarro (Schleier, "Tre dipinti mitologici di Nicola Vaccaro"). If Schleier is right, then the difference between the two paintings should be seen just as a vivid illustration of Shaftesbury's view of what makes for a successful history painting, rather than evidence of Shaftesbury's influence.

42. In addition to the large version of *The Choice of Hercules*, de Matteis completed two smaller versions, each with its own variations (SC 68–69). In the version currently in the Temple Newsome House in Leeds, Hercules's expression seems to me to be halfway between bemused and bored. In the version at Alte Pinakothek in Munich, Hercules is more consternated, both his face and body more intense and conflicted; for this reason, it seems to me that the Munich version conveys best the pivotal moment Shaftesbury wanted to capture. The Munich version also differs from (and, to my eye, is better than) the other two in that the distant spot Virtue is pointing to is a harsh mountaintop instead of a treed, grassy hill. The other difference is that in the Munich version, Pleasure shows a lot more skin, which Shaftesbury eventually came to think made her too attractive for his moral purposes.

## *Chapter 5: Writing*

1. I thought Shaftesbury made this story up. It sounded to me like something he'd make up. But no: he's describing a real person, one Franciscus Mercurius van Helmont the younger, who was a friend of Leibniz and whom Leibniz rose to defend. As Leibniz tells it, when Helmont was a prisoner of the Inquisition at Rome, he "took it into his head, in his solitude, to examine the function of the organs in pronouncing letters and thought he'd found how these characters are formed. I have known the same person unusually well, and I must do him the justice of saying that he was not as ignorant in the moral field as he seems here to be represented as being . . . Except for certain chimeras which remained with him from the impressions of his youth like a hereditary disease, he was an excellent man whose conversation was very instructive to all who could benefit from it. His works reveal only that part of him which was least praiseworthy" (Leibniz, *Philosophical Papers and Letters*, 631–632).

2. See also C 1.90. It's interesting that he classifies a limner, or face painter, as being of morally negligible status, akin to an anatomist rather than a history painter. It seems likely that Hume had in mind Shaftesbury's outlook, if not this very passage, when he said that his own work was more like that of an anatomist than that of a (history) painter (Hume, *A Treatise of Hume Nature*, 395 [3.3.3.6]; Hume, *Enquiry concerning Understanding*, 8 [1.8]). I'm not sure that Hume's comments about the painter and the anatomist are as in conflict with Shaftesbury as they might initially appear. Hume's point is that the work of an anatomist can help the work of a painter,

even if it's impossible to do both things at the same time. Shaftesbury acknowledges that true philosophers and moral painters can learn from other, more abstruse and abstract disciplines. He criticizes only those who stop at the abstruse and abstract, and never take the next step to developing a moral message (C 1.180). At least on the face of it, Hume's comments seem consistent with that.

3. The indispensable work on Shaftesbury and politeness is Klein, *Shaftesbury and the Culture of Politeness*.

4. Boyle, *Occasional Reflections upon Several Subjects*, 3 of unnumbered "Introductory Preface."

5. Boyle, *Occasional Reflections*, 1–2 of unnumbered "Introductory Preface."

6. Boyle, *Occasional Reflections*, 2 of unnumbered "Introductory Preface."

7. Boyle, *Occasional Reflections*, 18 of unnumbered "Introductory Preface." A hilarious parody of Boyle's reflections is Jonathan Swift's "A Meditation on a Broomstick."

8. Killegrew, *Mid-Night Thoughts*, 2 of unnumbered "To the Reader."

9. Hale, *Contemplations, Moral and Divine*, 1 of unnumbered "Preface."

10. Hale, *Contemplations, Moral and Divine*, 2 of unnumbered "Preface."

11. Culpeper, *Essayes or Moral Discourses on several Subjects*, 3.

12. The quotation is from Shaftesbury's instructions for the illustration (quoted in O'Connell, "Shaftesbury in Naples," 204–205).

13. Rivers, *Reason, Grace, and Sentiment*, 141

14. Boyle, *Occasional Reflections*, 2 of unnumbered "Introductory Preface."

15. Bayle, *Historical and Critical Dictionary*, 95–96.

16. PRO 30/24/46A/81.

17. For an entertaining and informative historical account of the idea of an opposition between honesty and outward displays of politeness, see Magill, *Sincerity*.

18. When discussing Shaftesbury's view of the naturalness of virtue, Mandeville writes, "[Shaftesbury] seems to require and expect Goodness in his Species, as we do a sweet Taste in Grapes and China Oranges, of which, if any of them are sour, we boldly pronounce that they are not come to that Perfect their Nature is capable of" (Mandeville, *The Fable of the Bees*, 323).

19. SC 198.

20. SC 198.

21. See earlier discussion in chapter 2, sections 1 and 6.

22. Frankfurt, *On Bullshit*.

23. Jaffro distinguishes "between a normative sense of 'being oneself' or 'remaining the same person,' and the metaphysical sense, that is, personal identity" (Jaffro, "Cyrus' Strategy," 158). I am discussing here what Jaffro calls the "normative sense."

24. SC 220; 247.

## *Conclusion*

1. Berkeley, *Alciphron*, 75.

2. Mandeville, *Fable of the Bees*, 331–332.

3. Mandeville, *Fable of the Bees*, 331.

4. For the alternative view that Shaftesbury was bedevilled by sexual feelings he abhorred, see Trumbach (*Sex and the Gender Revolution*, 441), Branch (*Rituals of*

*Spontaneity*, 264), Tierney-Hynes ("Shaftesbury's Soliloquy"), and Klein ("Cooper, Anthony Ashley, Third Earl of Shaftesbury").

5. V 141–2. See also C 2.76–77.
6. Astell, *Bart'lemy Fair*, 93–94.
7. Balguy, *A Letter to a Deist*, 36.
8. Balguy, *A Letter to a Deist*, 36. See also 8–10 and 13–14.
9. Balguy, *A Letter to a Deist*, 37.
10. Balguy, *A Letter to a Deist*, 37.
11. Astell, *Bart'lemy Fair*, 30.
12. Astell, *Bart'lemy Fair*, 31.

# BIBLIOGRAPHY

## Works by Shaftesbury

*Askemata*. Edited by Wolfram Benda, Christine Jackson-Holzberg, Patrick Müller, and Friedrich A. Uehlein, as part of the *Standard Edition* (II.6). Stuttgart-Bad Cannstatt: Frommann-Holzboog, 2011.

*Characteristicks of Men, Manners, Opinions, Times, with a Notion of the Historical Draught, or Tablature of the Judgment of Hercules and a Letter Concerning Design.* In three volumes. Indianapolis: Liberty Fund, 2001. The first number after the "C" represents the volume; the second number, the page.

*The Moralists, a Philosophical Rhapsody; The Sociable Enthusiast, a Philosophical Adventure*. Edited by Wolfram Benda and Gerd Hemmerich, as part of the *Standard Edition* (II.1). Stuttgart-Bad Cannstatt: Frommann-Holzboog, 1987.

Letters and other writings from the Shaftesbury Papers in the Public Record Office, the National Archive.

Shaftesbury, Anthony Ashley Cooper, the third Earl of. *The Life, Unpublished Letters, and Philosophical Regimen*. Edited by Benjamin Rand. London: Swan Sonnenschein, 1900.

*Second Characters*. Edited by Wolfram Benda, Wolfgang Lottes, Friedrich A. Uehlein, and Erwin Wolff, as part of the *Standard Edition* (I.5). Stuttgart-Bad Cannstatt: Frommann-Holzboog, 2001.

*An Inquiry Concerning Virtue, in Two Discourses*. London: A. Bell and S. Buckley, 1699.

Preface to *Select Sermons of Dr Whichcot. In Two Parts*. London: Awnsham and John Churchill, 1698.

## Works by Other Authors

Agliony, William. *Painting Illustrated in Three Diallogues*. London: John Gain, 1686.

Albee, Ernest. "Review of Shaftesbury's *Second Characters, or the Language of Forms*." *Philosophical Review* 25 (1916): 182–187.

Alderman, William E. "Bibliographical Evidence of the Vogue of Shaftesbury in the Eighteenth Century." *Transactions of the Wisconsin Academy of Sciences, Arts and Letters* 21 (1924): 57–70.

Allen, Stuart. *Wordsworth and the Passions of Critical Poetics*. London: Palgrave Macmillan, 2010.

Amir, Lydia. *Humor and the Good Life in Modern Philosophy: Shaftesbury, Hamann, Kierkegaard*. Albany: State University of New York Press, 2015.

Annas, Julia. *The Morality of Happiness*. Oxford: Oxford University Press, 1993.

Annas, Julia. "Virtue Ethics and the Charge of Egoism." In *Morality and Self-Interest*, edited by Paul Bloomfield, 205–221. Oxford: Oxford University Press, 2008.

Armitage, David. "John Locke, Carolina, and the Two Treatises of Government." *Political Theory* 32 (2004): 602–627.
Arreguie, Jorge V. and Pablo Arnau. "Shaftesbury: Father or Critic of Modern Aesthetics?" *British Journal of Aesthetics* 34, no. 4 (1994): 350–362.
Astell, Mary. *Bart'lemy Fair: or, an Enquiry after Wit; in which due Respect is had to a Letter concerning Enthusiasm, to my Lord ***. London: R. Wilkin, 1709.
Axelsson, Karl. *Political Aesthetics: Addison and Shaftesbury on Taste, Morals and Society*. London: Bloomsbury Academic, 2019.
Ayres, Philip. "Pope's *Epistle to Burlington*: The Vitruvian Analogies." *Studies in English Literature, 1500–1900* 30, no. 3 (1990): 429–444.
Balguy, John. *A Letter to a Deist*. London: John Pemberton, 1730.
Bayle, Pierre. *Historical and Critical Dictionary: Selections*. Translated by Richard H. Popkin. Cambridge, MA: Hackett, 1697/1991.
Beiser, Frederick. *Schiller as Philosopher: A Re-Examination*. Oxford: Clarendon Press, 2005.
Bentley, Richard. *A Confutation of Atheism from the Origin and Frame of the World*. London: H. Mortlock, 1693.
Berkeley, George. *Alciphron in Focus*. Edited by David Berman. London and New York: Routledge, 1752/1993.
Berman, David. "Deism, Immortality, and the Art of Theological Lying." In *Deism, Masonry, and the Enlightenment: Essays Honoring Alfred Owen Aldridge*, edited by J.A.L. Lemay, 61–78. London: Associated University Press, 1987.
Berman, David. "Disclaimers as Offence Mechanisms in Charles Blount and John Toland." In *Atheism from the Reformation to the Enlightenment*, edited by Michael Hunter and David Wooten, 255–272. Oxford: Clarendon Press, 1992.
Bernasconi, Robert. "Locke's Almost Random Talk of Man: The Double Use of Words in the Natural Law Justification of Slavery." *Perspektiven der Philosophie* 18 (1992): 293–318.
Bernasconi, Robert and Anika Maaza Mann. "The Contradictions of Racism: Locke, Slavery and the Two Treatises." In *Race and Modern Philosophy*, edited by Andrew Vails, 89–107. Ithaca, NY: Cornell University Press, 2005.
Bernstein, John Andrew. "Shaftesbury's Identification of the Good with the Beautiful." *Eighteenth Century Studies* 10 (1977): 304–325.
Bloom, Paul. *Against Empathy: The Case for Rational Compassion*. New York: Ecco Press, 2016.
Boeker, Ruth. "Shaftesbury on Persons, Personal Identity, and Character Development." *Philosophy Compass* 13, no. 1 (2018): e12471.
Boeker, Ruth. "Shaftesbury on Liberty and Self-Mastery." *International Journal of Philosophical Studies* 27, no. 5 (2019): 731–752.
Boyer, Abel. *The English Theophrastus: Or, the Manners of the Age*. London, 1702.
Boyer, Ernest J. "Schleiermacher, Shaftesbury, and the German Enlightenment." *Harvard Theological Review* 96, no. 2 (2003): 181–204.
Boyle, Robert. *Occasional Reflections upon Several Subjects*. London: Henry Herringman, 1665.
Branch, Lori. *Rituals of Spontaneity: Sentiment and Secularism from Free Prayer to Wordsworth*. Waco, TX: Baylor University Press, 2006.

Brewer, Holly. "Slavery, Sovereignty, and 'Inheritable Blood': Reconsidering John Locke and the Origins of American Slavery." *American Historical Review* 122, no. 4 (2017): 1038–1078.
Brown, John. *Essays on the Characteristics*. London: C. Davis, 1751.
Budd, Malcolm. "The Aesthetics of Nature." *Proceedings of the Aristotelian Society* 100 (2000): 137–157.
Burnet, Thomas. *The Sacred Theory of the Earth*. London: T. Osborn et al., 1759.
Butler, Joseph. *Fifteen Sermons Preached at the Rolls Chapel and Other Writings on Ethics*. Edited by David McNaughton. Oxford: Oxford University Press, 2017.
Cannon-Brookes, Peter. *The Painted Word: British History Painting 1750–1830*. Woodbridge: Boydell Press, 1991.
Carey, Daniel. *Locke, Shaftesbury and Hutcheson: Contesting Diversity in the Enlightenment and Beyond*. Cambridge: Cambridge University Press, 2006.
Carlson, Allen. *Aesthetics and the Environment*. London and New York: Routledge, 2000.
Carter, Allan L. "Schiller and Shaftesbury." *International Journal of Ethics* 31, no. 2 (1921): 203–228.
Cassirer, Ernest. "Schiller und Shaftesbury." *Publications of the English Goethe Society, New Series* 11 (1935): 35–59.
Chalmers, Alexander. *The General Biographical Dictionary*, vol. 7. London: J. Nichols and Son, 1812–1817.
Cohen, Alix. *Kant and the Human Sciences: Biology, Anthropology and History*. London: Palgrave Macmillan, 2009.
Collier, Jeremy. *A Short View of the Immorality and Profaneness of the English Stage*. London: S. Keble and R. Sare, 1698.
Collins, Anthony. *A Discourse of Free-Thinking*. London, 1713.
Corbeau-Parson, Caroline. *Prometheus in the Nineteenth Century: From Myth to Symbol*. London and New York: Routledge, 2020.
Crisafulli, Alessandro. "Montesquieu's Story of the Troglodytes: Its Background, Meaning and Significance." *PMLA* 49 (1937): 773–777.
Crisafulli, Alessandro. "Parallels to Ideas in the *Lettres Persanes*." *PMLA* 54 (1943): 372–392.
Crisp, Roger. *Sacrifice Regained: Morality and Self-Interest in British Moral Philosophy from Hobbes to Bentham*. Oxford: Oxford University Press, 2019.
Cudworth, Ralph. *The True Intellectual System of the Universe*. London: Richard Royston, 1678.
Culpeper, Thomas. *Essayes or Moral Discourses on several Subjects*. London: T. Longman, 1671.
Darwall, Stephen. *The British Moralists and the Internal 'Ought'*. Cambridge: Cambridge University Press, 1995.
De Quincy, Thomas. *Biographical Essays*. Boston: Ticknor, Reed, and Fields, 1850.
Dehrmann, Mark-Georg. *Das "Orakel der Deisten": Shaftesbury und die Deutsche Aufklärung*. Gottingen: Wallstein Verlag, 2009.
Dehrmann, Mark-Georg. "Transition: 'Pedagogy of the Eye' in Shaftesbury's *Second Characters*." In *New Ages, New Opinions: Shaftesbury in His World and Today*, edited by Patrick Müller, 45–60. Frankfurt: Peter Lang, 2014.

Den Uyl, Douglas. "Shaftesbury and the Problem of Modern Virtue." *Social Philosophy and Policy* 15 (1998): 275–316.
Derham, William. *Physico-Theology: or A Demonstration of the Being and Attributes of God, from his Works of Creation.* London: W. Innys, 1713.
Driver, Julia. "The History of Utilitarianism." *Stanford Encyclopedia of Philosophy*, edited by Edward N. Zalta. Winter 2014 edition. *https://plato.stanford.edu/entries/utilitarianism-history/*.
Echlin, Alexander and William Kelley. "A 'Shaftesburian Agenda?' Lord Burlington, Lord Shaftesbury and the Intellectual Origins of English Palladianism." *Architectural History* 59 (2016): 221–252.
Elson, Charles. *Wieland and Shaftesbury.* New York: Columbia University Press, 1913.
Emerson, Ralph Waldo. "Nature." In *Ralph Waldo Emerson: The Major Prose.* Cambridge, MA and London: Harvard University Press, 2015.
Epictetus. *The Discourses of Epictetus.* Translation by Robin Hard, with an introduction by Christopher Gill. London: Everyman, 1995.
Farr, James. "Locke, Natural Law, and New World Slavery." *Political Theory* 36, no. 4 (2008): 495–522.
Filonowicz, Joseph Duke. "Ethical Sentimentalism Revisited." *History of Philosophy Quarterly* 6, no. 2 (1989): 189–206.
Filonowicz, Joseph Duke. *Fellow-Feeling and the Moral Life.* Cambridge: Cambridge University Press, 2008.
Fleming, Suzannah. "The 'Convenience of Husbandry' in the Adaptation of the 3rd Earl of Shaftesbury's Garden and Park in Dorset." *Garden History* 43, no. 1 (2015): 3–32.
Fowler, Thomas. *Shaftesbury and Hutcheson.* London: Sampsom Low, Marston, Searle, & Rivington, 1882.
Frankfurt, Harry G. *On Bullshit.* Princeton, NJ: Princeton University Press, 2005.
Garrett, Aaron. "Seventeenth-Century Moral Philosophy: Self-Help, Self-Knowledge, and the Devil's Mountain." In *The Oxford Handbook of the History of Ethics*, edited by Roger Crisp, 229–279. Oxford: Oxford University Press, 2015.
Gatti, Andrea. "The Aesthetic Mind: Stoic Influences on Shaftesbury's Theory of Beauty." In *New Ages, New Opinions: Shaftesbury in His World and Today*, edited by Patrick Müller, 61–76. Frankfurt: Peter Lang, 2014.
Gill, Michael B. "The Religious Rationalism of Benjamin Whichcote." *Journal of the History of Philosophy* 37, no. 2 (1999): 271–300.
Gill, Michael B. *The British Moralists on Human Nature and the Birth of Secular Ethics.* Cambridge: Cambridge University Press, 2006.
Gill, Michael B. *Humean Moral Pluralism.* Oxford: Oxford University Press, 2014.
Gill, Michael B. "Shaftesbury on Politeness, Honesty, and the Reason to Be Moral." In *New Ages, New Opinions: Shaftesbury in His World and Today*, edited by Patrick Müller, 167–184. Frankfurt: Peter Lang, 2014.
Gill, Michael B. "Love of Humanity in Shaftesbury's *Moralists*." *British Journal for the History of Philosophy* 24 (2016): 1117–1135.
Gill, Michael B. "Shaftesbury on Life as a Work of Art." *British Journal for the History of Philosophy* 26 (2018): 1110–1131.
Gill, Michael B. "Hume on Moral Motivation." In *Humean Moral Philosophy and Contemporary Psychology*, edited by Philip Reed and Rico Vitz, 263–286. London and New York: Routledge, 2018.

Gill, Michael B. "Shaftesbury on Selfishness and Partisanship." *Social Philosophy and Policy* 37, no. 1 (2020): 55–79.

Gill, Michael B. "Shaftesbury's Claim that Beauty and Good Are One and the Same." *Journal of the History of Philosophy* 59 (2021): 69–92.

Gill, Michael B. "Lord Shaftesbury [Anthony Ashley Cooper, 3rd Earl of Shaftesbury]." *Stanford Encyclopedia of Philosophy*, edited by Edward N. Zalta. Fall 2021 edition. https://plato.stanford.edu/entries/shaftesbury/.

Glauser, Richard. "Aesthetic Experience in Shaftesbury." *The Aristotelian Society* suppl. vol. 76 (2002): 25–54.

Glausser, Wayne. "Three Approaches to Locke and the Slave Trade." *Journal of the History of Ideas* 51, no. 2 (1990): 199–216.

Gonthier, Ursula Haskins. "Persians, Politics and Politeness: Montesquieu Reads Shaftesbury." *Nottingham French Studies* 48, no. 2 (2009): 8–19.

Gould, Stephen Jay. *The Panda's Thumb: More Reflections in Natural History*. London: Penguin Books, 1980.

Gould, Stephen Jay and Richard Charles Lewontin. "The Spandrels of San Marco and the Panglossian Paradigm: A Critique of the Adaptationist Programme." *Proceedings of the Royal Society of London* Series B, vol. 205, no. 1161 (1979): 581–598.

Greene, Joshua. *Moral Tribes: Emotion, Reason, and the Gap Between Us and Them*. New York: Penguin Books, 2013.

Grote, Simon. "Shaftesbury's Egoistic Hedonism." *Aufklärung* 22 (2010): 135–149.

Haidt, J. and J. Graham. "When Morality Opposes Justice: Conservatives Have Moral Intuitions that Liberals May Not Recognize." *Social Justice Research* 20, no. 1 (2007): 98–116.

Hale, Matthew. *Contemplations, Moral and Divine*. London: William Shrowsbury, 1679.

Hamlin, J. Kiley, Neha Mahajan, Zoe Liberman, and Karen Wynn. "Not Like Me = Bad: Infants Prefer Those Who Harm Dissimilar Others." *Psychological Science* 24 (2013): 589–594.

Harris, James. *Three Treatises*. London: H. Woodfall, 1744.

Harris, James A. *Hume: An Intellectual Biography*. Cambridge: Cambridge University Press, 2015.

Hinnant, Charles. "Shaftesbury, Burke, and Wollstonecraft: Permutations on the Sublime and the Beautiful." *The Eighteenth Century* 46, no. 1 (2005): 17–35.

Hinshelwood, Brad. "The Carolina Context of Locke's Theory of Slavery." *Political Theory* 41, no. 4 (2013): 562–590.

Howell, Willliam. *The Spirit of Prophecy*. London, 1679.

Hume, David. *A Treatise of Human Nature: A Critical Edition*. Edited by David Fate Norton and Mary J. Norton. Oxford: Clarendon Press, 1739–40/2007.

Hume, David. *An Enquiry Concerning Human Understanding*. Edited by Tom L. Beauchamp. Oxford: Clarendon Press, 1748/2000.

Hume, David. *An Enquiry Concerning the Principles of Morals*. Edited by Tom L. Beauchamp. Oxford: Clarendon Press, 1751/1998.

Hume, David. "Of the Standard of Taste." in *Essays Moral, Political, and Literary*, edited by E. Miller, 226–249. Indianapolis: Liberty Fund, 1757/1987.

Hume, David. *Dialogues concerning Natural Religion*. Edited by Dorothy Coleman. Cambridge: Cambridge University Press, 1779/2007.

Hutcheson, Francis. *An Inquiry into the Original of Our Ideas of Beauty and Virtue.* Edited by Wolfgang Leidhold. Indianapolis: Liberty Fund, 1726/2004.

Hutcheson, Francis. *An Essay on the Nature and Conduct of the Passions and Affections, with Illustrations on the Moral Sense.* Edited by Aaron Garrett. Indianapolis: Liberty Fund, 1728/2002.

Irwin, Terence. *The Development of Ethics: Volume 2: From Suarez to Rousseau.* Oxford: Oxford University Press, 2008.

Jaffro, Laurent. "Shaftesbury on the 'Natural Secretion' and Philosophical Personae." *Intellectual History Review* 18 (2008): 349–359.

Jaffro, Laurent. "Cyrus' Strategy: Shaftesbury on Human Frailty and the Will." In *New Ages, New Opinions: Shaftesbury in His World and Today*, edited by Patrick Müller, 153–166. Frankfurt: Peter Lang, 2014.

Jaffro, Laurent. "Le choix d'Hercule: le problème artistique de l'expression du moral dans la tradition shaftesburienne." *DoisPontos* 11, no. 1 (2014): 39–65.

Jaffro, Laurent. "Psychological and Political Balances: The Third Earl of Shaftesbury's Reading of James Harrington." In *Shaping Enlightenment Politics: The Social and Political Impact of the First and Third Earls of Shaftesbury*, edited by Patrick Müller, 149–162. Frankfurt: Peter Lang, 2018.

Jaffro, Laurent and Christian Maurer. "Pathologia, A Theory of the Passions." *History of European Ideas* 39, no. 2 (2013): 207–220.

Jaspers, Karl. *Nietzsche: An Introduction to the Understanding of His Philosophical Activity.* Translated by C. Wallraff and F. Schmitz. South Bend, IN: Regnery and Gateway, 1965.

Jourdain, M. "Shaftesbury, the Boldest of the English Philosophers." *Open Court* 28 (1914): 367–375.

Kant, Immanuel. *Groundwork of the Metaphysics of Morals.* Translated by Mary Gregor and Jens Timmermann. Cambridge: Cambridge University Press, 1785/2012.

Kant, Immanuel. *The Metaphysics of Morals.* Translated by Mary Gregor and edited by Lara Denis. Cambridge: Cambridge University Press, 2018.

Killegrew, William. *Mid-Night Thoughts.* London: Benj. Clark, 1682.

Kinnunen, Aarne. "Luonnonestetiikka." In *Ymparistoesteiikka*, edited by Aarne Kinnunen and Yrjo Sepanmaa. Helsinkie: Gaudeamus, 1981.

Kistler, Mark O. "The Sources of the Goethe-Tobler Fragment 'Die Natur.'" *Monatsheft* 46, no. 7 (December 1954): 383–389.

Klein, Lawrence E. *Shaftesbury and the Culture of Politeness: Moral Discourse and Cultural Politics in Early Eighteenth-Century England.* Cambridge: Cambridge University Press, 1994.

Klein, Lawrence E. "Cooper, Anthony Ashley, Third Earl of Shaftesbury." *Oxford Dictionary of National Biography*, 2004. https://www.oxforddnb.com/view/10.1093/ref:odnb/9780198614128.001.0001/odnb-9780198614128-e-6209. Accessed February 19, 2022.

Leatherbarrow, D. "Character, Geometry, and Perspective: The Third Earl of Shaftesbury's Principles of Garden Design." *Journal of Garden History* 4 (1984): 332–358.

Legros, Rene P. "Diderot et Shaftesbury." *Modern Language Review* 19, no. 2 (1924): 188–194.

Leibniz, G. W. *Philosophical Papers and Letters: A Selection*. Edited by L. E. Loemker and Richard Sorabji. Dordrecht: Springer Netherlands, 1975.

Leiter, Brian. "Fatalism and Self-Creation in Nietzsche." In *Willing and Nothingness: Schopenhauer as Nietzsche's Educator*, edited by Christopher Janaway, 217–257. Oxford: Clarendon Press, 1998.

Leopold, Aldo. *Sand County Almanac, with Essays on Conservation*. Oxford and New York: Oxford University Press, 1949/2001.

Lepper, Mark, David Greene, and Richard E. Nisbett. "Undermining Children's Intrinsic Interest with Extrinsic Reward: A Test of the 'Overjustification' Hypothesis." *Journal of Personality and Social Psychology* 28 (1973): 129–137.

Lessing, Gotthold Ephraim. *Emilia Galotti*. Translated by Benjamin Thompson. London: Vernor and Hood, 1800.

Lessing, Gotthold Ephraim. *Laocoon*. In *Classic and Romantic German Aesthetics*, edited by J. M. Bernstein, translated by W. A. Steel, 25–130. Cambridge: Cambridge University Press, 2003.

Levy-Eichel, Mordechai. "'The Moral Arithmetic': Morality in the Age of Mathematics." *Intellectual History Review* 2020: 1–16.

Lewis, Douglas. "Locke and the Problem of Slavery." *Teaching Philosophy* 26 (2003): 261–268.

Liu, Yu. "The Possibility of a Different Theodicy: The Chinese 'Scharawadgi' and Shaftesbury's Aesthetics and Ethics." *Southern Journal of Philosophy* 42 (2004): 213–236.

Liu, Yu. *Seeds of a Different Eden*. New York: Columbia University Press, 2008.

Locke, John. *The Correspondence of John Locke*, vol. 5. Edited by E. S. de Beer. Oxford: Clarendon Press, 1979.

Locke, John. *Two Treatise of Government and A Letter concerning Toleration*. Edited by Ian Shapiro. Oxford: Oxford University Press, 1690/2003.

Locke, John. *The Reasonableness of Christianity: As Delivered in the Scriptures*. Edited by John C. Higgins-Biddle. Oxford: Clarendon Press, 1695/2000.

Magill, R. Jay. *Sincerity*. New York and London: Norton, 2012.

Mandeville, Bernard. *The Fable of the Bees: Or Private Vices, Publick Benefits*. Edited by F. B. Kaye. Indianapolis: Liberty Fund, 1732/1988.

Mannings, David. "Reynolds, Garrick, and the Choice of Hercules." *Eighteenth-Century Studies* 17 (Spring 1984): 259–283.

Martineau, James. *Types of Ethical Theory, volume 2*, 2nd edition. Oxford and New York: Clarendon Press and Macmillan and Company, 1886.

May, Joshua. "Does Disgust Influence Moral Judgment?" *Australasian Journal of Philosophy* 92, no. 1 (2014): 125–141.

McAteer, John. "Silencing Theodicy with Enthusiasm: Aesthetic Experience as a Response to the Problem of Evil in Shaftesbury, Annie Dillard, and the Book of Job." *Heythrop Journal* 57 (2016): 788–795.

Moore, C. A. "Shaftesbury and the Ethical Poets in England, 1700–1760." *PMLA* 31 (2): 1916: 264–325.

More, Henry. *An Antidote against Atheisme, Or an Appeal to the Natural Faculties of the Minde of Man, Whether There Be Not a God*. London: Roger Daniel, 1653.

More, Henry. *Enthusiasmus Triumphatus, or, A Discourse of the Nature, Causes, Kinds, and Cure, of Enthusiasme*. London: J. Flesher, 1656.

Mortensen, Preben. "Shaftesbury and the Morality of Art Appreciation." *Journal of the History of Ideas* 55 (1994): 631–650.
Muir, John. *Our National Parks.* Boston: Houghton Mifflin, 1904.
Muir, John. "An Unpublished Journal of John Muir." *North American Review* 245, no. 1 (1938): 24–51.
Muir, John. "A Near View of the High Sierra." In *The Mountains of California*. New York: Century Company, 1922, 48–73.
Müller, Patrick. "'Dwell with honesty & beauty & order': The Paradox of Theodicy in Shaftesbury's Thought." *Aufklärung* 22 (2010): 201–231.
Müller, Patrick. "Shaftesbury on the Psychoanalyst's Couch: A Historicist Perspective on Gender and (Homo)Sexuality in Characteristicks and the Earl's Private Writings." *Swift Studies* 25 (2010): 56–81.
Müller, Patrick. "'An Equal Commonwealth': Lord Ashley and the Republic Project of the Late 1690s." In *Shaping Enlightenment Politics: The Social and Political Impact of the First and Third Earls of Shaftesbury*, edited by Patrick Müller, 115–134. Frankfurt: Peter Lang, 2018.
Myers, Katherine. "Shaftesbury, Pope, and Original Sacred Nature." *Garden History* 39 (2010): 3–19.
Myers, Katherine. "'Wise Substitute of Providence!' The 3rd Earl of Shaftesbury's Stoic Philosophy of Nature in Estate Gardening." *Garden History* 45, no. 2 (2017): 193–212.
Nablow, Ralph Arthur. "Voltaire, 'Sesostris', and Prodicus' 'Choice of Hercules.'" *Romance Notes* 22, no. 1 (1981): 58–63.
Nehamas, Alexander. *Nietzsche: Life as Literature.* Cambridge, MA: Harvard University Press, 1985.
Newton, Isaac. *Opticks: Or, A Treatise of the Reflections, Refractions, Inflexions, and Colours of Light. The Second Edition, with Additions.* London: W. and J. Innys, 1713.
Nicolson, Marjorie Hope. *Mountain Gloom and Mountain Glory.* Seattle and London: University of Washington Press, 1959.
Nietzsche, Friedrich. *Human, All-Too-Human: A Book for Free Spirits.* Translated by R. J. Hollingdale. Cambridge: Cambridge University Press, 1878–79/1996.
Nietzsche, Friedrich. *The Gay Science.* Translated by Josefine Nauckhoff. Cambridge: Cambridge University Press, 1882 and 1887/2001.
Nietzsche, Friedrich. *Beyond Good and Evil.* Translated by Judith Norman. Cambridge: Cambridge University Press, 1886/2001.
O'Connell, Sheila. "Shaftesbury in Naples: 1711–1713." *The Volume of the Walpole Society* 54 (1988): 149–219.
Otteson, James R. "Shaftesbury's Evolutionary Morality and Its Influence on Adam Smith." *Adam Smith Review* 4 (2008): 106–131.
Paknadel, Felix. "Shaftesbury's Illustrations of *Characteristics*." *Journal of the Warburg and Courtauld Institutes* 37 (1974): 290–312.
Parsons, Glen and Allen Carlson. *Functional Beauty.* Oxford: Clarendon Press. 2008.
Peach, B. A. "Shaftesbury's Moral Arithmeticks." *The Personalist* 39 (1958): 19–27.
Pestilli, Livio. "Ut Pictura Non Poesis: Lord Shaftesbury's 'Ridiculous Anticipation of Metamorphis' and the Two Versions of 'Diana and Actaeon' by Paolo de Matteis." *Artibus et Historiae* 14, no. 27 (1993): 131–139.

Pfeffer, Michelle. "Paganism, Natural Reason, and Immortality: Charles Blount and John Toland's Histories of the Soul." *Intellectual History Review* 31 (2020): 563–583.

Plato. *Symposium*. Translated by Alexander Nehamas and Paul Woodruff. In *Collected Works*, edited by John M. Cooper, 457–505. Indianapolis: Hackett, 1997.

Prince, Michael. *Philosophical Dialogue in the British Enlightenment: Theology, Aesthetics and the Novel*. Cambridge: Cambridge University Press, 1996.

Prinz, Jesse. *The Emotional Construction of Morals*. Oxford: Oxford University Press, 2007.

Prinz, Jesse. "Against Empathy." *Southern Journal of Philosophy* 49, no. 1 (2011): 214–233.

Ray, John. *The Wisdom of God Manifested in the Works of the Creation*. London: Samuel Smith, 1691.

Richardson, Jr., Robert D. "Liberal Platonism and Transcendentalism: Shaftesbury, Schleiermacher, Emerson." *Symbiosis: A Journal of Anglo-American Literary Relations* 1 (1997): 1–20.

Ridge, Michael. "Reasons for Action: Agent-Neutral vs. Agent-Relative." *Stanford Encyclopedia of Philosophy*. edited by Edward N. Zalta. Fall 2017 edition. https://plato.stanford.edu/entries/reasons-agent/.

Rind, Miles. "The Concept of Disinterestedness in Eighteenth-Century British Aesthetics." *Journal of the History of Philosophy* 40 (2002): 67–87.

Rivers, Isabel. *Reason, Grace, and Sentiment: A Study of the Language of Religion and Ethics in England, 1660–1780—Shaftesbury to Hume*. Cambridge: Cambridge University Press, 2000.

Robb, Bonnie Arden. "The Making of Denis Diderot: Translation as Apprenticeship." *Diderot Studies* 24 (1991): 137–154.

Robertson, J. M. "Introduction." In *Characteristics of Men, Manners, Opinions, Times*. Edited by J. M. Robertson. Indianapolis: Bobbs-Merrill, 1964.

Rolston, Holmes III. *Environmental Ethics*. Philadelphia: Temple University Press, 1988.

Rorty, Richard. *Contingency, Irony, and Solidarity*. Cambridge: Cambridge University Press, 1989.

Rudd, M., K. D. Vohs, and J. Aaker. "Awe Expands People's Perception of Time, Alters Decision Making, and Enhances Well-being." *Psychological Science* 23, no. 10 (2012): 1130–1136.

Ryan, Robert M. "Keats's 'Hymn to Pan': A Debt to Shaftesbury?" *Keats-Shelley Journal* 26 (1977): 31–34.

Salteren, George. *A Treatise Against Images and Pictures in Churches*. London: William Lee, 1641.

Santayana, George. *The Sense of Beauty: Being an Outline of Aesthetic Theory*. New York: Charles Scribner's Sons, 1896.

Schleier, Erich. "Tre dipinti mitologici di Nicola Vaccaro." *Antichità Viva* 34, no. 3 (1995): 23–26.

Schneewind, J. B. *The Invention of Autonomy*. Cambridge: Cambridge University Press, 1998.

Sellars, John. "Shaftesbury, Stoicism, and Philosophy as a Way of Life." *Sophia* 55 (2016): 395–408.

Sidgwick, Henry. *Outlines of the History of Ethics*. London: Macmillan, 1902.

Slote, Michael. *The Ethics of Care and Empathy*. New York: Routledge, 2007.
Smith, Adam. *Essays on Philosophical Subjects*. London: Cadell and Davis, 1795.
Smith, Adam. *The Theory of Moral Sentiments*. Edited by D. D. Raphael and A. L. Macfie. Oxford: Oxford University Press, 1976.
Smith, Adam. *Lectures on Rhetoric and Belles Letters*. Edited by J. C. Bryce. Indianapolis: Liberty Fund, 1985.
Solomon, Harry M. "Shaftesbury's *Characteristics* and the Conclusion of 'Ode on a Grecian Urn'." *Keats-Shelley Journal* 24 (1975): 89–101.
Spurr, John. "'Rational Religion' in Restoration England." *Journal of the History of Ideas* 49, no. 4 (1988): 563–585.
Stolnitz, Jerome. "On the Significance of Lord Shaftesbury in Modern Aesthetic Theory." *Philosophical Quarterly* 43 (1961): 97–113.
Stolnitz, Jerome. "'Beauty': Some Stages in the History of an Idea." *Journal of the History of Ideas* 22 (1961): 185–204.
Stolnitz, Jerome. "On the Origins of 'Aesthetic Disinterestedness.'" *Journal of Aesthetics and Art Criticism* 20 (1961): 131–143.
Stolnitz, Jerome. "Locke and the Category of Value in Eighteenth-Century British Aesthetic Theory." *Philosophy* 39 (1963): 40–51.
Strohminger, Nina and Nichols, Shaun. "The Essential Moral Self." *Cognition* 131, no. 1 (2014): 159–171.
Stuart-Buttle, Tim. *From Moral Theology to Moral Philosophy: Cicero and Visions of Humanity from Locke to Hume*. Oxford: Oxford University Press, 2019.
Summerson, John. *Architecture in Britain, 1530 to 1830*. Melbourne and London: Penguin Books, 1953.
Sweetman, J. E. "Shaftesbury's Last Commission." *Journal of the Warburg and Courtauld Institute* 19 (1956): 110–116.
Swift, Jonathan. "A Meditation on a Broomstick according to the Stile and Manner of the Honourable Robert Boyle's Meditations." *A Complete Key to the Tale of a Tub*. London: E. Curl, 1713.
Thiel, Udo. *The Early Modern Subject: Self-Consciousness and Personal Identity from Descartes to Hume*. Oxford: Oxford University Press, 2011.
Thoreau, Henry David. *I To Myself: An Annotated Selection from the Journal of Henry D. Thoreau*. Edited by Jeffrey S. Cramer. New Haven, CT: Yale University Press, 2012.
Tierney-Hynes, Rebecca. "Shaftesbury's Soliloquy: Authorship and the Psychology of Romance." *Eighteenth Century Studies* 38, no. 4 (2005): 605–621.
Tiffany, Esther A. "Shaftesbury as Stoic." *PMLA* 38, no. 3 (1923): 642–685.
Tindal, Matthew. *Christianity as Old as the Creation: or the Gospel, a Republication of the Religion of Nature*. London, 1730.
Toland, John. *Christianity not Mysterious*. London: Sam Buckley, 1696.
Toland, John. *Letters from the Right Honourable the Late Earl of Shaftesbury to Robert Molesworth*. London: W. Wilkins, 1721.
Townsend, Dabney. "Shaftesbury's Aesthetic Theory." *Journal of Aesthetics and Art Criticism* 41 (1982): 205–213.
Townsend, Dabney. "Lockean Aesthetics." *Journal of Aesthetics and Art Criticism* 49, no. 4 (1991): 349–361.

Trianosky, Gregory W. "On the Obligation to Be Virtuous: Shaftesbury and the Question, Why Be Moral?" *Journal of the History of Philosophy* 16 (1978): 289–300.
Trumbach, Randolph. *Sex and the Gender Revolution, volume 1: Heterosexuality and the Third Gender in Enlightenment London*. Chicago: University of Chicago Press, 1998.
Tuveson, Ernest. "The Origins of the 'Moral Sense.'" *Huntington Library Quarterly* 11 (1948): 241–259.
Tuveson, Ernest. *The Imagination as a Means of Grace: Locke and the Aesthetics of Romanticism*. Berkeley: University of California Press, 1960.
Uehlein, Friedrich A. "Whichcote, Shaftesbury and Locke: Shaftesbury's Critique of Locke's Epistemology and Moral Philosophy." *British Journal for the History of Philosophy* 25, no. 5 (2017): 1031–1048.
Uzgalis, William. "'The Same Tyrannical Principle': Locke's Legacy on Slavery." In *Subjugations and Bondage: Critical Essays on Slavery and Social Philosophy*, edited by Tommy L. Lott, 49–79. Lanham, MD: Rowman & Littlefield, 1998.
Varsamaopoulou, Evy. "'Et in Arcadia Ego': Philosophical Aesthetics and the Origins of European Romanticism in Shaftesbury's *Characteristics* and Rousseau's *Reveries*." In *British Romanticism in European Perspective*, edited by Steve Clark and Tristanne Connolly, 45–68. New York: Palgrave Macmillan, 2015.
Voitle, Robert B. *The Third Earl of Shaftesbury, 1671–1713*. Baton Rouge and London: Louisiana State University Press, 1984.
Von Herder, Johann Gottfried. *Sammtliche Werke*, edited by Berhard Suphan. Berlin: Weidman, 1877–1913.
Walpole, Horatio. *A Catalogue of the Royal and Noble Authors of England, Scotland, and Ireland*, vol. 4. London: John Scott, 1806.
Walzel, Oskar. *Das Prometheussymbol von Shaftesbury zu Goethe*. München: M. Hueber Verlag, 1932.
Weiser, C. F. *Shaftesbury und das Deutsche Geistesleben*. Leipzig and Berlin: Druck und Verlag von B. G. Teubner, 1916.
Welchman, Jennifer. "Locke on Slavery and Inalienable Rights." *Canadian Journal of Philosophy* 25 (1995): 67–81.
Whichcote, Benjamin. *The Works*. 4 volumes. London: J. Chalmers, 1751.
Whichcote, Benjamin. *Eight Letters of Dr. Anthony Tuckney, and Dr. Benjamin Whichcote*. London: J. Payne, 1753.
White, David. "The Metaphysics of Disinterestedness: Shaftesbury and Kant." *Journal of Aesthetics and Art Criticism* 32, no. 2 (1973): 239–248.
Wiley, Basil. *The Eighteenth Century Background*. New York: Columbia University Press, 1940.
Wind, Edgar. "Shaftesbury as a Patron of Art." *Journal of the Warburg and Courtauld Institute* 2, no. 2 (1938): 185–188.
Winkler, Kenneth P. "'All is Revolution in Us': Personal Identity in Shaftesbury and Hume." *Hume Studies* 26 (2000): 3–40.
Wittkower, Rudolf. *Palladio and English Palladianism*. London: Thames and Hudson, 1974.
Xenophon. *The Shorter Socratic Writings*. Edited by Robert C. Bartlett. Ithaca, NY: Cornell University Press, 1996.

# INDEX

Abbt, Thomas, 160
Adams, John, 161
Addison, Joseph, 12
*Adept Ladys, The* (Shaftesbury), 179
aesthetics, 11–12, 37, 70, 160, 213n20.
    *See also* art; artistic beauty; beauty
affect, 37–38, 49, 57, 64, 68–69, 93, 132
afterlife, 26, 77
Agliony, William, 144
agriculture, 7, 21–22, 52
Akenside, Mark, 12
Albee, Ernest, 97
Allen, Stuart, 193n42
Amir, Lydia, 193n48, 205n46
Annas, Julia, 210n139, 213n30
Anne, Queen, 7
architecture, 20, 39, 49–50, 64, 123, 160
Aristotle, 65, 103
Armitage, David, 191n6
Arregui, Jorge, 212n20
art: appreciation of, 1, 119, 124, 129; criticism, 116, 142, 144–45; decoy reading of, 135–37, 215n56; instrumentalist interpretation, 124–29, 135–37, 140–42, 144, 167, 212n20; and morals, 118, 144, 155–56, 158, 161–62, 167, 197n57, 216n3; non-instrumentalist interpretation, 129–42, 167–68, 212n20; and truth, 89; and unity, 146–47, 151, 156; value of, 89, 129, 140, 160, 212n20. *See also* aesthetics; beauty; fine art; painting
art academies, 145
artistic beauty, 116–17, 119, 127, 138, 140, 146, 214n50. *See also* aesthetics
artists: beautiful mind of, 126; contemporary perceptions of, 87; definitions of, 88; and self-improvement, 104–7
Astell, Mary, 11, 187–88
atheism, 23–25, 27. *See also* daemonism; religion; theism
audiences, 12, 111, 116, 127, 135, 170, 186

Axelsson, Karl, 192n61, 193n36, 199n67, 209n30, 212n20
Ayres, Philip, 217n37

Balguy, John, 11, 187–88, 210n141
Bayle, Pierre, 6, 8, 179
beauty: as an end, 105, 107, 110, 117, 134; assessment of, 213n23; definitions of, 37, 67, 109, 125, 128, 131, 197–98n62; and enthusiasm, 129; and happiness, 142; and love, 38, 53; of the mind, 64, 66, 123, 125, 132, 155; of nature, 1, 39–56; and objectivity, 70; positive responses to, 37–38, 49, 57, 64, 68, 132; and the sublime, 160; and truth, 90, 178–79; and unity, 146, 217n34; value of, 65, 104–5, 117, 120, 132, 140; and virtue, 1, 109–10, 118, 122–23, 140. *See also* aesthetics; art; moral beauty; unity; virtue
beauty-good claim, 97–100, 130, 209n128. *See also* moral beauty; morals
Beiser, Frederick, 193n50
Bentham, Jeremy, 106, 108
Bentley, Richard, 199n66
Berkeley, George, 11, 97, 186–88, 197n62
Berman, David, 197n54
Bernasconi, Robert, 191–2n6
Bernstein, John Andrew, 98, 213n22
Biblical events, 34–35, 45, 143, 194n6, 197n57. *See also* Noah's flood; scripture
*Bicycle Thieves* (De Sica), 163–65, 167
Bloom, Paul, 205n33
Boeker, Ruth, 198n64, 205n42
Boyer, Abel, 212n18
Boyer, Ernest J., 12
Boyle, Robert, 174
Branch, Lori, 211n7, 219–220n4
Brewer, Holly, 191n6
*Bridge on the River Kwai* (Lean), 164–67
Brown, John, 12–13, 97
Budd, Malcolm, 200n90

[234] INDEX

bullshit, 181–82
Burnet, Thomas, 19–21, 34, 37, 50, 87, 195n30, 206n57
Butler, Joseph, 11, 207n73

Calvinism, 24, 65, 72, 86, 102
Cambridge Platonism, 81
Cannon-Brookes, Peter, 218n38
Carey, Daniel, 196n31, 205n15, 209n133, 214n29
Carlson, Allen, 200–201n90, 200n88
Carolina Colony, 5, 16–17, 191n5
Carracci, Annibale, 144, 146, 156–57
Carter, Allan, 193n50
Cassirer, Ernest, 193n50
Catholicism, 3, 145
Cesari, Giuseppe, 155
*Characteristicks of Men, Manners, Opinions, Times* (Shaftesbury): goals of, 121; illustrations in, 10–11, 56, 113, 212n19; praise for, 12; structure of, 2, 117, 184; writing style of, 14–15, 116. See also *specific works*
*Choice of Hercules, The* (Carracci), 147
*Choice of Hercules, The* (de Matteis), 145–160, 162–163, 218n42
*Christ and the Samaritan Woman* (Poussin), 158–59
Clarke, Samuel, 108, 210n141
cleanliness, 122
cognitive behavioral therapy, 177
Cohen, Alix, 205n44
Collier, Jeremy, 212n16
Collins, Anthony, 199n66
Cooper, Anthony Ashley. See Shaftesbury (Anthony Ashley Cooper, Earl of)
Corbeau-Parson, Caroline, 193n49
Cortona, Pietro da, 158
Crisp, Roger, 205n39, 207n64, 210n137
cross-references, 11
Cudworth, Damaris, 4
Cudworth, Ralph, 46
Culpeper, Thomas, 174

daemonism, 23–25. See also atheism; theism
Darwall, Stephen, 132
Darwin, Charles, 43, 56–58, 203n104
*David Garrick between Tragedy and Comedy* (Reynolds), 161

da Vinci, Leonardo, 144
Dehrmann, Mark-Georg, 127, 160, 193n46, 207n62, 212n20
deism, 29, 54–55, 196n44
Den Uyl, Douglas, 12, 103, 195n57, 213n27
deontology, 107–8, 110
Derham, William, 199n66
Descartes, René, 72, 111, 204n13
design argument for existence of God, 43–49, 56–57, 198–99n65, 199n66, 203n104
*Diana and Actaeon* (Cesari), 155
*Diana and Acteaon* (de Matteis), 161–62
Diogenes, 179, 181–83
Driver, Julia, 205n39
duty, 4, 107, 110

Echlin, Alexander, 217–18n37
egoism, 72–76, 78, 81, 103, 121, 204n30. See also selfishness
Emerson, Ralph Waldo, 23, 202n102
empathy, 79–80, 96
enthusiasm, 31–32, 54–55, 129, 134, 171
environmental philosophy, 23, 200n90, 201–2n99, 202–3n102
Epictetus, 117, 124–25, 140, 142, 212n19
Ewer, Jane, 8–9
Existentialism, 24, 27

farming, 7, 21–22, 52
Farr, James, 191n6
Filonowicz, Joseph Duke, 97, 205n12, 213n22–213n23
fine art, 11, 87–88, 145. See also art
Fleming, Suzannah, 211n15
foolish by a system, 173
footnotes, 9, 99, 120, 126, 134–35
Fowler, Thomas, 97
Frankfurt, Henry, 181–82

gardens, 51, 138, 201n93, 211n15
Garrett, Aaron, 205n46, 210n143
Gatti, Andrea, 201n94, 212n20
Giordano, Luca, 144
Glauser, Richard, 199n67, 213n50
Glausser, Wayne, 191n6
God: beauty of, 112, 125, 132, 142, 178; and evolution, 57; intentions for the Earth, 21–22; love for, 29, 36, 59; as perfect creator, 27–28, 44, 49; questioning

of, 30; worship of, 23, 25–26. *See also* miracles; religion
Goethe, Johann Wolfgang von, 18, 23, 90–91, 212n20
Gonthier, Ursula Haskins, 193n52
Gould, Stephen Jay, 203n104
Gray, Thomas, 13–14
Greene, Joshua, 81–82
Gregory I, Pope, 176, 178–79, 182–83
Grote, Simon, 204n30, 210n137

Haidt, Jonathan, 210n142
Hale, Mathew, 174
*Hamlet*, 168–69, 177
Hamlin, J. Kiley, 177–78
Harley, Robert, 9
Harris, James, 12, 160
Harris, James A., 11
hedonistic consequentialism, 106
Helmont, Franciscus Mercurius van, 218n1
*Hercules at the Crossroads* (Benvenuti), 149
*Hercules at the Crossroads* (Ricci), 150
Herder, Johann Gottfried, 12, 160, 212n20
herding principle. *See* partiality
*High and Low* (Kurosawa), 166–67
Hinnant, Charles, 160
Hinshelwood, Brad, 191n6
history painting. *See* painting
Hobbes, Thomas, 65, 72, 75–77, 81–83, 86, 102
homosexuality, 211n7
Howell, William, 196n46
humanity: compared to animals, 61–62, 73–75, 204n13; contempt for, 4, 59; harmony with, 67; love for, 25, 79–80, 112; as social, 59, 94–97, 209n113
human nature, 5, 18, 59, 75–76, 101–2, 179–81, 183, 195n30
Humboldt, Alexander von, 23
Hume, David, 11, 69, 75, 84, 87, 141, 198–99n65, 198n64, 206n57
Hutcheson, Francis, 5, 80–81, 84, 103
hyperbole, 158

identity, 41–42, 198n64
idolatry, 144–45
indexes, 9, 117
innate ideas, 101, 204n15, 209n133

*Inquiry Concerning Virtue, or Merit, An* (Shaftesbury), 4, 9, 12, 23, 27, 59, 92–98, 120–21, 135, 186–87
irony, 36
Irwin, Terence, 70, 210n138

Jaffro, Laurent, 160, 192n7, 198n64, 205n42, 212n20, 214n49, 215n56, 217n34, 219n23
Jaspers, Karl, 206n48
Jews and Judaism, 24, 137, 215n58
*Judgment of Paris, The* (Raphael), 148–49
justice, 141, 205n41

Kant, Immanuel, 85, 108, 120, 205n44, 210n141
Killegrew, William, 174
Kinnunen, Aarne, 200n90
Klein, Lawrence, 192n7, 197n61, 211n7, 212n20, 215–16n70, 219n3, 220n4
Kurosawa, Akira, 166–67

*Last Communion of St. Jerome, The* (Domenichino), 152
Lean, David, 164–65
Leatherbarrow, D, 201n93, 203n103
Le Brun, Charles, 144
Leibniz, Gottfried Wilhelm, 12, 218n1
Leiter, Brian, 206n48
Le Moyne, François, 144
Leopold, Aldo, 23, 202n102
Lepper, Mark, 177–8
Lessing, Gotthold Ephraim, 160
*Letter Concerning Enthusiasm, A* (Shaftesbury), 8
Levy-Eichel, Mordechai, 205n39
Lewis, Douglas, 192n6
Liu, Yu, 48
Locke, John, 3–5, 12, 21–23, 34, 37, 50, 111, 121–24, 191n6, 195nn30–31
love, 27, 53–54, 129, 131

Magill, R. Jay, 219n17
Mandeville, Bernard, 11, 81
manure, 52–53
marriage, 7–8, 113–14, 211n7
Martineau, James, 97, 210n136
*Massacre of the Innocents, The* (Raphael), 153, 158
mathematics, 38, 171–73

Matteis, Paolo de, 139, 145–46, 161–63, 167, 218n42
Maurer, Christian, 212n20, 214n49
May, Joshua, 210n142
McAteer, John, 48
melancholy, 27
Mendelssohn, Moses, 12, 160
*Mercury Escorting Psyche to Olympus* (Rubens), 150
Michelangelo, 144, 158
Mill, John Stuart, 13, 108, 207n64
miracles, 35, 44–46, 194n6. *See also* God
*Miscellaneous Reflections* (Shaftesbury), 135–36
Montesquieu, 12
moral beauty, 63–73, 78, 100–102, 109, 141, 209n134. *See also* beauty; beauty-good claim
*Moralists, The: A Philosophical Rhapsody* (Shaftesbury), 8, 29, 39–40, 54–64, 79, 92, 98, 108, 115, 120, 128–33, 181
morality: and art, 118, 127–28, 144, 158, 161–62, 167, 197n57, 216n3; moral judgment, 84, 102; and atheism, 25; and scripture, 35–36; and the self, 16. *See also* beauty-good claim; religion; virtue
moral realism, 68–72
moral sense, 24–26, 61–64, 68–72, 84–85, 204n14. *See also* moral sentiment
moral sentiment, 61–64, 68–72, 84, 108, 155, 205n44, 210n141, 213n23. *See also* moral sense
More, Henry, 196n45
Mortensen, Preban, 212n20
moviemaking, 155–57, 163–64
Muir, John, 23, 201–2n99, 202n102
Müller, Patrick, 48–49, 192n7, 211n7
mundane egg, doctrine of the, 20–21
Myers, Katherine, 201n92–201n93, 211n15

nature: beauty of, 1, 4, 22, 39–56, 120; and care for young, 73–74; and environmental degradation, 50–51; laws of, 45–46, 57, 194n6, 200n80; love for, 27, 57, 137, 201–2n99; as perfect, 26, 46–47; as a unified system, 1, 40–41, 43, 47–49, 63, 198n64, 202n102. *See also* wilderness
Nehamas, Alexander, 206n48
Newton, Isaac, 199n66

Nichols, Shaun, 16
Nicolson, Marjorie Hope, 194n1, 200n89
Nietzsche, Friedrich, 86–87, 90
Noah's flood, 19–21, 194n6. *See also* Biblical events

O'Connell, Sheila, 193n26, 219n12
original sin, 35
Otteson, James R., 194n57
overjustification hypothesis, 177–78

painting, 143–46, 148, 153, 155–58, 161–63, 168, 197n57. *See also* art
Paknadel, Felix, 10
partiality and herding principle, 73–81, 83, 205n33, 208n85
Pascal's Wager, 30
patriotism, 182
Peach, B. A., 210n137
Pestilli, Livio, 161–62
Pfeffer, Michelle, 197n54
philosophy: audiences of, 186; dedication to, 10; goals of, 115–16, 171–72; and literature, 14; prominent figures in, 11, 23, 65, 199n66; and soliloquy, 177–78; and virtuosoship, 131; writing styles of, 170–71
*Plasticks* (Shaftesbury), 215n64, 216n1
Plato, 65–66, 103, 113
poetry, 12, 91
Pope, Alexander, 12, 36
positive aesthetics, 200–201n90
Poussin, Nicolas, 144, 158–59
pretenses, 135–36
Prince, Michael, 200n87
Prinz, Jesse, 205n33, 210n142
Prometheus, 90–91, 207n62–207n63
punishment and reward, 26–28, 30, 77, 102, 185, 187–88
Puritans, 35, 144

Raphael, 144, 146, 148, 151, 154, 158
Rawls, John, 141
Ray, John, 199n66
religion: criticism of, 19–20, 29, 34; enforced forms of, 18; rationality of, 29–36, 43–50, 54–55, 196n44; and salvation, 35; and self-interest, 30; truth of, 34–35; value of, 29. *See also* atheism; God; morals; revelation; scripture; theism

religious emotion, 23–29, 195n44
revelation, 31–32. *See also* religion; scripture
reward and punishment, 26–28, 30, 77, 102, 185, 187–88
Ricci, Sebastiano, 150
Ridge, Michael, 205–6n47
Rind, Miles, 212n20
Rivers, Isabel, 11–12, 97–98, 178, 199n66, 204n14
Rolston, Holmes, 200n90
Romanticism, 23, 200n89
Rorty, Richard, 206n48
Rousseau, Jean-Jacques, 179
Rubens, Peter Paul, 144, 150
Rudd, M., 213n26

Sacheverell, Henry, 9
Salteren, George, 144
*Samaritan Woman at the Well, The* (Carracci), 156–57
*Samson and Delilah* (Van Dyck), 156–57
Santayana, George, 65
Sartre, Jean-Paul, 24, 27, 60
Schleier, Erich, 218n41
Schneewind, J. B., 70, 210n138
science, 38, 40–46, 52, 56, 75, 178, 199n67
scripture, 31–36, 196n46. *See also* Biblical events; religion; revelation
*Second Characters* (Shaftesbury), 11, 144, 148, 156, 158
self: authenticity of, 183; hiding of, 60; and morals, 16; and truth, 178; as a work of art, 84, 86–87, 90, 104. *See also* self-improvement; self-reflection
self-improvement, 84, 104–7, 110, 184
self-interest, 30–31, 103, 122
selfishness, 81–82, 102–3, 122, 131. *See also* egoism
self-reflection, 28, 85, 94–95, 107–8, 176–79, 181, 183, 213n23, 218n1
Sellars, John, 206n60, 212n20
*Sensus Communis: An Essay on the Freedom of Wit and Humour* (Shaftesbury), 8, 77, 92, 122, 194n65, 206n58
Shaftesbury (Anthony Ashley Cooper, Earl of): anti-Semitism of, 137, 215n58; audiences of, 2, 12, 111, 116, 127, 135, 170; critics of, 12–14, 97–98, 109, 179, 184, 186, 197n62, 198n64; early life of, 2–3, 137, 191n1; family responsibilities of, 2–4, 52, 112, 114; health of, 6–8, 10, 114–15; influence of, 11–14, 84, 160–61, 206n58; and marriage, 113, 211n7; political career, 5, 7, 9–10, 114, 192n7; praise for, 13, 160; private notebooks of, 36, 52–53, 59–60, 124, 137–38, 184, 212n19, 215n70; and slavery, 5, 16–17; social life, 4, 6, 59–60, 113; and working people, 186–87; writing style of, 9–10, 13–15, 18, 29, 36, 55–56, 85, 98, 116, 135, 175, 181, 184, 194n65. *See also specific works*
*Shakespeare between Tragedy and Comedy* (Westfall), 161
Sidgwick, Henry, 210n137
sin, 1, 21, 35
slavery, 5, 16–17, 191n5
Slote, Michael, 210n142
Smith, Adam, 13–14, 160
sociability of humans, 59, 73–75, 78–81, 93–97
social contract theory, 75, 78, 110
*Social Enthusiast, The* (Shaftesbury), 8
Socrates, 65–66, 113
*Soliloquy: or, Advice to an Author* (Shaftesbury), 9, 91–92, 108, 122, 170, 176
Solomon, Harry M., 193n40, 206n58
Spurr, John, 196n44
Stoicism, 103, 129, 131, 138–40, 177, 212n20, 214n30, 215n70, 216n71
Stolnitz, Jerome, 98, 212n20, 231n20
Stringer, Thomas, 115
Strohminger, Nina, 16
Stuart-Buttle, Tim, 195n31, 197n60, 199n67, 205n15, 209n133, 212n20, 214n42, 216n70
Sweetman, J., 215n68
Swift, Jonathan, 219n7
systems, 40–43, 47, 51, 53, 61, 68, 177. *See also* unity

theism, 23, 26–28, 54, 119. *See also* atheism; daemonism; religion
Thiel, Udo, 198n64
Thomson, James, 12
Thoreau, Henry David, 23, 202n102
Tierney-Hynes, Rebecca, 211n7, 220n4
Tiffany, Esther A., 97, 128, 137
Tindal, Matthew, 199n66
Toland, John, 5, 35, 45, 197n54
Tory Party, 3, 5, 7, 114. *See also* Whig Party

Townsend, Dabney, 212n20, 213–14n28
*Transfiguration of Christ, The* (Raphael), 154
Trumbach, Randolph, 211n7, 219n4
truth, 30, 89–90, 144, 146, 156, 158, 174–75, 178–79
Tuveson, Ernest, 195n31, 213n23

Uehlein, Friedrich, 195n31, 197n53, 209n133
unity, 1, 40–41, 47–49, 53, 63, 86–87, 146, 151–53, 156, 177, 184, 217n34. *See also* beauty; systems
Utilitarianism, 108, 205n39, 207n64
Uzgalis, William, 191n6

van Dyck, Anthony, 144, 156–57
Varsamaopoulou, Evy, 193n46
vice, 65, 93, 143, 148, 162, 187. *See also* virtue
virtue: and beauty, 109–10, 118, 122–23, 140; and happiness, 92, 99; and morals, 24, 65; motivations for, 26, 77, 92–94, 102–5, 117, 185; and motives, 69, 72; and privilege, 185–86; representation of, 91, 143, 151, 155; steps toward, 119, 123–25, 162; value of, 107, 124. *See also* beauty; morals; vice; virtuosos

virtuosos, 117–24, 131–32, 134, 138. *See also* virtue
Voitle, Robert, 11, 138, 191n1
Voltaire, 12, 160

Walpole, Horatio, 13
Walzel, Oskar, 193n50
Weiser, C. F., 193n49
Welchman, Jennifer, 192n6
Westfall, Stephen, 161
Whichcote, Benjamin, 35, 77, 81, 197n53
Whig Party, 3, 5, 7, 114, 192n7. *See also* Tory Party
White, David, 212n20
Wieland, Christoph Martin, 12, 160
wilderness, 1, 21–22, 50–51, 53, 195n30, 200n89. *See also* nature
Wiley, Basil, 210n136
William, King, 5, 7, 114
Wind, Edgar, 215n68
Winkler, Kenneth, 198n64
*Wit and Humour* (Shaftesbury). See *Sensus Communis*
Wittkower, Rudolf, 160
workmanship, 37, 45, 88, 175
writing, 176–79, 181

Xenophon, 65, 113, 146

GPSR Authorized Representative: Easy Access System Europe - Mustamäe tee
50, 10621 Tallinn, Estonia, gpsr.requests@easproject.com

www.ingramcontent.com/pod-product-compliance
Lightning Source LLC
Chambersburg PA
CBHW031434160426
43195CB00010BB/727